CORSICA

Authors:
Heike Mühl, Klaus Boll

An Up-to-date travel guide with 146 color photos
and 18 maps

First Edition
1996

Dear Reader,

Being up-to-date is the main goal of the Nelles series. To achieve it, we have a network of far-flung correspondents who keep us abreast of the latest developments in the travel scene, and our cartographers always make sure that maps and texts are adjusted to each other.

Each travel chapter ends with its own list of useful tips, accommodations, restaurants, tourist offices, sights. At the end of the book you will find practical information from A to Z. But the travel world is fast moving, and we cannot guarantee that all the contents are always valid. Should you come across a discrepancy, please write us at: Nelles Verlag GmbH, Schleissheimer Str. 371 b, D-80935 München, Germany, Tel: (089) 3515084, Fax: (089) 3542544.

LEGEND

✱ Place of Interest	♠	National Park	Four-lane road
■ Public or Significant Building	Calvi	Place Mentioned in Text	National Highway
■ Hotel	✈	International Airport	Major road
Church, Monastery, Castle	✈	National Airport	Main road
Tower, Lighthouse	M. Cinto 2706	Mountain Summit (Height in Meters)	Secondary Road
△ Campsite		Provincial Border	Track, Path
Inn, Mountain Hut			GR 20 - Hiking Trail
Beach	963 197	Route number	Railway
			Distance in Kilometers

CORSICA
© Nelles Verlag GmbH, 80935 München
   All rights reserved

First Edition 1996
ISBN 3-88618-036-0
Printed in Slovenia

Publisher:	Günter Nelles	**English Editor:**	Anne Midgette
Editor-in-Chief:	Berthold Schwarz	**Translations:**	Kent Lyon
Project Editor:	Heike Mühl		Robert Rowley
Editors:	Klaus Dietsch	**Cartography:**	Nelles Verlag GmbH
	Susanne Braun	**Lithos:**	Priegnitz, München
Picture Editor: K. Bärmann-Thümmel		**Printed by:**	Gorenjski Tisk

TABLE OF CONTENTS

GUIDELINES

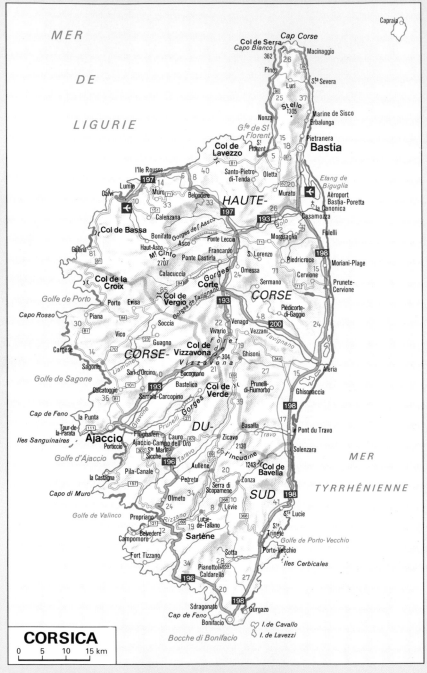

MER

DE

LIGURIE

Capraia

Cap Corse
Col de Serra
Capo Bianco
362 26 Macinaggio
Pino
Sta Severa
Luri
25 37
Stello
1305
Nonza
Marine de Sisco
Erbalunga
Gfe de St Florent
St Florent
15
18 Pietranera
5 Bastia
Col de Lavezzo

l'Ile Rousse
197 14
Lumio
Calvi
Muro 71
Belgodere
33
151
Calenzana
Col de Bassa
Bonifato
Gorges de l'Asco
Galeria
81
Haut-Asco
Mt Cinto
2707
Ponte Castirla
Calacuccia
Col de la Croix
84
Corte
Golfe de Porto
Col de Vergio
Porto Evisa
193
Capo Rosso
Piana
84
30
81
Vico
Cargese
14
Soccia
23
Guagno
Sagone
CORSE-
Col de Vizzavona
304
Vizzavona
Golfe de Sagone
San-d'Orcino
Bocognano
21
193
Bastelica
Col de Verde
Calcatoggio
101
Sarrola-Carcopino
36 81
Cap de Feno
la Punta
111
Tour-de-la-Parata
Ajaccio
Iles Sanguinaires
Porticcio
Ajaccio-Campo dell'Oro
302 Ste Marie-Sicche
Golfe d'Ajaccio
196
Pila-Canale
la Castagna
157
Capo di Muro
Petreto
Golfe de Valinco
Propriano
121
Belvedere 2
Campomoro
Sartène
Fort Tizzano
34
Pianottoli 859
Caldarello
196
20
198
Sdragonato
Cap de Feno
Bonifacio
Bocche di Bonifacio

HAUTE-
197
193
Santo-Pietro-di-Tenda
Oletta
Murato
820
26
Golo
Morosaglia
71
Francardo
S. Lorenzo
198
Piedicroce
Cervione
15
Prunete-Cervione
Omessa
71
Sermano
711
CORSE
Piedicorte-di-Gaggio
Gorges de Tavignano
24
Venaco
22
Vivario
48
Vezzani
Tavignano
200
24
Forêt de
19
Ghisoni
344
27
15
Aleria
39
Prunelli-di-Fiumorbo
Ghisonaccia
17
198
Basalla
le Pont du Travo
Zicavo
Travo
Solenzara
26 l'Incudine
2130
20
1243 Col de Bavella
Aullène
Zonza
Serra di Scopamene
Olmeto
268 10
Lévie
24
8
Ste Lucie
Lucie-de-Tallano
368
Ste Trinité
19
Golfe de Porto-Vecchio
Sotta
Porto-Vecchio
28
Iles Cerbicales
27
Gurgazo
I. de Cavallo
I. de Lavezzi

Oletta

MER

TYRRHÉNIENNE

Col de Lavezzo
Santo-Pietro-di-Tenda
Ponte Leccio
Aéroport
Bastia-Poretta
la Canonica
Casamozza
Folelli
Moriani-Plage
Piédicroce

Col de Vizzavona

Col de Verde

Flughafen
Cauro
Zicavo

Basalla

CORSICA

0   5   10   15 km

MAP LIST

CORSICA

The Greeks called Corsica *Kalliste*, "The Beautiful." Corsica is still known as *Ile de la Beauté*, "Isle of Beauty."

Hardly another Mediterranean region can offer so many contrasts within such a small area as this island: from fun in the sun to hiking and cultural activities, there's something here for everyone. In addition, there are the proud Corsicans who, in spite of tourism, have maintained their unique character and continue to adhere to their centuries-old traditions, far away from the coastal resorts.

Anyone who prefers an individual mode of travel and wants to familiarize herself with traditional lifestyles, on or off the coast, will probably end up making more than just one trip to Corsica. Hardly any vacationer leaves the island disappointed – Corsica is more than able to fulfill its great promise.

Geography

With an area of 3,401 square miles, (8,722 sq. km), Corsica is the fourth-largest Mediterranean island, after Sicily, Sardinia and Cyprus.

The island, geologically belonging to Italy and politically to France, extends from north to south between the 41st and 43rd northern parallels, which places it at the same latitude as Rome and Barcelona.

Seen on a map, the island looks something like a closed fist with an extended thumb; local craftsmen stylize it either as such or as an elongated, inverted triangle with an extended corner. The resulting pendants or charms, executed in silver

Preceding pages: Breakers pound Corsica's steep and rocky west coast. The hiking trail GR 20 crosses almost the entire island. Left: Narrow and winding, but gorgeous – the D 81 through the Calanche.

and gold, adorn the necks of many Corsicans. And it doesn't stop at pendants: watches, receptacles or coasters, the sky's the limit when it comes to "The Art of Corsica." Hard-core patriots even discover this shape in nature, in caves or rocks in the Corsican landscape.

The island is 113 miles (183 km) long and 51 miles (83 km) at its widest point. This approximately corresponds to the distances that separate Corsica from the French and Italian mainlands, 111 miles (180 km) and 49 miles (80 km) respectively. The 7-mile (12 km) wide Strait of Bonifacio lies between the southernmost tip of Corsica (Bonifacio) and Sardinia.

With a coastline more than 620 miles (1,000 km) long, complete with 186 miles (300 km) of beaches, there are plenty of alternatives to the east coast's broad but overpopulated (in August) sands. Visitors in search of tranquillity and seclusion can find idyllic bays along the mountainous west coast, in particular.

As early as the 19th century, the German geographer Friedrich Ratzel dubbed the island "a mountain in the sea," and that it is: Corsica is, in fact, the most mountainous Mediterranean island, with an average altitude of 1,864 feet (570 m). The highest mountain, Monte Cinto, is 8,848 feet (2,706 m) high – and that just 40 miles (25 km) from the sea. Twenty other mountain peaks reach heights of 6,540 feet (2,000 m) or more. This makes the island a popular holiday destination not only for sunbathers, but also for hikers and mountain climbers.

The main mountain chain takes the form of an "s," like a crooked spine running through the inner regions of the island. Leading across this central mountain chain are only four passes, which, in winter, are blocked by heavy snow: Col de Vergio, 4,829 feet (1,477 m); Col de Verde, 4,215 feet (1,289 m); Col de Bavella, 3,982 feet (1,218 m); and Col de Vizzavona, 3,803 feet (1,163 m). The mountain ridge is not only a water and weather divide, it also separates the island into two distinct cultural regions: *au-delà des monts* (the other side of the mountains, 48% of the terrain) and *endeçà des monts* (this side of the mountains, 52%) in the east. In both of these regions, traditions, lifestyles, and even the Corsican language have retained their differences from valley to valley.

Recent geological research has led to the assumption that the island represents the remains of a mountain range formed in the Paleozoic Era. It is bordered by fold mountains of the Tertiary period, the Pyrenees and the Apennines. Corsica thus comprises a leftover "in-between mountain range." As the Alps were in the process of being formed, other rock zones were being pushed up against the massif from the east at the same time as it was being lifted itself from below.

Corsica is differentiated into two rock zones: the Corsican crystal massif, which consists of crystallized preexisting rock (granite, gneiss and porphyry) and the main mountain chain, which forms the western and southern areas of the island, consisting mainly of slate. The adjacent regions of Castagniccia, Nebbio, Cap Corse and Casinca therefore have a distinctive low mountain range character.

Corsica's distinctive silhouette, rising out of the sea, was formed over several geological periods. This is the reason for the island's enormous geographical diversity within a relatively very small area. The advertising slogan "Island of Contrasts" is no exaggeration. Corsica offers alpine-like high mountain regions with impressive mountain chains that were once covered with glaciers; wild gorges and jagged ridges; and low mountain regions with more lush vegetation flourishing in wide valleys.

Two other characteristic zones are the valley of Corte, a geological basin between the granite massif and the slate mountain range, and the eastern coastal lowlands, 3-12 miles (5-20 km) wide, between Bastia and Solenzara. The latter was formed by recent alluvial sand deposits and includes a few large lagoons (Étang de Biguglia, Diane and d'Urbino). Mountainous country extends over 85% of the island's area; coastal lowlands make up the remaining 15%.

Climate

Like all the Mediterranean islands, Corsica is bathed in brilliant sunshine from June to October. There are, however, great variations in climate due to the extreme geographical differences on the island. A Mediterranean climate prevails along the coast and up to an altitude of nearly 650 feet (200 m). Anyone who drives up into the low mountains to an altitude of around 4,900 feet (1,500 m) will find a more temperate climate; while there is Alpine climate in the high mountains. Precipitation, often in the form of snow here, is much higher in the mountains than on the coast.

Ajaccio has the mildest climate of the entire island. The average high temperatures in July and August reach 86°F (30°C). Even in the coldest month, January, temperatures never fall below 41°F (5°C), and often, even at this time of year, stay between 50-55°F (10-13°C).

Wind often causes temperature fluctuations and weather inversions. Corsica, as an island, is extremely susceptible to winds, reflected in the fact that many winds have their own names in Corsican.

The most well-known wind is the *maestrale*, known and feared, in southern France, as the *mistral*. This cold, dry wind blows in from France to the northwestern part of the island after having lost much of its strength in crossing the sea. Despite this, it still manages to blast through Cap Corse, as does the north wind *tramontane*.

Right: Tourism is Corsica's most important industry (Sartène).

The *libecciu*, a west to southwest wind, often blows across Corsica. It can become violent and usually brings rain.

The east wind, the *levante*, and the southeast wind, the *sirocco*, are hot and humid; the former, however, can become quite unpleasant because of the sultry, greenhouse-like climate it brings with it. For its part, the sirocco, in addition to thunderstorms, sometimes brings sand from the Sahara desert.

Population

Approximately 40% of the 250,000 people on Corsica today inhabit the two large cities, Ajaccio and Bastia. This shows a population density of 5 - 75 people per square mile (2 - 30/sq. km), or an average of about 64 people per square mile (25/sq. km). These figures clearly illustrate the difference between Corsica and other Mediterranean islands. Malta, for example, has a population density of 2,500 per square mile (1,000 per sq. km), Sicily 437 (170), and Sardinia 146 (57).

The population was still rising continuously at the end of the 19th century, but with the recession in the 20th century, a wave of emigration set in, and more than 100,000 people moved to France or Italy, while other Mediterranean islands showed tremendous population growth (Sardinia, for example, grew by 73%).

There was no increase in population until the conditions after World War II led to improvements in the agricultural situation (one significant factor was the extermination of the anopheles mosquito, carrier of malaria, from the east coast).

Another contributing factor was tourism, which tripled between 1970 and 1990. Today, Corsica has 1.5 million visitors every year. This has made tourism the island's most important economic factor, although the figures have now stabilized. While there are plenty of visitors to Corsica, in short, you won't find here the kind of mass tourism you find on Mallorca; here, you can enjoy your own kind of vacation in a unique, very personal, environment.

HISTORY

Over a period of approximately 3,500 years, Corsica was continually at the mercy of other nations' invasions. It began with the Torreans, who stepped in and attacked the peaceful Megalithic civilization in 1600 BC. Then, one after the other, other well-known seafaring nations of the time also intervened: the Greeks, Etruscans and Carthaginians. Finally, the Romans conquered the strategically well-located island; they were able to hang onto it, tenaciously, for 700 years.

After the Vandals stormed throughout Europe on their pillaging crusades in the 5th century, not sparing Corsica, and the Moors laid waste to many of the island's coastal towns between the 9th and 12th centuries, Pisan rule, starting in 1077, ushered in a peaceful century. Following the Pisans, the powerful maritime nation of Genoa attempted to leave its own Italian stamp on Corsica for the next 500 years (1284-1768). The island has been in the hands of the French since 1769.

Visitors, however, will search in vain for signs of typical French or even Italian culture. The inhabitants of Corsica have maintained their original, proud character throughout the centuries, and have never succumbed to the force and suppression of foreign colonialists. Even those Corsicans who have emigrated to the mainland never quite develop into typical Frenchmen. Once a Corsican, always a Corsican...

Corsican Stone Age Civilization and the First Invasion

Until the mid-1950s, the early history of Corsica had essentially been ignored

Left: Memorial to the Corsicans who died in the two World Wars (Calvi).

by archaeological research, which was then itself scarcely 125 years old. With its Alpine mountain range and steep gorges, the island was considered too impassable; in addition, experts claimed that it could not have played a role in early Mediterranean history because of its lack of natural resources and raw materials.

One of the first visitors to suspect something about the island's mysterious prehistoric culture was Prosper Mérimée. Today known primarily as a writer, this Frenchman was sent to Corsica in 1834 as Inspector General for French antiquities. In 1840, he made public for the first time his claims that Corsica had been settled as early as the Stone Age. Despite this, his findings (among them the dolmen of Fontenaccia) were disregarded for a long time. Scientists understood these chamber tombs and menhirs, which were clearly visible even then, to be primitive stone sculptures that had supposedly been left behind by uncivilized shepherd tribes. Even the otherwise respected investigative historian Ferdinand Gregorovius assumed that the "Celtic tribes were the first and oldest inhabitants of Corsica."

Not until approximately 100 years later did the doyen of French prehistoric times, Abbé Breuil, started to guess at something of the island's magnificent history, and prompted exploration of it. His pupil, Roger Grosjean, began the laborious task in 1954, and gradually began to cast light into the "deep darkness that shrouds the early days of the island," as Mérimée wrote in 1840.

The last period of the Stone Age, the Neolithic period, began on the island extremely early. As a result, archaeologists have recently come to recognize that Corsica was an important link in the chain of early Mediterranean sea trade routes.

It is uncertain how the first hunters and gatherers reached the island. In all prob-

ability, they came over from Elba and settled in the south of Corsica, spreading out on up to the Gulf of Ajaccio. According to the accurate carbon-14 dating method, the earliest find dates back to 6750 B.C. It is the skeleton of a woman of around 35 years of age, dubbed the "Lady of Bonifacio," which was found in the Argiuna-Sennola cave near Bonifacio.

The Neolithic-period inhabitants, who kept up Mesolithic customs and lifestyles for a long time, made simple pottery with patterns of dots etched into the surface. Since the island was not very suitable for large-scale farming, herding played a pivotal role in the lives of the inhabitants. This lingers on today; the herds are driven on the old routes to the mountains in the summer and taken back to the coast in the autumn, just as they were 6,000 years ago.

Above: Remains of a Torrean complex in Filitosa. Right: Menhir with a depiction of a weapon, 2nd millennium B.C. (Filitosa).

In the early Neolithic period (5th - 4th millennium B.C.), people started breeding sheep and cattle, and building houses by layering small rocks on top of one another. At that time, there was an active trade in obsidian with the neighboring island of Sardinia. The people made knives and arrowheads out of this dark, vulcanized stone glass, which was very much sought after at the time and could not be found on Corsica itself.

Farming intensified around the middle of the 4th millennium B.C., a development which led to an astonishing rise in population. Some villages were now spread out over several acres. The question of whether the new inhabitants came from France, Catalonia or from the east remains a much-debated archaeological puzzle to this day.

These newcomers brought their own culture and religion based on nature with them; one relic of the latter are the impressive stone monuments which they erected around the island (Megalithic civilization).

From the very beginning, the people living on Corsica had placed funerary objects in the graves of the deceased, who were buried in cave dwellings. These offerings were often only pieces of food that quickly spoiled. The new religion based on nature was oriented towards permanence and immortality; the fact that houses were built for each person who died suggests that the people at that time had some sort of concept of the hereafter. Stone was for them the symbol of the everlasting; it became an expression for eternity, for the scat of divinity and bearer of supernatural powers. Eternal life was thus linked with the idea of an indestructible house for the deceased.

The Megalithic period is divided into three categories according to the size and type of the various monuments, dolmens and menhirs. In the beginning (1st Megalithic period), graves consisted of a type of tomb put into the earth at a depth of up to 6.5 feet (2 m) and covered with a mound of earth forming a barrow. Small menhirs, crudely carved, watched over the dead. The massive stone slabs, which megalithic man kept making taller and mightier over time, could also act as the repository of the soul or as a type of replacement body of the deceased.

In the next period of the Stone Age (2nd Megalithic period) the stones took on an increasingly human form. Head, neck and shoulder areas are clearly recognizable, and distinctive facial features can be made out on well-preserved specimens. In the same epoch, during the 3rd millennium, we see the gradual emergence of tombs built above ground in the form of dolmen. These *tumuli* (earthen mounds) have eroded away in the course of time, but there are still some 100 dolmens, more or less well-preserved, on Corsica.

In the 3rd Megalithic period (beginning around 2000 B.C.), the so-called *alignements* appeared. These are im-

pressive numbers of menhirs that are set up in a row or in several rows. All of these menhirs have their front side facing east, toward the rising sun. Since *alignements* have often been found near grave sites, most archaeologists today believe that these rows of stones were meant to express the hope of reincarnation.

Menhirs embossed with depictions of weapons begin to appear around 1600 B.C. Since weapons had been unknown to the peaceful megalithic peoples until that time, the archaeologist Grosjean inferred the invasion of a foreign civilization – that of the Torreans.

The Torreans, possibly identical with the seafaring people of Shardana, reached the southern part of the island around 1600 B.C., forced the megalithic peoples out of their villages, and drove them inland and to the north. They took over the conquered dwellings, moved in, and built stone towers several yards high which served as places of worship; it was, in fact, because of these towers that

CRATERE A COLONNETTE
DIT 'DES VENDANGES'
PEINTRE DE PAN
V s av. J.C

Roger Grosjean gave their civilization the name we use today (*torre* means tower in Corsican).

Excavations in Filitosa have yielded clear evidence of warlike conflict between Torreans and megalithic peoples.

Traces of both civilizations disappear around 800 B.C. The megalithic peoples had retreated to the north, and from there, their trail goes cold. The Torreans most likely left Corsica to go to Sardinia; this did away with the need for importing the valuable obsidian, which was a difficult process. The tower-shaped *nuraghi* found on Sardinia very much resemble the Torrean towers on Corsica.

The Corsican Iron Age

The research of the Iron Age on Corsica still shows large gaps. Countless finds, some of which are displayed today

Above: Red-figure krater from the 5th century B.C. – relic of the Greek colony Alalia (Museum of Aléria).

in the archaeological museums in Sartène and Levie, reveal that Corsica was an important trading post during the early Iron Age. The inhabitants dealt in ceramics, metal objects and foodstuffs. The Stone Age civilizations had already helped develop the art of bartering with the obsidian trade. Even the form of settlement in the Iron Age was not significantly different from that of the Megalithic period; some people even settled in the same fortifications.

Corsica's inhabitants, numbering some 30,000, were now concentrated inland, somewhat more isolated, and were divided into well-organized tribes. The tribal name Corsi dates back to the second half of the 1st millennium. It was applied to the original Corsicans, who developed common social institutions; evidence of this are identical tombs found in both the north and south of the island. Their good strategic position did not, however, protect the islanders from more invasions. Aggressors streamed to Corsica from all sides: Ligurians from the north, Iberians from the west; Libyans landed in the south, and Phoenicians on the east coast.

First Attempt at Colonialization: The Greeks

Not until the 6th century B.C. do we find written documents about Corsica; from this point on, historians can structure their research and hypotheses around reliable dates.

The first attempt to colonize the island was the work of Greeks from Phocaea, a city in Asia Minor. Threatened by the Median king, Harpagos, the Phocaeans decided it would be better to emigrate to a foreign country with all of their possessions than to become slaves. After they had founded the city of Massilia (present-day Marseilles) as early as 600 B.C., they came to rest on the east coast of Corsica (Kyrnos in Greek), where they settled and built the city of Alalia in 565 B.C.

For nearly 30 years the Phocaean Greeks and Corsicans were able to live peaceably side by side. The colonists hardly ventured inland because of the rough terrain of the island; in general, they remained on the east coast, leaving the Corsicans alone.

Although they brought their gods, language, and olive trees and grapevines to the island – these last two, especially, are still very important today – the Phocaeans never managed to attain the power they hoped for over the Tyrrhenian Sea.

In his *Histories*, the Greek historiographer Herodotus (5th century B.C.) gave the following reason for the downfall of the Greek colony on Corsica: "during that period they [the Phocaeans] caused to much annoyance to their neighbors by plunder and pillage, that the Tyrrhenians (Etruscans) and Carthaginians agreed to attack them with a fleet of 60 ships apiece. The Phocaeans manned their own vessels, also 60 in number, and

sailed to meet them in the Sardinian sea. In the engagement which followed the Phocaeans won, but it was a Cadmeian sort of victory with more loss than gain, for 40 of their vessels were destroyed and the remaining 20 had their rams so badly bent as to render them unfit for service."

Since this laborious victory of the Phocaeans was equal to a defeat and they were no longer safe on what they had dubbed "The Isle of Beauty," they decided to leave the island. They found new homes in Massalia and Rhegium (Reggio di Calabria, Italy).

Alalia, however, remained a port under Greek influence and was one of the most important trading centers in the western Mediterranean; a range of ceramic finds attest to this.

Etruscans and Syracusans founded bases on the island. Towards the end of the 3rd century B.C., the Carthaginians became interested in the island and settled here. And Rome, too, soon became aware of this superb Mediterranean base, which was a perfect point of departure for the coasts of all the countries which they hoped, someday, to conquer.

Roman Rule

The Romans could not allow the Carthaginians to have supremacy over Corsica, so in the first Punic War (264-241 B.C.) in which the Romans battled against the Carthaginians, the Roman consul Lucius Cornelius Scipio started off by conquering Aléria, and razed this once-flourishing trading center to the ground. Rome emerged victorious from these Carthaginian conflicts, and just 30 years later was able to establish itself firmly on the east coast of Corsica.

Aléria was not rebuilt as a city until much later, under Sulla (80 B.C.), who settled it with his veterans. During the reigns of the emperors Caesar and Augustus, Aléria was enlarged considerably and equipped with the standard large-scale buildings of a Roman city. Under Augustus, the city of 20,000-30,000 people was given the name Colonia Julia and was made the capital of the province of Corsica.

Unlike other conquered Roman territories, such as Gaul, Roman soldiers and Corsican natives did not gradually mingle on Corsica. Mistrustful of life on the coast, the natives retreated inland and fought with all their might against the Roman colonization. Only after ten military campaigns, which reduced the Corsican population by nearly half and made slaves out of them, could the Romans claim power over the island.

The pride of the Corsicans, however, remained intact. The Romans limited their settlements to the military colonies of Aléria and Mariana at the mouth of the Golo River and to the coastal towns of Sagone, St-Florent and Ajaccio. The Corsicans were able to retain their impermeable mountainous country.

Corsica did not become a Roman province until the 6th century A.D. With the decline of the Western Roman Empire, Rome's interest in Corsica diminished. Aléria was half abandoned, and a large fire around the year 420 A.D. finished off the work; whatever was left of the once-magnificent city after this was destroyed by the marauding Vandals in 456 A.D. The Goths then arrived on the scene, followed by Byzantines who governed Corsica, together with Sardinia, as an eastern Roman province from 534-725 with only a brief interruption. Afterwards, the Lombards made a short appearance on the island until they were driven away in 758 by the king of the Franks, Pépin the Short.

Evidence of Christianity appears on Corsica around the 3rd century. A Christian oil lamp and engraved early Christian symbols have been found in Aléria.

Right: Pope Urban II in a 17th-century Spanish painting.

The Christians could not escape from the cruel persecutions of the Valerians and Diocletian. The three best-known martyrs are Saint Restituta, whose sarcophagus is in the church near Calenzana, Saint Devota, and Saint Julia, who is honored in Nonza on Cap Corse.

Churches, Nobility and Pirates

In 754 A.D., Pépin the Short conferred the island to the papal court. Charlemagne, his son, confirmed the gift of the former Byzantine regions shortly thereafter, in the year 774.

Yet the desired peace still failed to come. Corsica was caught up in a state of chaos: laws no longer meant anything, and complete anarchy prevailed.

Ever since Spain had been in the hands of the Moors, the Saracens swept across all the Mediterranean islands, thieving, plundering, and even sometimes settling down and dominating many places for years on end.

And Corsica was not spared, either. Between the 9th and 11th centuries, the Saracens invaded it, driving the inhabitants out of the coastal towns, plundering towns, and abducting a considerable number of Corsicans. In addition, they supposedly brought malaria with them, which "spread like wildfire" and could not be completely eradicated until after World War II.

The rest of the population retreated to the most remote areas of the island. They built their houses closely together for protection, preferring inaccessible mountaintops which served as excellent vantage points from which to espy oncoming danger. Place names such as Campo-*moro*, *Moro*saglia, and *Mor*siglia are modern-day reminders of the barbaric period of the Moors' plundering rampages.

But even after the Saracens finally left Corsica, the islanders had little chance to catch their breath. The next problem was

feudalism, which began developing in the 11th century. The wild and greedy aristocrat class, only a small percentage of which was of Corsican origin, was scattered about the entire island. These "noblemen" were often Italian nobles who had fled from the Barbarians; they also included Lombard, Gothic or Frankish vassals who had rendered outstanding services in fighting against the Saracens and been rewarded with land and feudal titles. Little by little, powerful dynasties began to develop which, from their fortresses up on the hills, tyrannized the poor Corsicans.

Anarchy prevailed again; constant fighting and bloody feuds were regular elements of daily life.

Peace Under Pisa

As there was no end in sight to the tyranny of the powerful *Signori* (noblemen) over the island, the desperate Corsicans turned to Pope Gregory VII for help. In 1077, accordingly, he transferred all rights to the island to Landolfo, the Bishop of Pisa; and Pope Urban II confirmed this gift in 1092.

Landolfo and the Pisans brought order, peace, and tranquillity back to the island. Historians praise their rule as wise and just.

The new rulers introduced laws and proclaimed a new community constitution. From this point on, Corsica was divided into parishes (*pieve*), determined by either geographical or historical considerations. Each pieve's center was the parish church, which was considered to be an institution for both religious and secular affairs. Justice, for example, was also administered in Corsican parish churches.

Under the Pisans, a large number of Romanesque churches were built on Corsica. The researcher Geneviève Morachini-Mazel, who has done intensive investigations into the individual buildings, estimates them to number more than 300; however, only a few of these simple but impressive churches are in good condi-

tion. Most of them are ruins upon which you unexpectedly stumble while walking through the maquis.

Before long, the maritime nation of Genoa, Pisa's rival, became jealous of the latter's success. After a few quarrels, Pope Innocent III stepped in and divided up the six existing dioceses in 1133. The archbishoprics of Ajaccio, Aléria and Sagone were to remain with Pisa, while Accia, Nebbio and Mariana were put under the rule of Genoa. Power-hungry Genoa was not satisfied with this division, and planned an occupation of the island. Gradually, through repeated invasions and attacks, the Genoese were able to establish and strengthen their position on the island. This caused, in turn, increasing strife on the island itself: the islanders sided either with the Pisans or the Genoese, while the *Signori* (nobility) cared only for their own interests.

Above: Pisan Romanesque west portal of S. Maria Assunta (La Canonica). Right: Genoese fortress in Bonifacio.

For this reason, the Pisans had their hopes set on a Corsican nobleman who had emigrated to Pisa, Giudice della Rocca. They appointed him judge and count of the island, and sent him to Corsica with a few ships in 1280. For a short time, he and his followers were able to overthrow the Genoese faction and justly and wisely rule the island under Pisan supremacy.

However just four years later, in 1284, the big sea battle of Meloria took place. Pisa suffered a devastating defeat at the hands of Genoa and lost almost its entire fleet. After more than 100 years of disputes, Pisa had to turn over its supremacy over Corsica to its rival, Genoa.

Five Centuries of Genoese Rule

The powerful Genoese also had a difficult time with the rebellious Corsicans, who did not so readily want to accept the new Italian domination.

Genoese supremacy on Corsica lasted from 1284 to 1768, with only sporadic

interruptions by Corsicans and other nations.

The rulers of Cinarca fought against the new rulers right from the beginning. Pope Boniface VIII also refused to accept the victory of the Genoese over the Pisans, perhaps because he also feared the mighty sea republic. As he was still in possession of the old, unresolved feudal rights to the island, he decided, in 1297, to transfer Corsica and Sardinia to the king of Aragon, Jacob II, who was more than happy to accept this gift.

This generated confusion once again; the peasants and, even more, the island's powerful aristocrats were divided into two or even three camps. The new Aragonese rule suited some of the people just fine; others came down on the Genoese side; and a small minority fought for themselves.

First result of this discord was the disintegration of the social order. In this period, for instance, a peculiar, wild sect, virtually akin to early communists, started to take root on Corsica, while making themselves felt in Italy at the same time. Basing themselves in the area around Carbini, they made "headlines," so to speak, under the name of the *Giovannali*, fighting especially with the worn-out Corsican noblity. The Pope excommunicated the sect, while the bishop of Aléria did his part by having its members persecuted as heretics.

The bloody conflicts everywhere caused waves of emigration. During this period, many Corsicans emigrated to the Italian mainland to settle in Pisa or Livorno.

Already under a heavy burden, the population was threatened to the marrow of their existence by the plague epidemic in 1348. Practically one-third of the island's population lost their lives to the feared "Black Death."

The enmity between Aragon and Genoa was not limited to Corsica alone, although the island was a bone of contention; rather, it was felt throughout the entire Mediterranean region. In 1376, the Spanish dared to make a first move and

commissioned the Corsican Arrigo della Rocca, son of Giudice della Rocca, who had already served the Pisans, to take steps against the Genoese to bring the island into the possession of Aragon. After a stay in Aragon, della Rocca left for Corsica in 1392; he soon became quite popular among the people, proclaimed himself a count, and for the next four years ruled Corsica unchallenged, but with an iron hand. As a result, even a number of Corsicans asked the Genoese to step in and intervene against Arrigo della Rocca. The seafaring nation turned this task over to a group of five *nobili*, who called themselves *Maona*. However, they didn't manage to get very far, and Arrigo della Rocca drove them from the island in a bloody battle.

Genoa asked the French for help in 1396. Thus strengthened, they managed to expel Arrigo, after which they were

Above and right: Bridges and watchtowers – testimony to years of Genoese rule on Corsica.

able to rule Corsica again for some time. However, Aragon did not give up. Arrigo was soon replaced by a new man, Vincentello d'Istria, scion of a noble Corsican family who had been educated in the court of Aragon.

Commissioned by King Alfonso V of Aragon, he started, in 1404, to conquer Corsica. After several expeditions of conquest, he was crowned viceroy of the island in 1420. In the 14 years of his reign, he conquered the most important Corsican coastal cities, among them Bonifacio, and by constructing the citadel of Corte, he was able to secure his rule inland as well. In 1434 he was taken prisoner and killed as the result of a Genoese conspiracy.

After his death, Corsica's aristocrats attempted yet again to take control of the island; now one, now another had himself dubbed the Count of Corsica. Unfortunately, the poor common Corsican people were afforded no peace; the constant battling meant they had to keep on defending themselves, time and again.

Since the Genoese were unable to keep the situation on the island under control, they took the recommendation of the Corsican nobility and sold the island to the Bank of San Giorgio in Genoa in 1453; in return, the bank covered Genoa's debts. This financial institution, which had its own army, judiciary and administration at its disposal, had already been lending the republic of Genoa money for 40 years and receiving certain public revenues in return, by way of security.

By moving in and immediately taking vigorous action, the Bank of San Giorgio was the first power that managed to bring peace to the island and rule it without any notable conflicts for decades. The fruits of this calm period, which led to a notable economic upswing, are still evident today. First, the citadels in the most important coastal cities (Bonafacio, Calvi, Bastia, St-Florent and Ajaccio) were reinforced. In these fortified citadels, surrounded by ramparts and moats, the bank erected splendid government buildings and palaces. The well-preserved governor's palace in Bastia is a fine example of such edifices. Afterwards, a network of roads was laid out over the entire island; notable relics of this transportation system today are the picturesque arches of stone bridges, often overgrown with maquis.

To protect themselves from attacks of foreign powers, the Genoese had some 150 watchtowers built along the coast of Corsica. Communities had to provide their own skilled workers and building materials for the ingenious warning system, which was not completed until around 1700. It was therefore much cheaper for the Bank of San Giorgio to protect Corsica from more invasions in this manner than it would have been to establish a naval fleet.

Despite a few minor conflicts between various noble families from Milan, Genoa and the insurgent Corsican no-

bility, the bank managed to secure its rule on the island.

It was during this reasonably peaceful period that the rebellious and proud Sampiero Corso came onto the scene. Along with Pasquale Paoli, he is the most notable freedom fighter of the island; his goal was never a royal title or sole rule for himself, but rather, above all, freedom for Corsica. His name adorns legion Corsican restaurants, pubs, hotels and street signs today.

Sampiero Corso

Sampiero was born in Bastelica on May 23, 1498; unlike other Corsican heroes, he was from an ordinary family. He was of "great stature, sinister and warlike in appearance, a proud creature... His gaze was piercing, and his speech was short, firm, and powerful," reported Gregorovius. Very early on, he left for the mainland of Italy to get an education. After in 1536, he fought under the French flag of King François I, who appointed

him colonel of the Corsican regiments. Sampiero showed great courage in the war between France and Spain, but never forgot about the fortunes of his home island during all those years of absence. When he went on to save the life of Henri II, the heir to the throne, his reputation as a hero was assured.

Sampiero Corso did not return to Corsica until 1547, when he took the beautiful Vanina d'Ornano, who was from one of the oldest and best houses on the island, to be his wife.

Genoa feared the return of the successful commander to such an extent that shortly after the wedding he was thrown into the dungeon for something trivial. This only intensified Sampiero's hate for Genoa. Freed with the help and intervention of influential French friends, he immediately made his way to France to persuade Henri II to liberate Corsica.

Above: Sampiero Corso, fighter for Corsica's freedom. Right: Andrea Doria, portrait by Agnolo Bronzino, 16th century.

It was easy to persuade the king to take action, since for one thing, he realized that the island had an excellent strategic location in the Mediterranean, and for another, this would mean fighting against Emperor Charles V, who was an ally of Genoa. Marshall Thermes was commanded to conquer Corsica, and in 1553 he sailed to the island together with a fleet of his country's Turkish allies under their commander, Dragut.

Meanwhile, Sampiero had called upon the Corsicans to help fight against Genoa with great success; popular hatred of Genoese rule had continued to increase.

Bastia was the first to surrender and Corte could also be taken quite easily. Wherever Sampiero appeared, gates were gladly opened for him. Only Calvi, Ajaccio and Bonifacio remained loyal to Genoa; but with Turkish assistance, strategy and toughness, the defenders of Ajaccio and Bonifacio were finally forced to surrender.

Genoa, however, could not be persuaded so easily to lay down its arms; first, it transferred command to the famous 86-year-old general Andrea Doria. On November 20, 1553, Doria arrived in the Gulf of St-Florent; he was able, at least temporarily, to chalk up great successes against Genoa. At the same time, there was some friction between Sampiero and Thermes, which led to them both being called back to France to justify their behavior.

When Sampiero was finally able to return to his native island, some cities, including Bastia, had already returned into Italian hands. Undaunted, Sampiero continued to fight for many years, supported by the French.

In 1557 in Vescovato, Giordano Orsini, Marshall Thermes' successor, declared that Corsica was annexed to the Kingdom of France. But just two years later, Henri II made peace with Philip of Spain in the Treaty of Cateau-Cambrésis and ceded the island back to Genoa. The

population of Corsica had once again become a pawn of the major European powers. Thanks to a simple sheet of paper, they were now at the mercy of Genoa's revenge.

Sampiero Corso, however, refused to recognize this treaty. Over the next four years, he traveled throughout Europe to plead the case for Corsica's freedom, voyaging to Catharine de Medici in Navarre (which then belonged to France) and to the dukes of Florence. He even sailed to Algiers to see Barbarossa and hurried on to Constantinople to Sultan Suleiman.

Informed about Sampiero's endeavors, Genoa tried, wherever possible, to throw a wrench in the works. For example, by means of a trick, the Genoese managed to lure Sampiero's wife, Vanina, to Genoa. When her husband heard of this betrayal in 1563, he sailed home immediately, found his wife and killed her with his own hands because she had allowed herself to be outwitted by the Genoese. In spite of this murder, he continued to gain

further support, and even found financial backers in the French court. In June, 1564, he sailed with only two ships, a handful of Corsicans and Frenchmen, and a full load of built-up resentment to Corsica, which Genoa had since taken back from the Bank of San Giorgio in 1561.

His reputation here was still such that Sampiero Corso was soon able to gather a large army, which meant that over the next two years of battles against Genoa, many of the combats were decided in his favor. Finally, the only way the Genoese could come up with to bring down Sampiero was maliciously to murder him. For this they could count on the support of the d'Ornano family, which had sworn a vendetta, blood revenge, since Sampiero had murdered their relative, Vanina Sampiero.

On January 17, 1567, Sampiero was surrounded in the Prunelli Valley town of Cauro and brutally slaughtered. He just barely managed to order his followers and his son Alfonso to flee.

In memory of Sampiero Corso, his son relentlessly continued to fight against the Genoese for the next two years, until both parties were exhausted from the years of battles and finally conceded that they had to come up with some kind of solution to their conflict.

Finally, a treaty was written: Corsica remained in Genoese hands, but total amnesty was granted to Alfonso and his Corsican followers, and political prisoners were set free. In addition, every Corsican was granted the option of emigrating to Italy with all his or her possessions and without any problems. Alfonso left for France and served under Charles IX; many other Corsicans, on the other hand, emigrated to Venice.

160 Years of Peaceful Genoese Rule

For the next 160 years, Genoa was untroubled by Corsican independence

Above: Corsica shown as a Genoese possession on an Italian map of 1700.

movements, but the people on the island lived in increasing misery and poverty.

The island was ravaged, and its population decimated by wars and the ongoing waves of emigration. The remaining inhabitants were threatened by the plague and pirates who attacked the villages and abducted many Corsicans to serve as slaves.

To counteract the depopulation, in 1676 the Genoese allowed Greek refugees to settle on the west coast, on the Gulf of Sagone. The Corsicans envied and hated the Greeks: for one thing, they worked hard and knew how to put the land they had been given to good agricultural use; for another, they were on the side of Genoa.

By contrast, the Italian rulers gradually deprived the Corsicans of the liberties and rights they had initially guaranteed them. They were driven out of all secular, military and religious offices, which were then filled with Genoese. During this relatively "peaceful period" – since everything was in the hands of the Genoese – the island experienced a slight economic upswing. But the Corsican people, so long beleaguered by catastrophes, were not to have peace for a long time.

The 40-Year War of Independence 1729 - 1769

At the beginning of the 18th century, repeated crop failures, large tax burdens and famine finally drove the Corsicans to organize an armed revolt against their oppressors.

First, they chased the tax collectors out of the Castagniccia in 1729 and plundered the lower city of Bastia. In a plebiscite in 1730, the Corsicans designated Andrea Colonna Ceccaldi and Luigi Giafferi as their generals.

Genoa, always wary of new agitators among the people, asked Emperor Charles VI of Austria for assistance. In 1731, he sent an army of 8,000 men to the island, equipped with the best weapons. At first, the Corsicans had a difficult time against such a contingent. Inland, however, where they had the advantage of being on their home turf, they were able to protect themselves amazingly well, whereas the Hapsburg troops suffered great losses. As a result, both parties signed a peace treaty in Corte on May 11, 1732. A general amnesty was to be granted and they would waive the costs of war reparations. Tax debts for the Corsicans were waived, and they would again be allowed to assume public office. After the Austrians pulled out, however, the Genoese violated the treaty; the Corsicans therefore revolted again and proclaimed the independence of Corsica in the Orezza monastery on January 6, 1735.

To lead the new nation, they elected Luigi Giafferi, Colonna Ceccaldi and Hyacinthe Paoli, a brave man from Castagniccia, who was to become a good speaker and statesman. In a plebiscite

they placed their country under the protection of the holy Virgin Mary and dedicated to her the Corsican national anthem, *Diu vi salva Regina*, which still makes proud Corsican hearts beat faster today.

Genoa reacted with a sea blockade. This hit the Corsicans hard because the island lacked all the raw materials to be able successfully to conduct a war against Genoa.

Fortunately, a ship under the British flag landed on the coast of Aléria on the morning of March 12, 1736. Theodor von Neuhoff, a German baron, was on board. His arrival ushered in a seven-month-long, involuntarily amusing chapter of Corsican history.

Theodor, born in Cologne toward the end of the 17th century, was an adventurer par excellence. In his youth he had served at the court of the Duke of Orléans, had been a courtier in Spain, and returned to France to the court of Louis XIV. Neuhoff led an unsteady life between pageantry and ruin.

As chance would have it, he happened to be in Livorno at the same time as Giafferi and Ceccaldi. Both had journeyed here to obtain the weapons they lacked and the necessary staples and supplies for their war of independence. They were quickly dazzled by the baron's striking appearance and convincing air. Impressed, the Corsicans signed an agreement with Neuhoff in which he ensured he would come to Corsica with help, weapons, shoes, food supplies and, together with them, lead the battle against the Genoese. To repay him, the Corsicans were to crown him King of Corsica.

He landed as promised on Corsica with all the supplies. One month later, on April 15, 1736, the Corsicans kept their promise and crowned him sole king of the island with a wreath of laurel and oak twigs in the monastery of Alesani (Castagniccia). Theodor I resided in the nearby former palace of the Bishop of

Cervione, but remained without extensive political functions. He had a council of 24 men selected from the people as well as a parliament, without whose agreement no decision could be made. This meant that legislation remained in the hands of the parliament and the people.

In spite of this, everything at first went exactly according to Theodor's wishes. He named Giafferi and Paoli as his first ministers and was generous in distributing the titles of count and marquis. He also took care of the economic needs of the island; he had weapons factories and salt mines built and minted gold, silver and copper coins. At first, even the battles against Genoa went in favor of the Corsicans: Sartène and Porto-Vecchio were conquered. However, the supplies he had brought with him were quickly being exhausted. Powerful Genoa had

Above: The ruins of the monastery of Orezza. Right: Gian Pietro Gaffori, Corsican freedom fighter from Corte.

better diplomatic connections, and turned to France for help.

Meanwhile, the Corsicans put the pressure on Theodor I. He then promised them to take steps to obtain new help and ammunition from England. On November 11, 1736, on the pretext he would search for assistance himself, Neuhoff sailed out of Aléria under the French flag and went to Livorno, Italy. From time to time, he managed to have some relief goods sent to Corsica, which kept the Corsicans, although already half-demoralized, loyal to him.

In 1738, the Corsican king managed yet again, with the help of the Dutch, to assemble a respectable fleet of cargo ships to bring war provisions to Corsica. Yet what he found was a Corsican people completely exhausted from the wars they had already lost to Genoa and hardly able to take advantage of his help. Unable to gain any support even from the nobility, he left the island, deeply hurt. He died ignominiously in a London debtors' prison in 1756.

The 15,000 well-armed Frenchmen who came to the aid of the Genoese had an easy job with the weakened Corsicans. After the French had emerged victorious, they left the island's inhabitants to the strict and cruel regime of the Genoese. The Corsican leaders, among them Giafferi and Paoli with his 14-year-old son Pasquale, left Corsica and fled into exile in Italy.

Yet opposition to the Genoese continued to brew. In spite of all their defeats, the tenacious Corsicans were as determined as ever to fight for their independence.

Since 1745, the Corsicans had had a new leader, Gian Pietro Gaffori, a doctor from Corte. Gaffori became the terror of Genoa. He cleverly organized the Corsican resistance and called the former freedom fighters back from exile. With their help, he was quickly able to drive back the enemy; only a few coastal cities remained in Genoese hands.

On his campaigns, Gaffori was utterly ruthless, even with regard to his own family: when he stormed the citadel in Corte (1746), the Genoese seized his son and tied him to the wall of the citadel to force his father to cease fire. Without blinking an eye, Gaffori ordered his men to fire. Miraculously, Gaffori's son survived unharmed.

At an assembly in Orezza in 1753, the people elected Gian Pietro Gaffori General of the Nation. The triumphant euphoria lasted but a short time. The Genoese again felt seriously threatened and resorted to a tried and true method: on October 3, 1753, they lured Gaffori into an ambush and murdered him.

Pasquale Paoli – 14 Years of Independence

The death of Gaffori only served to bring the Corsicans, who had now declared an all-out war on Genoa, closer together.

A suitable replacement for Gaffori was quickly found: the youngest son of Hyacinthe Paoli, Pasquale. Born in Morosaglia on April 6, 1725, Pasquale Paoli (in French, one also sees the name spelled Pascal) is still considered today to have been Corsica's most effective freedom fighter – as well as its most beloved one. He is affectionately referred to as *Babbu di u patria*, Father of the Fatherland.

His father took the young Paoli into exile with him, to Naples, and had him educated with great care. He learned Latin, Italian, English and French at the university. While there, he read Montesquieu's book *L'Esprit des Lois* (1748), in which the author proposes the system of separation of powers, a principle which has since been worked into the constitution of every modern democracy.

It was his brother, Clemence, who finally wrote Pasquale in 1755 requesting that he return to Corsica because his people needed him. As a result, Pasquale immediately resigned from his service as

an officer in Naples and sailed back to the island of his birth. In the same year, on July 13, 1755, the Corsican people elected him General of the Nation.

The achievements of this 30-year-old freedom fighter over the next 14 years, from 1755 to 1769, in reforming an island that had been continually plagued and battered with wars, clan feuds and vendettas, is exemplary in the history of Europe.

Paoli's Government

When drawing up the Corsican constitution, Paoli started from the principle that the people are the sole source of power and laws. All citizens over 25 years of age were eligible to vote in elections for the *Consulta*, the general assembly. For every 1,000 inhabitants, there was one elected community repre-

Above: Pasquale Paoli, Corsican freedom fighter and statesman. Right: Paoli encouraged the cultivation of chestnuts.

sentative. The Consulta was comprised of representatives from the community, the clergy, and provincial officials. Resolutions needed a two-thirds majority to become law.

The supreme councilor of state, the *Consiglio Supremo*, was elected from the Consulta. Nine men (similar to ministers) from the nine free provinces (Nebbio, Casinca, Balagna, Campoloro, Orezza, Ornano, Rogna, Vico and Cinarca) comprised the executives, represented the general assembly in external political affairs and could intervene in important cases with their veto rights. The president of the Consiglio Supremo was Pasquale Paoli, who was responsible to the state council; this body, in turn, was controlled by the Consulta.

The Consulta also named the five *Syndici*. The civil servants of the Syndicate traveled through the provinces to hear and handle complaints about administration and justice. In addition, all civil servants selected by the general also had to report to the Syndicate.

The central ideas of Paoli's constitution were based on a self-governing population, the citizen's participation in state and public affairs (people's sovereignty) and on the principle of the separation of powers, or balance of power. These advanced democratic principles were later (1774) to serve as the foundation for the American and French revolutionaries' constitutions.

Paoli also built up the economic sector again. He had extensive parts of the swamps drained, popularized potato growing, and encouraged the cultivation of olive trees and chestnut trees, as well as corn.

To educate the Corsicans better, Paoli had elementary schools built, and in 1765, he founded a university in Corte, his seat of government. At the time, it accommodated 300 Corsican students of theology, philosophy, law, mathematics and medicine.

To continue boosting the economy, he founded a printing press and had coins minted. The latter were embossed with the head of a Moor; and the black Moor's head is still the best-known symbol of Corsica today. On November 24, 1762, Paoli decided the Moor's head should, as a symbol of resistance, adorn the country's official coat-of-arms.

The origin of the symbolic depiction of the Moor's head has been a headache for many a historian. The king of Aragon already had this symbol on his coat-of-arms. In the past, the Moors had supposedly blindfolded their prisoners with a white band as a symbol of slavery. Paoli then had the white blindfold pushed up onto the Moor's forehead as a symbol of freedom.

Paoli's Struggle Against Genoa and France

Parallel to all these revolutionary reforms, Paoli continued the fight against the weakened Genoese. The first thing he did was to expand Paoliville (the present-day Ile Rousse) into a harbor which could rival that of Calvi, a town still loyal to

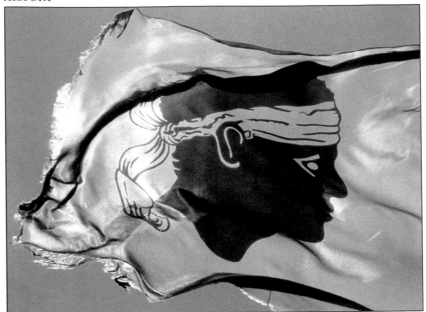

Genoa. Except for a few bases, the Corsicans soon managed to drive the Genoese from the island and stabilize their independence. As a result, the Genoese senate decided to sell its rights to the island to France. On May 15, 1768, the two powers sealed the deal in the Treaty of Versailles.

One can easily imagine that the Corsicans felt like "a herd of sheep being sold." Just a week after the treaty had been signed, Paoli called a national assembly. It was unanimously decided that the island would defend itself to the utmost and that war should be declared on France. The most fervent speaker at this gathering was Carlo Bonaparte, Paoli's secretary and Napoleon's father.

Under the command of Marbeuf, the French invaded Corsica. Paoli quickly assembled a militia of 4,000 men, and initially fought against the French in the north. Even the strongest and bravest Corsicans, however, hardly had a chance against the powerful and, more importantly, better-equipped Frenchmen; Cap Corse was, therefore, soon captured by the French.

Paoli and his troops retreated in the direction of Corte to seal off the capital. On May 8, 1769, the French defeated the Corsicans in a large-scale attack (15,000 soldiers!) near Ponte Novu at the lower reaches of the river Golo. After this defeat, Paoli attempted to prevent the French from penetrating into Casinca and the Castagniccia, but in June, 1769, the Corsican people were ultimately defeated by the French. The Corsican freedom fighters had to flee into exile, among them Paoli, who spent the next 21 years in England.

French Rule

In 1769, a year marked by the chaos of war and Corsica's defeat, Napoleon Bo-

Above: The Moor's head with the band of freedom on the Corsican flag. Right: Napoleon Bonaparte was born on Corsica in 1769.

naparte, the future emperor, was born in Ajaccio on August 15.

At the time, the island was under the administration of Count Marbeuf, who was glad to support the offspring of families with French sympathies by granting them scholarships. Letizia, Napoleon's mother, was richly blessed with eight children and quickly became friends with Marbeuf. He sent three Bonaparte children, Napoleon among them, to France with scholarships. Even Letizia's husband, Carlo, once an advocate of Corsican liberation, quickly saw which way the wind was blowing and went over to the flag of France.

Corsica's enthusiasm for Napoleon, today found mainly in his native town, is difficult to comprehend. After Napoleon had gotten a taste of the wide world, he did virtually nothing for his native island. On the contrary: he accelerated the process of centralism in 1811 by making Corsica a *département* with Ajaccio as its sole capital. Corsica is still suffering from this today.

In addition, he did everything to make Corsica as French as possible. For instance, he sent gifted Corsican young people to schools and universities in France so that they would be imprinted with a lasting impression and the influence of that country.

After he left Corsica, he visited the island only twice, in 1793 and 1799, and then turned his back on it forever to make a career in France.

Paoli, on the other hand, never forgot his island. He returned to Corsica during the French Revolution, at which time every Corsican in exile was granted an amnesty. After 21 years he landed at Cap Corse in Macinaggio and was given a grand reception by the people. Because of his services, the French revolutionary government even designated him chief administrator of Corsica.

Paoli, however, soon fell out of favor with Paris because he could not warm up to the bloody politics of the revolutionaries. He then asked England for help in 1793, and together with Admiral Nel-

son's navy he was able to drive the French out of St-Florent, Bastia and Calvi. In 1794, Corsica was declared part of the British Empire. The British king George III, however, appointed Sir Elliot viceroy and not Paoli, much to the Corsicans' disgust.

Under pressure from the French, the British left the island again two years later. Paoli had no choice but to return to his London exile. He died there on February 5, 1807, and was ceremoniously buried in Westminster Abbey. His corpse was transported to Corsica 82 years later (1889); he now rests in his birthplace in Morosaglia in the Castagniccia, in a chapel built especially for him.

In the 19th century, France paid virtually no attention to her island. Accordingly, the conditions became chaotic again: clan feuds and vendettas were in

Above: The French represented Corsican resistance as banditry (newspaper of 1900). Right: The tourist industry – too much in French hands?

full swing. The stronghold of the blood feuds at the time was Sartène, where entire city districts were fighting against each other. This left no time to improve the country's economy.

Napoleon III made initial attempts to help Corsica. He tried to drain the swamps on the east coast, hoping to keep malaria in check and thus help agriculture to flourish there again. In addition, he expanded the road system. The ban he placed on bearing arms, in an attempt to bring the vendettas and feuds under control, was virtually futile. The miserable situation resulted in an emigration wave which practically depopulated several villages.

Not until France marched into battle against Germany in World War I did anyone remember the fighting Corsicans. Approximately 30,000 of them died under the French flag in this war; that was close to a quarter of all halfway adult men. The listings on monuments to those killed in action, which can be found in almost every little village, are often longer than those of the current lists of inhabitants.

In the aftermath of war, the island's economy continued to decline. There were hardly any men at all in the villages, the women found no one to marry, and the younger generation had little or no interest in recultivating the devastated fields and repairing the houses that had fallen into ruin. Once again, hordes of Corsicans left their island; during this time, the nearby town of Marseilles grew to become the world's largest Corsican enclave. Many sons of the island served in the French colonial army, mostly in North Africa.

Although the island had still not recovered from World War I when World War II broke out, Corsican men were again supposed to fight and die for France, a country they hardly knew. Charles de Gaulle ordered a mobilization of all Corsican men between the ages of

20 and 28 to send them to battle for the *Grande Nation*.

After 1942, German and Italian troops occupied the island. On the east coast, Germans and Americans engaged in battle. At that time, Bastia was bombed, and then the railway line, just completed in 1935, was also destroyed; it's never been rebuilt. The first French *département* to be liberated, Corsica was freed by French troops, with the help of the resistance movement, on September 10, 1943.

The Americans tried to help the Corsicans back to their feet after World War II by the extensive use of DDT, which finally eliminated malaria from the island, and by draining the swamps.

In the mid-1950s, Corsica had reached an absolute low in population; barely 160,000 inhabitants were counted, compared to 270,000 in 1880. Displaced colonial Frenchmen from Tunisia, Algeria and Morocco – some of Corsican heritage – reacted quickly and began taking hold of the now cultivable land on the

east coast; with the help of government subsidies, they created flourishing, modern farmlands there. Among Corsicans, this gave rise to envy and a sense of being infiltrated from without. In addition, many Maghreb farm workers entered the country, following in the footsteps of the *pieds noirs* (former colonial Frenchmen).

After poor economic decisions had hurt the island and the sense of national identity had reached rock bottom, the pendulum began to swing back: the following years saw the beginnings of strivings for Corsican autonomy, which continue to the present day.

In the eyes of local patriots, the island's politics and economy – particularly the tourist industry – are much too strongly dominated by France. The radical Corsican National Liberation Front, FLNC – now divided and fighting among itself – has repeatedly underlined its desire for independence with bombings. The background of this *Corsica Nostra* movement is explained in a feature on page 220.

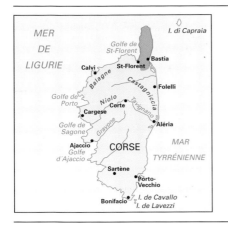

BAROQUE BASTIA, RUGGED CAP CORSE

BASTIA

CAP CORSE

ST-FLORENT

PATRIMONIO

BASTIA

"In Bastia you work, in Ajaccio you live." That is how the citizens of Ajaccio poke fun at their eternal rivals – and if this comment sounds spiteful, there is probably a grain of truth in it, since Bastia is the most prosperous city on Corsica. Since the end of the 19th century, its port has been the largest on the island: well over half of Corsica's trade goes in and out of Bastia's port, and this is also where most ferry passengers disembark. This makes Bastia one of the most important ports in the Mediterranean.

An adjacent residential and industrial area (cigarettes, food and furniture industries) extends 12 miles (20 km) to the south. It is part of the ten communes comprising greater Bastia, where lives half of the entire population of the province Haute-Corse.

With a population of 38,000, Bastia is significantly smaller than Ajaccio, but the Bastians refuse to accept this. If you inquire at the city information office about the number of inhabitants, the woman behind the counter will answer self-confidently: "Bastia is certainly larger than Ajaccio... and if the figures say something different– well, Bastia *seems* larger in any case."

One thing is certain: Bastia is the Corsican city with the most Italian flair. The Genoese built the first walls here to found a city, and even today, Bastia maintains important trade relations with Genoa, Livorno, La Spezia and Piombino.

Archaeological finds confirm that the first human settlement here was around 1500 BC. The Romans founded the small colony of *Mantinon* here, and it was abandoned in the 6th century because it could not stand up to the Vandals' attacks. At the beginning of Genoese colonialization, Biguglia, today a small village in the countryside south of Bastia, was the seat of the Genoese governor. After the rebelling Corsicans had burned the former capital to the ground, the Genoese searched for another location on the coast, which would allow them easier access to their homeland. Governor Leonelli Lomellini chose the natural fishing harbor of Cardo in 1380 and had a *bastiglia* built on the easily defensible southern cliff; this "little bastion" gave rise to the name of modern-day Bastia. It wasn't until 1480 that Tomasino Campofregoso reinforced and expanded the bastion into a city.

Preceding pages: Bastia is Corsica's busiest city (views of the old and new harbors). Left: Parlor under the plaintains (Place St.-Nicolas).

Since then, the quarter around the old harbor and the extension to the north has been called Terra-Vecchia, while the area around the citadel goes by the name of Terra-Nova.

Under Genoese rule, Bastia was raised to the status of capital. The population rose from 1,500 towards the end of the 15th century to 10,500 in 1686 – quadrupling, in short, within two hundred years. This considerable population growth is clear indication of the good trade relations Bastia enjoyed with Genoa. The harbor was the link between Genoa and the richest economic regions of the island: Cap Corse, Balagne and the east coast plains. Even today, the town's large Baroque churches and splendidly decorated chapels attest to its former wealth.

During the Corsican wars of independence, in 1730, a peasant army 4,000 men strong plundered the lower part of the town, and the inhabitants fled to the island of Capraja.

After the French Revolution had triumphed all over Corsica, there began a wave of religious persecutions. In 1798, a revolt began in the Golo region, led by the 80-year-old Agostino Giafferi, as a reaction against the suppression of the church and its priests. As am identifying symbol, the followers of the movement wore a small white cross, for which reason the uprising was dubbed *La Crocetta.* Napoleon's brother Lucien, a politician with anti-clerical views, had the rebellion in Bastia put down. Giafferi was taken prisoner and shot to death on Place St-Nicolas in Bastia.

In 1796, the central French government divided Corsica into two departments, which made sense from an administrative point of view: Golo in the north, with Bastia as its capital, and Liamone in the south, with Ajaccio as its capital. The Emperor Napoleon, however, made his native Ajaccio the island's sole capital in 1811. Despite this degradation, Bastia

grew to be an important trade and industrial center.

In the 19th century, in the northern city district of Toga, iron foundries were built to process ore from the island of Elba. The iron was then exported to the steel mills near Lyon, France. However, these factories, with a total of 200 employees, were forced to shut down in 1885 because of rising transport costs. Work on the new harbor began in 1885, but it was not completed until approximately 50 years later. In 1975 the island was again separated into two departments, a division which has continued until today: Haute-Corse and Corse-du-Sud, with Bastia and Ajaccio as the respective capitals. Since then, the inhabitants of Bastia

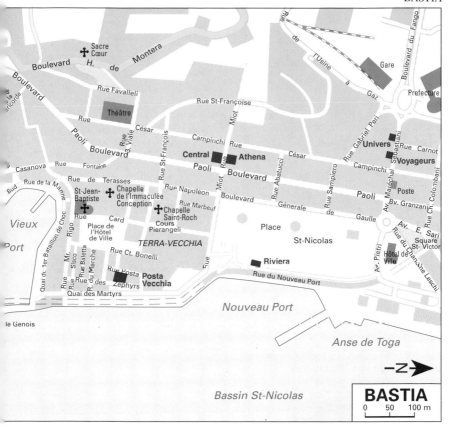

City Sightseeing Tour

After you've completed the long crossing on the night ferry, and the ship's belly has finally finished discharging its cargo of cars onto the dock of the new harbor, a wise move is to find the neighboring **Place St-Nicolas**, the main square, where you can partake of croissants and café au lait in the first rays of the morning sun. An hour or so later, the flow of tourists will have subsided, as the newly-disembarked caravans of mobile homes, automobiles, motorcycles, and bicyclists will have started on their way to Col de Teghime on the west coast or to the sandy beaches farther south on the east coast. All that will remain will be a few people curious enough to start out with a look round the city, and the Corsican retirees who observe the hustle and bustle every morning from benches located a safe distance away.

Large Place St-Nicolas, lined with plane and palm trees, completed in the late 19th century, is an important meeting point for young and old alike. Two statues stand at the north and south ends of the square: a monument to the victims of the two World Wars, and Napoleon, rather sentimentally attired as Caesar, en-

can again proudly claim to live in a capital city, and can be more self-assured in their frequent arguments with their Ajaccio rivals.

church was built between 1636 and 1666; its interior is a typical example of Bastian Baroque. The interior decoration of the three-aisle basilica dates primarily from the 18th century: gold-leaf stucco work, carved choir stalls from 1781, and multi-colored marble work. The splendid main altar from Northern Italy dates back to 1844. The murals were done in the illusionist *trompe-l'oeil* technique, mainly depicting subjects relating to the church's patron saint, John the Baptist. The walls are decorated with marvelous paintings from the Fesch collection. There is a large bell hanging in front of the sacristy in the northern side aisle. If you ring it, the friendly pastor will let you enter the sacristy with its beautiful carved chestnut-wood furniture from the 18th century.

Leaving the church by the west portal, you can walk down the narrow steps to the **Vieux Port**, the old harbor. The picturesque little marina with yachts and sailboats is semi-circular in shape; it's a pleasant place to sit and unwind, watching the fishermen folding their nets while you drink a cup of coffee or sample an *aziminu*, the Corsican bouillabaisse, Algerian couscous, or Moroccan *tagine* in one of the inviting harborside restaurants. The crumbling facades, the exposed electric wiring and the obviously added-on bathrooms all give the scene a certain melancholy charm – renovations, however, are already underway. Allowing your gaze to roam across the house facades, you see Bastia's landmark, the Baroque facade of St-Jean-Baptiste with its twin towers. If you want to photograph its unusual southern facade, which rises up above the harbor like a theater backdrop, you're likely to find the best angle from which to capture it on film at the citadel.

Following the **Quai du Sud** into the Terra-Nova quarter, you can go halfway up a flight of stairs to a small park on the left, the **Jardin Romieu**, or keep going

circled by palm trees. There is also a small pavilion for music ensembles in the center of the square. A small rectangular building at the square's north end houses the tourist information office.

Those who would rather take home a genuine Corsican specialty than a plastic Napoleon should not miss the *Cap Corse* store, located west of the square on **Boulevard Général de Gaulle** amidst delightful street cafés. Leaving the square from the south side, you can walk across the **Cours Pierangeli** to the **Place de l'Hôtel de Ville**. The former city hall is on the west side of the square. Many Bastians meet here every morning to shop at the busy market, which makes it a great place to listen in on conversations to get a taste of the Corsican idiom.

On the west side of the market square is the church of **St-Jean-Baptiste**, supported by flying buttresses. This parish

Above: Tower of the Genoese Governor's Palace. Right: Market on the Place de l'Hôtel de Ville in Bastia.

up the stairs to the top and go left through a gateway completed during the reign of Louis XV to the **Place du Donjon**. This centrally located square was named after the city's first defensive tower. Located here is the former **Governor's Palace** (1530), which now houses the **Ethnographic Museum of Corsica**; the latter provides an informative introduction to a Corsica trip.

The first room presents the geology of the island with a few mineralogical exhibits, such as various types of marble, porphyry, serpentine, alabaster and granite. Archaeological findings are displayed in the following rooms, among them an unusual, marble child's sarcophagus. The various stages of Corsica's history are illustrated with objects and documents from the 18th and 19th centuries. In the last room, you're afforded an interesting view into traditional life on Corsica with a Nativity scene, or crèche, made of woven palm leaves. Stairs lead up to the second floor, where the Carlini collection is exhibited. Carlini, a former

mayor of Marseilles, donated this collection, which includes paintings from the Ancien Régime, the Revolution, and the Empire. In spite of the interesting exhibits, don't pass up the opportunity to glance out of the window. The governor's palace offers the best view of the old harbor and St-Jean-Baptiste church. The conning tower of the submarine *Casabianca* can be seen in the courtyard; commanded by Captain Herminier, it made history in the battle to liberate Corsica in 1944.

You can reach the church of **Sainte-Marie** by way of Rue Notre Dame. Today, it is still popularly called a "cathedral" because it carried out that function from 1570 until the seat of the bishop was moved to Ajaccio in 1801. The body of it was built between 1570 and its consecration on July 17, 1625. Notice the different colors of stone in the interior: white marble from Carrara, blue from Corte and red from Oletta. The impression here is of a harmonious Baroque ensemble of the 17th and 18th centuries. Above the

high altar, there's a painting by Leonoro d'Aquiladie depicting the *Assumption of the Virgin* (1512). In the right side chapel there is an intricately carved marble statue of the Virgin Mary and child, which once stood in the former cathedral, La Canonica. The attraction in the right side aisle is the beaten-silver relief of the Assumption of the Virgin Mary, which is kept behind glass; a work of the Sienese artist Gaetano Macchi, it dates from 1856. The beloved Madonna is carried in an annual procession through the citadel and Terra-Vecchia every August 15. The church's large organ was manufactured by the firm of the Serassi brothers in Bergamo, and was installed and dedicated in 1845. In addition, there are a few paintings by Italian artists from the Fesch collection.

Upon leaving the church and taking an immediate right onto Rue de l'Evêché, you reach the inconspicuous entrance

Above: Attempts to save the city's original buildings are coming at the eleventh hour.

gate to the **Chapelle Sainte-Croix** after approximately 55 yards (50 m). The French writer Prosper Mérimée, who was in Corsica in 1840 as *Inspecteur Général des Monuments Historiques de France*, put this Rococo gem under historic preservation in the same year. Visitors are received in a blue-and-gold room with stucco decor in the style of Louis XV. These marvelous appointments were added in the course of renovations beginning in 1758. Of interest is the altarpiece; a depiction of the Annunciation by Giovanni Bilivert (1633). But the actual attraction in this small chapel is the *Christ des Miracles*, a blackened wooden crucifix flanked by two figures of fishermen. According to legend, in 1428 this holy cross was burning and drifting about in the sea when it was recovered by the two sardine fishermen Camulgi and Giuliani, and then borne in an improvised procession to the cathedral. It is certain that there has been a chapel on this location since 1490 and that, since then, a procession through the citadel has been held every year on May 3, when the fishermen sacrifice their first catch of the year – as tradition demands.

Before leaving the citadel, make sure you take the time to stroll across idyllic **Guasco Square**, located about 110 yards (100 m) further on, in the direction of the museum. By way of the Jardin Romieu and the old harbor, you can return to the quarter of Terra-Vecchia.

Located at the end of Rue des Terrasses is the humble-looking **Chapel of the Immaculate Conception**; construction was begun in 1589. The rich interior decoration, with wooden paneling and wine-colored damask and velvet wall coverings from Genoa, dates from the 18th century, and is not unlike the auditorium of an elegant theater. Most interesting object here is the chapel's main altar, which dates from 1624.

The altarpiece depicts the Immaculate Conception of the Virgin Mary and was a product of the school of the Spanish Baroque painter Bartolomé Murillo. On the left side there is a statue of the Madonna, which is ceremoniously carried in a procession through the old city to the church St-Jean-Baptiste every year on September 8. The sacristy, also to the left of the altar, contains a small museum of religious art objects from the 15th to the 19th centuries: a couple of the more interesting displays include a luminous missal from 1685 sitting on a lectern in the form of an angel, or the 18th-century statue of St. Erasmus, patron saint of fishermen. It's here, in the sacristy, that you'll find the light switches for the otherwise dark chapel.

Just a few steps farther down Rue Napoleon is the **Saint-Roch Chapel** from 1604, with works by Ligurian masters and an altar by the Florentine artist Giovanni Bilivert.

Continuing down the street, you reach Place St-Nicholas again after a few minutes. But don't end your sightseeing tour just yet; there are still the city's two main shopping streets, the **Boulevard Paoli** and **Rue César Campinchi**, to explore, crowds and all. Not far away, at the intersection of Boulevard Paoli and Avenue Maréchal Sébastiani, is Bastia's main post office. Heading out of the city, Avenue Sébastiani runs past the train station after about another 220 yards (200 m). From here, you can take the legendary Corsican railway to Corte, Ajaccio and Calvi.

Driving along the Boulevard Paoli in the opposite direction, to the south, you can glimpse another noteworthy building: the 19th-century Palais de Justice, with its colonnade of blue marble.

CAP CORSE

Rugged **Cap Corse** (*Capi Corsu*) is often described in travel literature as the thumb of a fist or as a compass needle pointing directly north. It could just as well be called Corsica in miniature, since the geography of this large peninsula is certainly comparable to that of the rest of Corsica. Among other things, Cap Corse is notorious for the strong winds that blow virtually at any time of day or night, especially at the northern extremity of the peninsula. In the winter, the winds are usually humid – the *sirocco* and the *grecale* – and blow from the southeast and northeast, while at other times of year you can test your endurance against the southwest wind (*libecciu*) or the north wind (*tramontane*). These winds are also responsible for the severe fires which rage through the landscape every year. The last two devastating fires, which didn't even spare the gardens of houses, happened in 1990 and 1994.

As in the main part of Corsica, there is a central mountain ridge of crystalline slate running through Cap Corse; highest point is **Monte Stello**, measuring 4,273 feet (1,307 m). This ridge, serving as both a watershed and a meteorological divide, drops in the south to the pass of

Teghime (1,752 feet/536 m), which is traversed by the D 81 from St-Florent to Bastia. This road also forms the southern border of Cap Corse.

To the east and west, the countryside here is crisscrossed with brooks and streams; to the east, as they flow toward the sea, they create lovely valley landscapes. The towns on Cap Corse adapted to geographic conditions, and most of the communities are divided into two parts. The original towns are located high in the mountains at the sources of the streams, while their respective harbor settlements developed at the point where these streams flow into the sea; in Corsican, these harbor towns are called *marina*. Narrow roads link each *marina* with its sister town in the mountains. Most of the roads leading inland from the coast of Cap Corse are dead-ends, ending in whichever town is associated with a given marina.

If you're driving around Cap Corse, there are only two short-cuts, and these are only in the north. One of them is near Santa Severa, where the D 180 leads from the east coast through Luri to Pino. The second one is located some 4 miles (7 km) farther north. From Marina de Meria, you can take the D 35 to Morsiglia and continue on to the west coast. To drive around Cap Corse, you should allow either one very long day or, proceeding at a more relaxing pace, plan to take two days with an overnight in Macinaggio or Centuri-Port.

Although it is only about 70 miles (110 km) around Cap Corse from Bastia to St-Florent, it is very difficult to make good time – mainly because of the narrow, winding roads on the west coast. Only a small percentage of tourists to Corsica spend their vacation on Cap Corse, which explains why there are so few hotels, hardly any gas stations, and virtually no banks at all.

Leaving Bastia in a northerly direction, you pass through the industrial area of **Toga**, where huge blast furnaces once stood and where today's cork-processing industry is located. Traffic lets up within a few miles, and you pass Bastia's beautiful villa suburbs located directly on the coast.

The first easily accessible beach is in **Miomo**. It can boast a well-restored and photogenic Genoese tower at the north end. Shortly thereafter, you pass through the town of **Lavasina**, a small pilgrimage town with the 17th-century church of **Notre-Dame-des-Grâces**. Unfortunately, a concrete bell tower was added to this church in the 20th century. On the inside, there is a Renaissance painting from the school of Perugino (16th century) hanging above the monumental black-and-white marble altar. The painting depicts the Madonna of Lavasina, and attracts flocks of Corsicans in a pilgrimage every September 8.

Take your first break of the day in the little fishing village of **Erbalunga**. You can safely leave your car in the large parking lot on the left side of the road; from here, it's an easy walk to the picturesque town, where cars are not allowed. The magnificent houses testify to the former wealth of Cap Corse. As early as the Middle Ages, the inhabitants of the cape maintained trade relations with Pisa, and later with Genoa, Livorno, Marseilles and other European ports. Control of the cape was divided between the Avogari di Gentile family of Erbalunga and the Da Mare family of Rogliano. Both of them were loyal vassals of Genoa.

Even today, you can clearly distinguish elements of the Tuscan dialect in the local brand of Corsican, and visitors from northern Italy are often more easily understood on Cap Corse than the French. Trade, especially with Genoa, brought prosperity to the area. Natural mineral resources were mined, such as copper near Cardo and antinomy near Luri, Meria and Ersa. An iron foundry

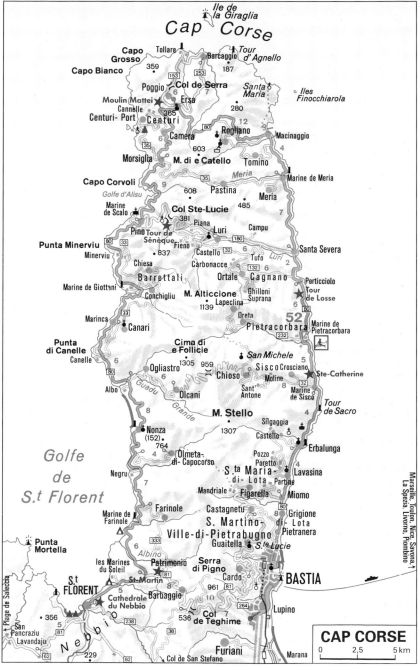

Ile de la Giraglia

Cap Corse

Capo Grosso
Tollare
Barcaggio
Tour d' Agnello
Capo Bianco
359
187
153
253
Poggio
Col de Serra
Santa Maria
Iles Finocchiarola
Moulin Mattei
Ersa
6
7
Cannelle
365
280
Centuri- Port
Centuri
Camera
Rogliano
12
80
Macinaggio
603
4
35
6
Morsiglia
M. di e Catello
Tomino
Capo Corvoli
Meria
Marine de Meria
9
608
Pastina
35
Meria
Golfe d'Alisu
485
7
Marine de Scalo
Col Ste-Lucie
381
Piana
Luri
Campu
Pino
Tour de Sénèque
Fieno
180
Punta Minerviu
80
33
6
Castello
32
Luri
Santa Severa
Minerviu
837
Tufo
2
Chiesa
Carbonacce
132
6
Barrettali
Ortale
Cagnano
Marine de Giottani
Ghilloni
Porticciolo
Conchigliu
M. Alticcione
Suprana
Tour de Losse
1139
Lapeclina
6
80
Marinca
33
Oreta
52
Marine de Pietracorbara
Canari
Pietracorbara
232
Punta di Canelle
Cima di e Follicie
San Michele
Canelle
1305
959
Sisco
Crosciano
6
Ogliastro
Chioso
Moline
Ste-Catherine
80
6
Sant'
8
Marine de Sisco
32
Albo
Olcani
Antone
Tour de Sacro
8
M. Stello
4
Nonza
Sisgaggia
(152)
1307
764
Castello
Olmeta-di-Capocorso
Erbalunga
4
Pozzo
Golfe de S.t Florent
Poretto
Lavasina
Negru
S.ta Maria-di-Lota
4
7
Partine
Mandriale
Figarella
Miomo
Farinole
80
Marine de Farinole
Castagnetu
Grigione di- Lota
Punta Mortella
S. MARTINO-
Pietranera
VILLE-DI-PIETRABUGNO
333
6
Guaitella
S.te Lucie
les Marines du Soleil
Albino
Patrimonio
Serra di Pigno
BASTIA
St-Martin
81
8
Cardo
S.t FLORENT
Barbaggio
961
81
Cathédrale du Nebbio
Lupino
356
536
Col de Teghime
264
5
81
Nebbio
238
38
San Pancraziu
Lavandaju
229
Furiani
Marana
62
82
Col de San Stefano

CAP CORSE

0   2,5   5 km

processed ores from the island of Elba. The Corsicans exported wine, oil, wood and fish, trading these for fabric, construction materials and grain, which was ground in one of Cap Corse's numerous windmills. Until the end of the 19th century, this area was among the richest in all of Corsica. Afterwards, trade slowly came to a standstill; in addition, a plague of phylloxera practically brought wine export to a complete halt. It was no longer lucrative to mine natural resources because of the high transportation costs. This resulted in a large population exodus. There are still visible traces of this today: abandoned manor homes in the inland areas and overgrown fields. Not until just recently did people begin producing wine here again. The local vintage is more impressive for its quality than for its quantity, and it boasts the sought-after AOC distinction.

Above: "Non-smokers will die sometime, too." Right: Genoese watchtower in Miomo, Cap Corse.

Erbalunga used to be the most important export harbor on Cap Corse. The quiet fishing town, which has only a small pebble beach to show for itself, is known for its *Cerca* procession on Good Friday. The 4-mile (7 km) procession begins in the **St-Erasme** church at 7 am and goes through all the communities of the Brando district. In the evening, the faithful move in torchlight formations of traditional shapes, such as the *Granitola*, a spiraling shape resembling a snail, or the shape of a cross.

After Erbalunga, the countryside becomes wilder and the population sparser. Because of the annual fires in the dry period late in the summer, the slopes are mainly covered with bushy *garrigue* vegetation, a lower-growing variety of maquis with fewer species of plants.

When weather conditions are favorable, you can see the island of Capraja out in the sea to the east. A couple of miles north of **Marina de Sisco**, you can sometimes make out a statue of St. Catherine on the side of the island facing

away from the sea. A road branches off here and leads to a 15th-century Romanesque chapel of the same name. Anyone who wants to take a break from sightseeing and go for a refreshing dip in the sea can seek out the bathing cove, which curves for several hundred yards, in **Marina de Pietracorbara**.

Genoese Watchtowers

Not far past Marina de Pietracorbara, an excellently preserved example of a Genoese watchtower appears on your left, the **Tour de Losse**.

Similar Genoese watchtowers line the Corsican coast with pleasing regularity. Approximately 150 of these round towers were built between the rule of the Bank of St. Giorgio in the 15th century and the beginning of the 18th century. In this period, pirates from northern Africa were causing havoc on the island. In the 16th century alone, 6,000 Corsicans are said to have been abducted and taken to Algeria as slaves. Genoa was concerned about its revenue from its Corsican colony and decided to build towers around the whole island. They did little, however, in terms of financing the project. After the Genoese governor had chosen the individual locations, the communities had to provide the workers and come up with the building materials themselves. It was also the responsibility of the Corsicans to provide the guards (*torregiani*) to man the towers, and furnish them with weapons and provisions.

When an enemy ship appeared off the coast, the guard blew a conch-shell horn (*conca*). With this timely warning, the population could retreat to the hills or, as on Cap Corse for instance, seek refuge in a square tower in the interior of the island. The guards' next duty was to spread the news to the next tower by means of a signal fire, since the towers were positioned in sight of each other. This made it possible to send a warning around the entire island within a few hours.

Generally round, these towers (*torre*) were always built according to the same plan. Consisting of two rooms one above the other, they are between 39 and 55 feet (12 and 17 m) high and between 26 and 45 feet (8 and 14 m) in diameter. There is an opening in the middle, about 16 feet (some 5 m) up. Thus, you could only enter the tower by means of a ladder, which was pulled up whenever danger seemed to be threatening. The small room, with embrasure-type openings, was manned by at least two guards at all times. There is a cistern in the lower part for longer sieges. Square towers such as those in Nonza or Porto are exceptions, or date from the Pisan epoch.

There are still approximately 90 watchtowers along the coast of Corsica today; some however, are no more than picturesque ruins. Not until a few years ago did the French government place them under historic preservation. Since that time, they have either been sold or leased to private individuals under strictly imposed conditions for renovation. Even the popular and much-photographed Tour de Losse is privately owned.

Before long, you reach the town of **Santa Severa**. Here, you have your first chance to cross over to the west coast by taking the D 80. If, instead, you follow the D 180 farther along the east coast, you arrive at the small tourist town of **Macinaggio** with a marina, restaurants and cafés. The harbor was an important military base until well into the 18th century because it was better protected than the harbor in Bastia. During the wars of independence, Pasquale Paoli besieged the natural harbor in 1757, but he was not able to conquer it until four years later. In 1761, Paoli started expanding the town of Macinaggio to convert it into his naval base. It was from here that, on February 16, 1767, with an expedition army of 200 men, he launched an attack on the island

of Capraja, which was still in the hands of Genoa. His victory over the Genoese on Capraja marked the end of Genoese rule on Corsica.

Some 29 years later, on July 14, 1790, Paoli returned to Macinaggio on his way back from his exile in England. The Corsicans greeted Paoli enthusiastically and escorted him to Bastia. There are memorial plaques with names of famous visitors on the old houses along the wharf: Pasquale Paoli 1790, Napoleon Bonaparte, May 10, 1773, and Empress Eugénie, December 2, 1869. The generously proportioned harbor, capable of accommodating 500 yachts, is also worth seeing.

Leaving the east coast, the road now wends its winding way towards the west coast. Lining the road here are strawberry trees (*arbousier*), which are eye-catching in autumn when they're hung with their red fruit. After a short drive you see the picturesque village of **Rogliano** on the left, clinging to the slope of **Monte Poggio**, 1,461 feet (447 m) high. The mighty towers and terraced fields of this somewhat sleepy hamlet are reminders of its great history and the wealth it once possessed.

First settled by the Romans, the town was initially named – after the Roman emperor Aurelian (3rd century) – *Pagus Aurelianus*. The modern-day name Rogliano is probably a derivative thereof. Rogliano was the main residence of the Da Mare family from the 12th to the 16th centuries; their 12th-century fortress, **San Colombano**, is nothing but a ruin today. Directly adjacent to it is the **St. François Monastery**, which dates from the 16th century. More and more of the town's trim little houses are being renovated as vacation homes, making the town a lively place – at least in the summer months. For access, follow the one-way D 53, which is also known as the *Chemin de l'Impératrice* (The Empress's Path).

Right: Centuri-Port on Cap Corse in the light of sunset.

The French empress Eugénie, Napoleon III's wife, paid Rogliano a visit on December 2, 1869. She was returning from the inauguration of the Suez Canal on her yacht, *L'Aigle*. A storm forced her to go ashore in Macinaggio and the empress walked to the town of Rogliano: after this strenuous activity, she financed the paving of the road out of her own pocket.

Shortly before you reach the west coast, you can, in **Ersa**, turn off to make the trip all the way to the northernmost tip of the island. This little tour to the tip of the island and back to Ersa is 9 miles (15.5 km) long and takes you through the lonely fishing village of **Barcaggio**, which has a small sandy beach and a hotel known for its tasty seafood. From Barcaggio, there is a good view of the small island of Giraglia and its lighthouse.

From Ersa, the D 80 brings you quickly to **Col de Serra**. Here, you should take a short walk and visit the **Mattei Mill**, the only remaining windmill on Cap Corse. The aperitif company Mattei renovated it for advertising purposes and uses it as a kind of billboard. While the mill is certainly picturesque, the frequent winds that buffet this exposed point, 1,321 feet high (404 m), make picnicking here an adventurous and not very pleasant endeavor.

For this reason, the nearby town of **Centuri-Port** is a better place to eat, or simply hang out. This affluent town, which mainly lives off crayfish and tourism, is reachable by following the D 80 for approximately 1 mile (1.5 km) and then taking the narrow D 35, which branches off towards the sea. This fishing village, which was mentioned by the Roman historiographer Pliny and which Paoli expanded into a military base, is one of the most beautiful places on Cap Corse. Finding accommodations is not a problem here, and one has the impression that there is a restaurant or café in every house.

Continuing the trip farther south, after almost 2 miles (3 km) you can see on the hillside the Monastery of the Annunciation (16th century), which has been abandoned since 1907. As you drive along the delightful, scenic countryside on the coast you cannot help noticing the large, square towers that were built as refuges against Saracen attacks.

Once in Pino, it is worth taking a little detour to the **Seneca Tower**. Upon entering the town, take the D 180 towards the east coast, and after 3 miles (5 km) you'll reach the **Col de Ste.-Lucie** (1,245 feet/381 m). To get to the foot of the Seneca Tower, take the small road directly behind the chapel, through the laricio pines; before long you'll come to a dilapidated building that housed a children's home from 1925 to 1985. From this point on you have to proceed on foot along a clearly visible path. You should allow about an hour to walk there and back. From the tower you have a breathtaking view out over the Gulf of Aliso and the northernmost tip of the island. On a clear day you can see the islands of Capraja and Elba off in the hazy distance.

The philosopher, politician and poet Lucius Annaeus Seneca was exiled to Corsica in 41 A.D. at the age of 39 by emperor Claudius because he ostensibly seduced Claudius's niece. According to legend, Seneca is said to have spent his eight-year exile in this tower; but this is, in fact, hardly possible, as the tower was not built until the 15th or 16th century. The Stoic, accustomed to Roman comforts, was more likely to have lived in the colonies of Aléria or Mariana. A type of Mediterranean stinging nettle that grows here is called *Ortica di Seneca*. According to Corsican tales, the moral philosopher was caught in an intimate moment with a young Corsican beauty by the relatives of the woman in question, and they punished him by whipping him with stinging nettles.

Right: Nonza sits on a cliff 200 meters above the ocean.

Large eucalyptus trees welcome you back to **Pino**. In the gardens there are huge family mausoleums, some of which are more impressive than the residential buildings. These, as well as eulogies to the dead, illustrate the significance of death, ancestry, and heritage in Corsican tradition.

The 15-mile stretch (25 km) between Pino and Nonza is perhaps the wildest one on Cap Corse. The narrow road, more than 325 feet (100 m) above the sea in some places, winds its way along the coastline.

Shortly before arriving in Nonza you pass a large, deserted factory – an asbestos mine that has been sitting inoperative since 1965. Its slag and run-off, which the locals claim is perfectly "safe," color the dark beaches along this section of coast.

You can see **Nonza** from a good way off. The town stands alone in all its splendor on top of a 654-foot-high (200 m) cliff towering out of the sea. The square Genoese tower made of greenish serpentine rock is not only a landmark, but also the center of attraction. After a steep, ten-minute climb up to the tower, you are rewarded with a fabulous view of the dark-gray pebble beach, which extends for miles.

The history of the tower is closely linked to the Corsicans' passionate, and heroic, love for their country. When the French came to Nonza in 1768, they assumed that 200 of Paoli's followers were hiding in this tower. In fact, only the aged captain Casella had barricaded himself inside. Tricky as he was, he fired all the guns simultaneously, thereby instilling obedient respect into the 1,200 French soldiers. He negotiated with the French, who guaranteed him that he and his army would be escorted to Paoli's headquarters with military honors. Casella agreed to this deal, surrendered, and left the tower by himself, as the perplexed Frenchmen looked on.

Nonza's 16th-century church, **Ste-Julie**, has a Baroque marble altar of Italian origin (1694), as well as a painting of the crucified Julia, the patron saint of Corsica. Supposedly a girl from Nonza, she is said to have been tortured to death under Diocletian in the 4th century for steadfastly refusing to participate in a pagan festival. Her breasts were cut off and fell to the ground, and on this very spot a miraculous spring appeared. The 154 steps opposite the church lead to the gray beach, and you reach the refreshing spring after only 54 steps.

ST-FLORENT

The fishing village of St-Florent, with almost 1,400 inhabitants, lies on the **Gulf of St-Florent** at the deepest part of the inlet. The Romans founded the city of *Nebium* on this spot, which had already been settled since the Neolithic period. The Genoese built a citadel at the malaria-infested mouth of the Aliso River in 1439 and enlarged the harbor into a base for its naval and merchant fleet. Strategically speaking, **St-Florent** (*San Fiurenzu*) has an advantageous maritime location, which is why it has always been bitterly fought over. The town served as a garrison for Genoa until the seafaring republic gave it up in 1667 because of the constant danger of war and malaria infestation. St-Florent then remained deserted for 200 years. Napoleon III started draining the swamps, but the malaria mosquitoes prevailed until World War II.

The **marina**, built in 1971, contributed to St-Florent's rising from the ashes to flourish as a tourist town. From May to October, the harbor promenade and the alleyways of the old city are teeming with visitors. There is a sandy beach 1.2 miles (2 km) south of the harbor.

The old **Nebbio Cathedral**, Santa Maria Assunta, is located about half a mile (1 km) east of the city and is worth a visit. You can get the key to the south portal from the tourist office by leaving an ID card as security. The church of Santa Maria Assunta was the seat of the

bishop from the 4th century until into the 19th century. Not until 1814 was the diocese affiliated with Ajaccio. Along with La Canonica on the east coast, it is one of the most important Pisan Romanesque buildings on Corsica. The edifice was built in the first half of the 12th century on the site of an early Christian basilica that had been destroyed by the Saracens in the 8th century. The elegant, harmonious proportions of the current building are noteworthy. The capitals on either side of the main entrance are executed in high relief: on the right is a reclining, snarling lion; on the left there are two snakes wound around each other. Each of the basilica's three aisles is separated from the next one by six pillars or columns, where most of the decorative sculpture is concentrated. The capitals have various reliefs: snakes, ram's heads, lions, shells and buds. Parts of the marvelous frescoes from the 14th and 15th centuries have been freed from underneath the Baroque stucco work that adorns the vaulted apse.

Here, too, is the wooden figure of San Fiurenzu (St. Flor), whose remains are kept in a glass reliquary in the right aisle. The identity of the saint is controversial; Saint Flor was either the first bishop of Nebbiu, who missionized throughout this region in the second century, or the skeleton belongs to a Roman warrior who was martyred by Diocletian at the end of the 3rd century. Whoever he was, San Fiurenzu is the patron saint of both cathedral and city. The abbreviation C.S.F.M. inscribed on the reliquary stands for *Clément à Saint-Florus Martyr*.

The most inviting beach in the area, **Plage de Saleccia**, is hidden in the barren foothills of the **Agriates**: you get to it by going 7 miles (12 km) along a side road that branches off from the D 81 at Casta. This extremely poor route leads to the picturesque sandy cove of Saleccia (campground with café).

Above: The remains of St. Flor in the cathedral of the Nebbio near St-Florent. Right: The Patrimonio is known for its wines.

NEBBIO AND PATRIMONIO

The **Nebbio** region encompasses the countryside of the Aliso River basin (9.3 by 2.4 miles/15 x 4 km), and is surrounded by mountains with altitudes of between 1,960 and 4,900 feet (600 to 1,500 m). The Nebbio region is bordered by the Gulf of St-Florent, the Teghime Pass, the Stefano Pass and the Asto mountains. Its name derives from the Latin word *nebula*, morning fog, since cloud formations often pile up over the mountain crest of southern Cap Corse. This area, known for its mild climate, good soil, and protected from strong winds, is ideal for wine-producing, olive groves and fruit orchards. No wonder the locals call it *Conca d'Oru* (shell of gold).

On the edge of this fertile shell-shaped basin winds a narrow, enticing little road, the D 62. Combined with the D 81 (starting in St-Florent) and the D 82 on the way back, this forms part of a pleasant Nebbio round-trip. It leads through the old Nebbio villages of **Santo-Pietro-di-Tenda** (with a Romanesque church), **Piève** (menhirs next to the parish church) and **Rapale** (the dilapidated 13th-century mountain chapel of San Cesario). From here, you can also take a detour to the famous church of San Michele at Murato (for description, see page 68). Crossing the **Col de San Stefano** (1,203 feet/368 m), you pass the nicely situated village of **Oletta**, the monastery ruins of St. François, and a renowned pottery before returning to St-Florent.

The **Patrimonio wine-growing region** (*Patrimoniu*) is located at the northern end of the Nebbio region and on the southern foothills of the Cap Corse slopes. It is famous for its fine location and its excellent red, rosé, white and muscatel wines. In the prosperous village of **Patrimonio** itself, there is a wine-tasting bar in practically every house; don't miss the opportunity to do some wine-tasting.

The seven-foot-tall (2.29 m) limestone menhir **Nativu** is reminiscent of the Corsican Megalithic period, some 3,000 years ago. It stands at the entrance to the town on the left, well-protected by a sheltering roof. The menhir, found during construction work in 1964, had been underground for centuries and is therefore in excellent condition; you can still see shoulders, ears, nose and chin. It is dated to the first millennium B.C. At that time, the Torreans had already driven the megalithic peoples from the southwest to the north, where they peacefully settled; for this reason, this menhir doesn't display any depictions of weapons.

Picturesquely located on a hill at the edge of the village of Patrimonio is the church of **St-Martin**. Because of its exposed position, it is one of the most-photographed churches on Corsica; the best perspective is a bit farther uphill from the D 81. Construction is thought to have started in 1570, but the church was thoroughly renovated between 1801 and 1810. The bell tower dates from this period. While the side and east facades are plain and without decoration, the west side has Baroque forms which confer a unique note upon the whole church. The numerous holes on the facade were there to support the scaffolding during construction, and were simply left uncovered after the church was completed.

If you want to end your Cap Corse round-trip in Bastia, continue on the D 81 – a magnificent road for panoramic views – over the **Teghime Pass**, 1,270 feet (536 m) high, which separates the Nebbio mountains from the Cap mountains. A memorial at the pass commemorates the liberation battles against the German occupation. A beautiful view opens up here: the Gulf of St-Florent, Patrimonio and the eastern coastal plains with the Étang of Biguglia and Bastia.

From the Col de Teghime, two lovely, winding mountain roads branch off here: the D 338 goes up to the look-out point of **Serra di Pigno**, while the D 38 leads back down to Oletta in the Nebbio region.

BASTIA
Accommodation
LUXURY: **Thalassa**, 39, Route du Cap, tel. 95315663, **L'Alivi**, Route du Cap, tel. 95316185. *MODERATE:* **Posta Vecchia**, 3, Rue Posta-Vecchia, tel. 95323238, **Voyageurs**, 9, Avenue Maréchal-Sébastiani, tel. 95310897/95316103, **Central**, 3, Rue Miot, tel. 95317112, **Napoléon**, 43-45, Bd Paoli, tel. 95316030/95317783. *BUDGET:* **Riviera**, 1 bis, Rue du Nouveau-Port, tel. 95310716, **Univers**, 3, Avenue Maréchal-Sébastiani, tel. 95310338.

Restaurants
There are good fish restaurants all along the old harbor. Fish specialties: **Chez Huguette**, le Vieux Port, tel. 95313760. Local cuisine: **Bistro du Port**, Rue Porta Vecchia, tel. 95321983. **La Taverne**, Rue Général Carbuccia, tel. 95311787

Museum
Musée Ethnographique, Citadel, Palais des Gouverneurs, Place du Donjon, tel. 95310912, opening times: summer: daily 9 am-noon and 2-6 pm, winter: daily 9 am-noon and 2-5:30 pm.

Transportation
BY AIR: **Air France/Air Inter**, 6, Avenue Emile Sari, tel. 95545495. Aéroport Bastia-Poretta, tel. 95545454.
BY BOAT: **harbor**, tel. 95310715, **S.N.C.M.**, Nouveau Port, tel. 95546699/95546688. **Corsica Ferries**, 5, Bd. Chanoine-Leschi - B.P.239, tel. 95311809. **Moby Lines**, S.A.R.L. Colonna D'Istria et Fils, 4, Rue Commandant-Luce-de-Casabianda, tel. 95314629/ 95316247.
BY TRAIN: station / SNCF, Square Maréchal Leclerc, tel. 95328061/95326006. Trains run to Ajaccio, Corte and Calvi 4 times a day.
BUS: **Les Rapides Bleues/Eurocorse Voyages**, 1, Rue Maréchal Sébastiani, tel. 95310379.
TAXI: **Taxi de L'Aéroport**, tel. 95360465. **Radio Taxi Bastiais**, Place St-Nicolas, tel. 95340700.
RENTAL CAR: **Avis Ollandini**, Rue Salicetti, tel. 95325730, airport, tel. 95360356. **Budget**, Port de Toga, tel. 95317731, airport, tel. 95300504. **Hertz-Filippi Auto**, Square St-Victor, tel. 95311424, airport, tel. 95300500. **Eurodollar**, 5, Rue du Ch. Leschi, tel. 95326118, airport, tel. 95360364.

Hospital
Centre Hospitalier Général Paese Nuovo, Route Impérial, tel. 95551111.

Police
Tel. 95545022.

Sports
DIVING: **Neptune Club Bastiais**, 3, Rue du Commandant L'Herminier, tel. 95335635. **Campoloro Plongée Club**, Rue des Sérenades, tel. 95303115.

GOLF: **Bastia Golf Club - Castellarèse** - Route de L'Aéroport, 20290 Borgo, tel. 95383399.
MOUNTAIN BIKES: **Corsica Loisirs Aventures**, 31, Avenue Emile Sari, tel. 95325434.
RIDING: **Société Hippique Urbaine de Bastia**, Montesoro, tel. 95335308/95303762.
SAILING: **Club Nautique Bastiais**, Quai Sud du Vieux Port, tel. 95326733. **Plaisance Service Location**, Port de Toga, tel. 95314901.
SQUASH: **L'Orange Bleue**, Route du Fort de Toga.
TENNIS: Information: **Ligue Corse de Tennis de la Haute Corse**, 43, Rue César-Campinchi, tel. 95311400.

Tourist Information
Place Saint-Nicolas, tel. 95310089/95318134.

CAP CORSE
Accommodation
LAVASINA: *MODERATE:* **Les Roches**, tel. 95332657.
ERBALUNGA: *MODERATE:* **Castel Brando**, B.P.20, tel. 95301030/95339805.
MARINE DE SISCO: *MODERATE:* **U Pozzu**, tel. 95352117. *BUDGET:* **Hotel de la Marine**, tel. 95352104.
PORTICCIOLO: *MODERATE:* **Le Caribou**, tel. 95350233. *BUDGET:* **Torra Marina**, tel. 95350080. **U Patriarcu**, tel. 95350001.
MACINAGGIO: *MODERATE:* **U Libecciu**, Route de la Plage, tel. 95354322. **U Ricordu**, tel. 95354020. *BUDGET:* **Les Iles**, tel. 95354302.
BARCAGGIO: *MODERATE:* **La Giraglia**, tel. 95356054.
NONZA: *BUDGET:* **Auberge Patrizi**, tel. 95378216.

Campgrounds
MARINE DE SISCO: **Renajo**, tel. 95352114, 200 spaces. **A Casaiola**, tel. 95352150, 80 spaces.
SANTA SEVERA: **Santa Marina**, tel. 95320286, 100 spaces.
MACINAGGIO: **Camping de la Plage**, **U Stazzu**, Route de la Plage, tel. 95354376.
MORSIGLIA/CENTURI: **L'Isulottu**, tel. 95356281.

Restaurants
LAVASINA: *Corsican*: **Chez Auguste**, tel. 95332540.
ERBALUNGA: *Traditional*: **Chez Jo**, tel. 95339465. **U Fragnu**, tel. 95339323. **La Petite Auberge**, tel. 95332078. *Pizzeria*: **A Piazzetta**, tel. 95332869. **Pizza Anto**, tel. 95339470.
MACINAGGIO: *Corsican*: **U Colombu**, tel. 95354507. **Maison Bellini**, tel. 95354037. **La Vela d'Oro**, tel. 95354246. *Pizzeria*: **La Giraglia**, tel. 95354049. **U Lampione**, tel. 95354487.
PINO: **Les Platanes**, tel. 95351229.

NONZA: *Traditional*: **Le Pirate**, Route de la Plage, tel. 95378347. **U Franghju**, tel. 95378469.

Sports
DIVING: **Club Bleu Marine Compagnie**, Morsiglia, information at the campground L'Isulottu, tel. 95356046.
MOUNTAIN BIKES: **Technic Azur**, Macinaggio, tel. 95354499.
PARAGLIDING: **Cap Corse Parapente**, Canari, tel. 95378481/95378170, not for beginners.
RIDING: **U Cavallu Di Brandu**, Erbalunga, tel. 95339402. **U Cavallu Di Ruglianu**, Route de la Plage, Macinaggio, tel. 95354376.

ST-FLORENT
Accommodation
LUXURY: **Hotel du Golfe**, D 82 at the southern entrance to the city, with tennis courts and swimming pool, tel. 95371010. **Bellevue**, at the northern edge of the city, with tennis and swimming pool, tel. 95370006.
MODERATE: **Madame Mère**, swimming pool, tel. 95371420. **Tettola**, swimming pool, on the beach, tel. 95370853. *BUDGET:* **U Liamone**, Route de Treperi, tel. 95371281. **Le Montana**, Route d'Oletta, tel. 95371485.

Campground
Kalliste, Route de la Roya, on the beach, tel. 95370308. **D'Olzo**, northern entrance, tel. 95370334.
U Pezzo, Route de la Roya, tel. 95370165.
La Pinede, Bord de l'Aliso, tel. 95370726.

Restaurants
You'll find a number of changing restaurants, especially ones specializing in seafood, lining the promenade along the harbor and in the alleyways of the old city.
La Marinuccia, a good fish restaurant with terrace built right out over the sea. At the end of the harbor, follow a narrow street to the right down to the sea. Tel. 95370436.

Night life
La Conca D'Oru, Route d'Oletta, tel. 95370046.
L'Etable, Route d'Oletta, tel. 95370128.

Sports
BIKES: **Sun Folies**, Plage de la Roya, tel. 95370418.
BOAT RENTALS: **Dominique Plaisance**, motorboats, tel. 95370708.
DIVING: **Neptune Club**: C.E.S.M., Route de la Roya, tel. 95370061.
RIDING: **Le Ranch**, Route de la plage de la Roya.
TENNIS: **Tennis Club du Nebbiu**, toward Oletta, tel. 95370552.

Tourist Information
D 81, toward Patrimonio, B.P.29, tel. 95370604.

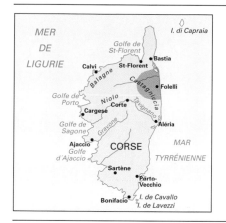

FROM BASTIA INTO THE CASTAGNICCIA

BIGUGLIA

SAN MICHELE

LA CANONICA

THE CASTAGNICCIA

HIKES IN THE CASTAGNICCIA

BIGUGLIA

The highway between Bastia and Bonifacio is the only national highway on Corsica where motorists can truly test the abilities of their car engines. A good section of the nearly 12-mile (20 km) stretch of the N 193 from Bastia to Casamozza is a two-lane road; note, however, that traffic tie-ups are frequent during peak hours.

From Casamozza, the N 193 leads along the Golo River, through Ponte Leccia and Corte to Ajaccio. To reach Bonifacio and the southern tip from Casamozza, take the N 198. The 100-mile (150 km) stretch is as straight as an arrow and gets you there in two to three hours.

Leaving the capital city of the north and heading towards Bonifacio, you first drive through a long housing and industrial area. After a few miles, you see on your left the stadium that collapsed during the soccer game between Olympique Marseilles and Bastia on May 5, 1992. Seventeen people were killed and more than 2,500 were injured.

With an area of 4,000 acres (1,600 ha), Corsica's largest lagoon is located two

Preceding pages: A ruler is often called in to referee a game of boules. Left: Enigmatic ornamentation – San Michele near Murato.

miles (4 km) south of Bastia. The **Étang de Biguglia** is about six miles (10 km) long and up to two miles (3 km) wide. While the lagoon is only about three feet (1 m) deep today, it was originally an excellent natural harbor. However, the powerful sea currents running northwards gradually built up a sandy spit of land.

In the lagoon, where the salt content varies according to rainfall and evaporation, eels are bred today. The lagoon is also interesting for ornithologists because migratory birds stop off here every spring and autumn on their trip to and from the south. Unfortunately, the sand spit is also used by noisy sunbathers; furthermore, the lagoon lies directly under the flight path of the Bastia-Poretta airport. For these reasons, nature lovers fear that the days of the bird paradise are numbered.

Around 6 miles (10 km) past Bastia, the town of **Biguglia** (population ca. 4,000) snuggles up against the hillside. It is hard to believe, but under the Pisans this town once served as the capital of Corsica; they moved the seat of government from Mariana on the coast to this spot. The Genoese governors also had their headquarters in Biguglia until 1372. After that, the town slipped back into its provincial slumbers.

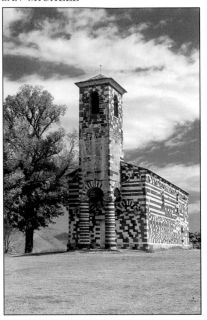

SAN MICHELE

Just after Biguglia, the D 82 branches off on the right toward St-Florent. The road goes across the **Défilé de Lancone** and over the **San Stefano Pass** (1,203 feet/368 m); it's definitely worth taking an excursion at least to the latter. From there, it is only 3 miles (5 km) on the D 5 to the Pisan Romanesque Church of **San Michele** near **Murato**, one of the most attractive, and thus most photographed, churches on Corsica.

According to the archaeologist Geneviève Moracchini-Mazel, who has conducted excavations for Roman and Christian artifacts on Corsica since 1951, there were once more than 300 Pisan Romanesque churches on the island. Unfortunately, only a small number of them remain. Some have been beautifully restored, such as San Michele in Murato, others appear as romantic ruins, overgrown with maquis, along solitary hiking trails.

During their peaceful rule over Corsica, the Pisans divided the island into six dioceses, and these were subdivided into parishes, known as *pieve*. Pieve were determined in part by geographical and in part by historical considerations, and the Pisans appointed chief magistrates and community leaders.

The parish church played a very special role in the community; it was not only responsible for religious duties, but for secular tasks as well, such as tax affairs and the administration of justice. This also explains the unusual iconography at many church entrances. In Aregno and Murato, for example, two human figures on the west facade symbolize the medieval separation of powers of church and state: the sculpture holding an object resembling a rod depicts an allegory of the law (scroll), and the figure wearing a long dress represents the clergy (church robe).

The close ties to Pisa are clearly reflected in elements of the church's architecture. Modern art historians now assume that Corsican craftsmen worked together with Pisans in building the churches. The Corsican influence can be seen mainly in the somewhat naive, but lovely sculptural work.

Of all the Romanesque churches on the island, San Michele has the greatest wealth of sculptural ornamentation. In 1840, Prosper Mérimée considered it to be the "most elegant church of the island." Especially notable is the sometimes asymmetrical, polychromatic stonework. In building the parish church, the bricklayers used a dark-green type of rock (serpentine) with a fine, solid grain which was easy to work with, and therefore ideal for sculptural work. The white stone is limestone, which is just as easy to cut. The bell tower is the only thing that slightly disturbs the harmonious proportions; it wasn't built until restoration

Above: San Michele, Corsica's most elegant church, in Pisan Romanesque style.

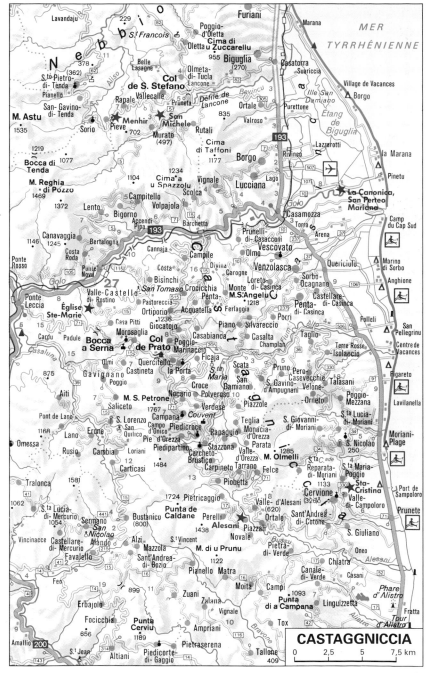

CASTAGGNICCIA

0   2,5   5   7,5 km

work in the 19th century. All of the consoles on the west facade depict four-legged animals in motion, done in high relief. The exceptions are the two outermost sculptures: these are the allegorical figures with the rod and long robe described above.

At the east end of the northern side wall, the recessed window shows a charming naive depiction of The Temptation of Eve. The leaves of the tree of paradise are shaped like clover leaves. Eve covers her naked body with her right hand and stretches out her disproportionately large left hand (reflecting the hand's importance rather than accurate perspective, something common in medieval art) toward the snake and the fruit. Adorning the frieze on the window's lower ledge is a scene that's particularly hard to explain: on the left, there is an angel with large wings, a frail body and a fat head, who is pointing with its bent right arm to a heavily-laden grape vine and holding a knife in its raised hand – perhaps an illustration of the Biblical passage Genesis 3:23-24. The ledge under the window in the western part of the wall shows the Lamb of God holding the cross and standing between two bellowing creatures. This reminds us of the battle between good and evil, perhaps, in an allegorical sense, even of the victory of the Crusaders over the Saracens in the 11th century.

The facade of the southern side wall is mainly adorned with decorative ornamentation and animals (snakes, birds, and other creatures). The symbolism has not yet been explained in detail, so its significance is left to the viewer's imagination. One thing is certain: in terms of architecture and symbolism, there are definite links between the churches at Aregno and Murato. If you want to look around inside, you can get the key from

Right: "La Canonica," or Santa Maria Assunta, consecrated in the 12th century.

Mr. Murati in Murato, in the Villa Patronale (tel. 95 37 60 70).

LA CANONICA

Another church from the same era worth seeing is the old **Cathedral of Santa Maria Assunta**, also popularly called **La Canonica**. In the little roadside village of Crocetta, 10 miles (17 km) south of Bastia, turn left off N 193 and then take an immediate right onto the D 107 toward Plage de Pinto (be careful not to get on the D 507 toward the airport by mistake). Another 3.5 miles or so (5.5 km) will bring you to the church. It is built on the foundations of the former Roman settlement of Mariana. There are still remains of the walls of a bath, mosaics and thermal baths.

At the beginning of the 4th century, Christianity was able to gain a foothold here. The foundation walls of a small basilica date from this period, as well as a baptistery with mosaics depicting Christian symbols: fish, dolphins, geese and deer. In keeping with the function of a baptistery, the four corners of the room sport four bearded heads of men personifying the four rivers of paradise. As they carry the water of life throughout the world, the rivers of paradise are associated with baptism.

Because of the frequent Saracen attacks and the constant threat of malaria, Mariana was abandoned in the 9th century. It wasn't until Pope Gregory VII (1077) put the island under the bishopric of Pisa that people began to settle near the coast again. As an enticement, Pisa had the churches there rebuilt – including Santa Maria Assunta. Around the turn of the millennium, Mariana rose to the status of a diocesan town, seat of a bishopric; and Pisa's archbishop consecrated the church into a cathedral in 1119.

The bitter battles between the two rivals, Pisa and Genoa, completely destroyed the town center in the 13th cen-

tury, so the clergy moved the seat of the bishopric to Vescovato. The canonical councils continued to maintain the church, whence its nickname of *La Canonica*. In its layout, the 83-foot-long (35 m) basilica resembles the former cathedral of Nebbio of the same name. The building materials came by ship from the quarries of Cap Corse, Sisco and Brando. The rough blocks were delivered in Mariana and were cut and worked on the spot. The scaffolding holes were probably intentionally left untreated, since they create a lively play of light and shadow on the otherwise practically unadorned exterior.

On the west facade, the keystones of the tympanum arch are adorned with a sculpted frieze of animals executed in high relief. The tympanum itself is bare today, but it was originally ornamented with a fresco. The side facades are virtually unadorned, with the exception of the southeast corner. Here you can make out an ornamentation of inlaid stone which was originally decorated in color –

a Tuscan motif. There may have been plans to decorate the whole exterior, but if so, they were never carried out. There are also remains of the bell tower wall at the same corner. They are overgrown with purple oleander bushes and contrast beautifully with the gold color of the stones, especially in the late afternoon.

The road to Prunete on the east coast has little to offer as far as culture and history are concerned. But it does give you plenty of chances to relax on the long sand beaches or participate in the extensive sport programs offered by the various vacation facilities. The towns of Moriani-Plage and Prunete are perfectly suited as starting points for excursions into the Castagniccia region.

THE CASTAGNICCIA

If you look at the history of Corsica, it quickly becomes clear that the **Castagniccia** region has always effectively formed the island's political and cultural heartland. In the north, the N 193 forms

the border of this Chestnut Country, running along the magnificent gorge of the Golo River from Casamozza to Ponte Leccia. Toward the plains of the east coast, the Golo has been canalized in order to irrigate vegetable fields and vineyards. To the west, where it extends toward the basin of Corte, this region is bordered by the San Quilicio Pass. The Tavignano River and N 200 mark the southern boundary.

The Castagniccia and the northeasterly area of Casinca, with the principal town of Vescovato, have preserved their own distinctive characters up to the present day. Groves of chestnut trees run wild cover countless hills; scattered between these are hundreds of small villages and hamlets, with a few stately houses indicating the area's past wealth. This was once the most populous area of Corsica;

Above: The gorse scrub of the Castagniccia. Right: Coppa, made of pork from the chestnut woods of the Castagniccia, is a particular delicacy.

today, however, emigration threatens to depopulate the villages altogether. Not even the lucrative tourist industry has been able to get a foothold in these remote valleys, even though there's an extensive network of roads; accommodations, therefore, are rare. Only a few visitors to the east coast – who comprise only one-quarter of all tourists to Corsica – plan day-trips into the hinterland. Therefore, you can still discover valleys and villages in the Castagniccia where every day the grocer and the baker drive up, sound their horns and inquire about the current local gossip in Corsican dialect.

The name Castagniccia derives from the chestnut trees which thrive here, growing to heights of some 65 feet (20 m) tall and more than 6 feet (2 m) across. The French word for chestnut is *chataigne*. The Genoese had the chestnut trees planted on a large scale in the 15th century. They had already tested the qualities of the chestnut in the Apennines and wanted to make it indigenous to Corsica. The Genoese governor signed a de-

cree in 1584 stating that all landowners and farmers were required under penalty of heavy fines to plant four trees every year (fig, olive, or chestnut). Afterwards, Castagniccia experienced an economic upswing; at the end of the 17th century, there were already close to 250 people per square mile (100 per sq. km). Towards the end of 1770, 70% of the area was planted with chestnut trees.

Today – as in the past – chestnuts are processed into flour which is used to bake excellent cakes and bread. Since flour was a staple, the chestnut tree was also called the bread tree. The wood from the tree was well suited for making wine casks and scaffolding. Breeding pigs used to be a natural economic sideline, since the animals were happy to stuff themselves on their wanderings through the chestnut groves. Even today, the half-wild, legendary Corsican pigs hunt through the overgrown chestnut groves for fallen nuts and, after they're slaughtered, turn into the fabulous Coppa and Lonzu hams. Today, however, many of

the chestnut trees have been affected by diseases; harvesting chestnuts, furthermore, is too laborious to be worthwhile. The chestnuts are therefore used predominantly for flour production and private consumption.

The Castagniccia played a historically important role in the 18th century. During the wars of independence, the most important rebels lived here. The patriots often gathered in the regional monasteries for meetings. The Corsicans declared the war of liberation against the Genoese in the Orezza monastery; the German baron Theodor von Neuhoff proclaimed himself king of the Corsicans and was crowned in the monastery of Alesani, while Pasquale Paoli was elected General of the Nation in the monastery of Rostino.

The Castagniccia region is also the crib of great Corsican patriots: Pasquale Paoli was born in Morosaglia, Louis Giafferi in Talasani and Paoli's friend, Antoine Salicetti, a delegate to the French National Assembly, was born in Saliceto.

City Tour

The best place to start a tour through the Castagniccia is in **Casamozza**. From there, follow the N 193 to Ponte Leccia, where you turn onto the D 71 heading directly to the low mountain range of the Castagniccia. After you've completed the route, you get off the D 71 after Cervione; in Prunete you can get back onto the east coast "race track" of the N 198.

On the way from Casamozza to Ponte Leccia, in **Ponte Novu**, just 5 miles (8 km) before Ponte Leccia, you come upon one of the most significant historic places on Corsica, although all that remain today are the ruins of a bridge and a monument. It was here that, on May 8, 1769, the French confronted the Corsican freedom fighters for the last time and won once and for all. With their huge, well-equipped army, the French sallied

Above: A specialty of the Castagniccia – sweets made of sweet chestnuts. Right: The village bar is a convivial meeting place.

out from the Nebbio toward the Golo River. The Corsican freedom fighters retreated toward the Golo, since most of their positions in the Casinca region had already fallen and they wanted to protect the route towards Corte. In the so-called "Disaster of Ponte Novu," the French army, far outnumbering the Corsicans, destroyed them utterly. Corsica's 14 years of independence, unique in the history of an island which had always been controlled by foreign powers, was thus ended; Paoli fled to London in exile.

From **Ponte Leccia**, an important railroad and highway junction, follow the narrow, winding D 71 towards Cervione. After 9 miles (14.5 km) and crossing the **Bocca a Serna** (2,276 feet/696 m), you reach **Morosaglia**. Morosaglia, with nearly 900 inhabitants, is one of the largest and also best-known towns in the Castagniccia. Three of the most prominent Corsican freedom fighters were born here: Pasquale Paoli, his brother Clément, and their father, Hyacinthe. There is a monument to Pasquale at the city entrance and his **birthplace**, now a public museum, is in the district of Stretta. He was born on April 6, 1725. The museum contains various personal souvenirs, documents and fragments of his first book, *La justification de la révolution corse*, which was printed in Oletta in 1758. His funerary urn, which was brought here from England on September 2, 1889, now rests in the lowest level of the house.

Little Paoli was baptized in **Santa Reparata**, a Romanesque church which has been renovated and altered several times since. Today's village school once housed the **Monastery of Rostino**, where the Corsicans elected Paoli General of the Nation; his brother Clément also died here in 1793.

Up to now, there have been plenty of views of the **Aiguilles de Popolasca**; on the other side of Morosaglia, however, you penetrate more deeply into the chest-

nut woods of the region. The road winds its way up to the **Prato Pass** at an altitude of nearly 3,300 feet (1,000 m). Under favorable weather conditions, a magnificent panorama opens up over the hilly countryside with Monte San Petrone (5,778 feet/1,767 m), the highest point of the Castagniccia, and the Tyrrhenian Sea.

About a half-mile (1 km) after the pass, a small road (D 405) branches off towards Stoppia Nova and Quercitello. Beyond Quercitello, the D 515 leads down the slopes to the next destination, **La Porta**, a little village of 300. Here, in the middle of the peaceful Castagniccia, you're often treated to a concert of the horns of tourist buses, which, much to the enjoyment of their passengers, blare almost ceaselessly as they negotiate the winding roads to warn oncoming traffic of their presence.

The reason for the surprising crowd of international tourists is the extraordinary church of **St-Jean-Baptiste** with its oversized bell tower. Constructed between 1648 and 1680, the building, as

well as its ocher- and white-painted facade from 1707, was designed by the Milan architect Domenico Baina. The elegant pilasters, columns and volutes (scrolls) of the facade harmonize with the interior which, however, was mainly executed in the 19th century.

Despite the size of the huge *Campanile* (bell tower), it appears light, largely because of the way it is divided into five stories and topped off with a diamond-shaped roof. Baina died before his plans for the tower could be carried out, so the execution was put into the hands of the architect Pompci de Quercitello. The tower was finished in 1720; in 1979, a good 250 years later, it had to be restored.

From La Porta, motorists, now accustomed to the "Country of 1,000 Curves," get back on the D 515 and proceed uphill and through the hamlet of Croce until they finally rejoin the D 71 again. After nearly 4 miles (6 km) in the direction of **Piedicroce**, there is a ruin on the left, which, with its picturesque vegetation and romantic location, could serve as a

stage set. Once an important monastery, the 18th-century Franciscan **monastery of Orezza** has been secularized since the French Revolution. The building served as the local police station until the roof collapsed in 1934. Afterwards, the Italians used it to store ammunition, and it was finally destroyed during a German attack in World War II.

During the wars of independence 200 years earlier, the monastery had been considered an important bastion of resistance. It was here, after several extensive consultations, that the war of liberation against the ruling Genoese was proclaimed on April 20, 1731. In June, 1751, the council voted here on a new constitution, and transferred the executive powers of office to Jean-Pierre Gaffori. Today, surrounded by grazing cows, visitors delight in the beautiful view the site commands over the **Orezza Valley**.

Above: Well-preserved frescoes in the chapel of Santa Christina near Cervione. Right: Paragliding competition in Cervione.

The name Orezza can be found on the label of mineral-water bottles on practically every Corsican dining table: it is the name of a mineral water spring known ever since antiquity. To get to this spring, follow the D 506 which branches off in Piedicroce. You can fill your water bottle at a fountain free of charge.

After a long drive towards Cervione on the D 71 you come to the village of **Valle-d'Alesani**. Immediately past it, turn off to the right on the D 217 in the direction of **Piazzali** and then onto D 17 heading for **Perelli**. Almost 4 miles (6 km) down the road you arrive at the somewhat run-down Franciscan monastery of **Alesani**, which the monks abandoned as recently as the beginning of the 1980s. Inside the church (which is locked most of the time) there is a captivating copy of a valuable painting from the Sienese school: *The Virgin of the Cherry* (1450).

On April 15, 1736, Theodor von Neuhoff from Cologne, Germany had himself crowned King of Corsica here.

Back on the D 71, it's another 10 miles (17 km) to **Cervione**, a picture-book village snuggled up against the hillside. Only 3 miles (5.5 km) from the plains of the eastern coast, it still towers 1,100 feet (336 m) above it. The old **St-Érasme Cathedral** (1584) in the center is considered to be one of the first Baroque churches on Corsica. In one wing of the city hall you'll find the **Ethnographic Museum**, which features exhibits and historic scenes relating to the lives of residents of Cervione and the Castagniccia.

The nearby Romanesque chapel of **Santa Cristina** is well worth a look. Upon leaving Cervione, drive towards San Nicolao for a short distance, then turn right onto the D 71 toward Prunete. After almost 1 mile (1.5 km), follow the route signposted for *Chapelle Santa Cristina – Le Port*, then make a sharp left and continue for another few hundred yards (600 m) on an unpaved yet passable dirt road. Magnificently-preserved frescoes from 1473 await the visitor in the church's twin apses. These double

apses can probably be explained by the church's double patronage (St. Christina and St. Hippolytus). In the left apse there is a depiction of Christ as Pantocrator flanked by the Virgin Mary and St. Christina; at his feet is a monk, possibly the donor. On the right, you can see Christ surrounded by the four symbols of the Evangelists, and a crucifixion scene is in the middle of the arch. The central nave was built as early as the 9th century, while the two apses date from a phase of reconstruction in the 15th century.

After so much art, a swim in the Mediterranean might be a welcome change of pace. **Prunete** and **Moriani-Plage** are very enticing with their clean, sand beaches, campgrounds, and wind-surfer and sailboat rentals.

HIKES IN THE CASTAGNICCIA

The French IGN maps on a scale of 1:25,000, with hiking trails marked in red, are very helpful for hiking in this region. For the Castagniccia, you need

maps 4349 OT and 4351 OT; these can be obtained in bookstores on Corsica (Bastia) or ordered from your local bookstore before you go.

Monte San Petrone

Hiking fans should undertake a tour of the highest mountain in the Castagniccia and ascend the 5,778 feet (1,767 m) of Monte San Petrone. There is hardly another high mountain on Corsica that is as easy to climb, since the well-marked and easy-to-see trail leads mainly through a shady forest. The hike begins at Col de Prato (3,220 feet/985 m) on the D 71 between Morosaglia and Piedicroce. From there, the trail leads right between two houses at the top of the pass. This path across the field forks after a few hundred yards; one path goes straight ahead, the other, marked in red, goes to the left

Above: Agriculture, Corsican style – even pigs that seem to be running wild always belong to someone.

(southwest) towards the forest – this is the one you want to follow. After roughly an hour's march uphill, the trail declines briefly. This is where you leave the forest trail and take the one marked in red leading to the left, heading south, continuing uphill. After some 1.5 hours, you come across a spring on the edge of the path. Keep going southwest for another half-hour; you'll come to open plateau with a fabulous view, from where the trail heads east, then, shortly afterwards, turns again to the north and back into the forest. Not far from the peak, the ascent becomes somewhat more strenuous as the steep path winds in serpentine curves.

After hiking 2 to 3 hours, and fairly tired out, you reach the peak and are rewarded for your pains with a truly magnificent view. The panorama extends from the east coast plain and the Tyrrhenian Sea across the rolling hills of the Castagniccia to the Balagne in the west and on into the Nebbio region. The highest mountains of Corsica are also in sight: the Monte Cinto massif and Monte Incudine (6,978 feet/2,134 m), the south-ernmost mountain over 2,000 meters.

A Stroll to the Church of Santa Maria di Riscamone

This short walk through the maquis can be lengthened, or you can culminate it with a picnic in a peaceful spot by the church. The best way to reach the starting point is to take the N 193. About half a mile (1 km) past Ponte Novu as you go toward Ponte Leccia, a small road, the D 615, leads off to the left towards **Valle-di-Rostino**. Almost 550 yards (500 m) before reaching the village an unpaved road turns off sharply to the right, marked with a somewhat weathered signpost bearing the legend: "Chemin des Ruines - Église Ste-Marie."

You can park here and walk the rest of the way. After 650 yards or so (600 m), where the route curves slightly to the left, a newly-lain path branches off to the right, leading down the hill. Another couple of hundred yards and you'll happen upon the ruins of **Santa Maria di Riscamone** (Église Ste-Marie) and the **Baptistery San Giovanni Battista**, overgrown with maquis and pic-turesquely perched up above the Golo with a view of the 6,540-foot (ca 2,000 m) Aiguilles de Popolasca, which keep their caps of snow until early summer. The church dates from the early Roman-esque period, built in the 10th century, while the large octagonal baptistery is from the 12th century. The door lintel of the baptistery, which now lies on the ground, shows a primitive depiction of the Fall of Man. It is presumed that this relief was actually made much earlier, and was brought here later as a spoil of war. Part of the baptismal font can be found among the ruins of the church. If you look closely, you can make out a mysterious human face in relief on one side of the font. Both buildings are in poor condition and are being restored.

NORTHERN EAST COAST
Accommodation

CASAMOZZA: *MODERATE:* **Chez Walter**, very good mid-priced hotel with pool and tennis courts, good Corsican cooking, tel. 95360009.
CERVIONE/PRUNETE: *LUXURY:* **Ori-zonte**, on the beach, pool, tennis, tel. 95380104.
FOLELLI: *MODERATE:* Holiday resort **San Pellegrino**, Plage de San Pellegrino, tel. 95369061.
MORIANI PLAGE: *MODERATE:* **Monte Cristo**, tel. 95384538/ 95315682.
MARINE DE BRAVONE/SAN NICOLAO: *MODERATE:* **Sotta-Torra**, swimming pool, tennis, tel. 95388103/95388146.
TAGLIO ISOLACCIO: *MODERATE:* **Mare e Sole**, also offers furnished apartments to rent by the week, tel. 95368590.

Campgrounds

PRUNETE: **Calamar**, tel. 95380354, **Olmello**, tel. 95380321. **Tropica**, Linguizetta, R.N.198, nude beach **MORIANI PLAGE**: **Merendella**, tel. 95385347.
STE-LUCIE-DE-MORIANI: **U Punticchiu**, tel. 95385779.
TAGLIO ISOLACCIO: **Paul Pietri Arepos**, rental bungalows, tel. 95369090.

Car rental

MORIANI-PLAGE: **Europcar**, Elf gas station, tel. 95385043. **Hertz-Filippi Auto**, Relais de Ta-vagna, tel. 95384140.

Sports

DIVING: **Club Plongée Bastiais**, Villa Capullo, tel. 95333128.
SAILING: **U.C.P.A. Borgo-V.V.F.**, Route du Cordon Lagunaire, tel. 95337722. Prunete, Cer-vioni, **U.C.P.A. Prunete**, tel. 95380021.

CASTAGNICCIA
Accommodation

PONTE LECCIA: *BUDGET:* **Las Vegas**, tel.95476159. **Des Touristes**, restaurant, tel. 95476111.
CERVIONE: *BUDGET:* **Saint-Alexandre**, restaurant, tel. 95381083.
PIEDICROCE: *BUDGET:* **Le Refuge**, restaur-ant, tel. 95358265/95358108.
SAN NICOLAO: *BUDGET:* **L'Ile d'Or**, tel. 95385116.

Sports

PARAGLIDING: Cervione, **Cime Ale**, École Agrée, Casa Comunale, tel. 95381344. *RIDING:* La Porta, **Centre de Tourisme Equestre S.C.S. Soliva**, tel. 95392256/95392292. Ponte Leccia, **Centre Equestre "A Stalla,"** Haras de Codole, Route de Saint-Laurent, tel. 95476525.

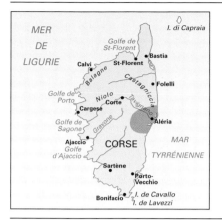

MER
DE
LIGURIE

I. di Capraia

Golfe de St-Florent
•Bastia
Calvi St-Florent
Balagne Castagniccia
•Folelli
Golfe de Porto Niolo Corte
Cargese
Golfe de Sagone Gravone Tavignano •Aléria
Ajaccio CORSE MAR
Golfe d'Ajaccio TYRRÉNIENNE
•Sartène
•Porto-Vecchio
Bonifacio• *I. de Cavallo*
I. de Lavezzi

TRACES OF ANTIQUITY ON THE EAST COAST

ALÉRIA
FIUMORBO
OYSTER FARMING

The central section of the **east coast**, which you can drive through quickly on the Corsican "race track," the N 198, is dominated by modern agriculture and touristy seaside resorts. Cultivated in the wide **Plaine Orientale**, the coastal lowland of eastern Corsica, are citrus fruits and wine, grown on large *Domaines*. This section of the coast attracts nearly 20% of all vacationers to Corsica; it has broad sandy beaches, ideal for families; charming bungalow villages for holiday occupancy; and a wide range of sporting activities. Yet even in August the beach of **Bravone** is not overrun; and even when the weather's at its hottest, there's always a cool breeze at the ice-cream café *La Tour Bravone*, which sits on a slight elevation of land.

ALÉRIA

The excavation site of Aléria and the museum in the Genoese Palazzo Fort Matra rank among the most interesting sights on Corsica. Aléria is perched up on a plateau between 130 and 200 feet (40 to 60 m) high and more than a mile (2 km)

Preceding pages: Unlike the mountains, the east coast plains boast modern methods of wine cultivation. Left: The wind blows offshore along the beaches of the east coast.

long, some 2.5 miles (4 km) from the sea. From the museum grounds you can see the Étang de Diane and the mouth of the Tavignano River. The village of 2,000 people is at the junction of N 198 and N 200; the latter leads inland along the Tavignano Valley as far as Corte. As well as the excavations and museums on the (unshaded) plateau, there are also some crafts shops; and after you tour the area, you can savor tasty Corsican specialties in one of the two inviting cafés.

Long before the Romans managed to take control of this area, other cultures had settled here. The history of Alalia/Aléria goes back more than 2,500 years. The earliest finds here date from the Neolithic period. The first inhabitants lived off seafood, farming, stock-breeding, and the obsidian trade with nearby Sardinia. Finds from the Bronze and Iron Ages confirm that the plateau was continuously inhabited through the years. But even in Antiquity, Corsica was at the mercy of countless, and repeated, enemy invasions. It is no overstatement to see in this fact the initial origins of the struggle for independence that still goes on today; the will to resist and stand up for oneself has, it seems, been passed down from one generation to the next.

First colonists here were the Phocaean Greeks, who tried to set up their colony

in 565 BC. They were forced to leave their city of Phocaea in Asia Minor under pressure from the expanding Persians. After founding their trade colony of Massilia (present-day Marseilles) shortly before, they built the city of Alalia on the easily defensible plateau up above the mouth of the Tavignano River. This started a Greek-Roman heyday that lasted almost 1,000 years, until the Vandals destroyed the city in 456 A.D. Following additional Phocaean immigration waves, the Greeks expanded Alalia from 540 to 535 B.C. and it became their capital. Corsica had a strategically advantageous location which made Alalia one of the most important intermediate stops in Mediterranean seafaring trade.

The Phocaeans brought a highly-developed civilization to Corsica with them, as well as their latest agricultural achievements. First of all, the Greeks made the grape vine, olive tree and wheat

Above: Orange-growing is an important local industry.

indigenous to the fertile east coast. They also made clever use of the products that were virtually lying in their front yard: seafood and sea salt. They soon began mining the valuable raw materials inland; these included copper and iron in the Venaco and Corte regions, as well as argentiferous lead. And one cannot overlook their flourishing wood trade, which would not have been possible without Corsica's extensive forests. They also spread their writing, arts and crafts, and the newest agricultural techniques of that time, which may still be contributing to the quality of Corsican wine, even today. No one has yet satisfactorily explored the question of what kind of relationship – good or bad – they had with the native Corsicans. The Greeks referred to them as *Kurniens*, while the Corsicans called themselves *Corsi*. From gravestone inscriptions, however, we do know that some Corsicans must have lived in Alalia, perhaps worked there as well, and were certainly buried there.

The Greek city's heyday was interrupted in 535 B.C., when the allied Etruscans and Carthaginians fought against the Phocaeans in the sea battle of Alalia. The Phocaeans managed, with difficulty, to win the battle, but it was hardly better than a defeat. As a result, the weakened inhabitants of Alalia moved their capital to Massilia and left Corsica, for the most part, altogether; although they still kept the city as a base for Mediterranean trade for a time. On the basis of excavations of ceramic shards and pots, it's been established that some Etruscan influence made itself felt here; but 15 years later, it was the Carthaginians who had the upper hand over Alalia's sea trade. In 259 B.C., in the course of the first Punic War (264-241 B.C.), the Romans, under the command of the consul Lucius Cornelius Scipio, landed on Corsica and drove away the resident Carthaginians.

From their base on the east coast, the invaders also set out for the hinterland of

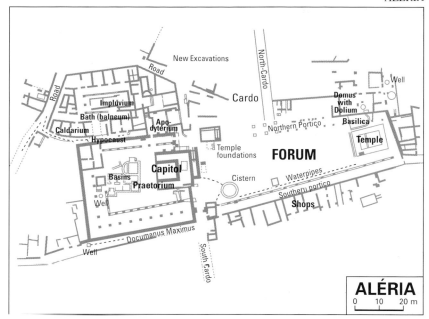

ALÉRIA

0   10   20 m

the island and had to fight against the fierce resistance of the Corsicans on their campaigns. By the year 230 B.C., the Romans were firmly established on the east coast, yet the Corsicans defended themselves with great courage and were far from being defeated.

By 163 A.D., the Romans had managed to put down all of the revolts, and the population of Corsica had been reduced by half. Even the Corsican slaves proved a handful for the colonialists: they either offered passive resistance or committed suicide. Archaeologists have found the skeleton of a Corsican in chains in Aléria; the manuscripts of contemporary Roman historians also report on the difficult conditions at that time. In a lighter vein, another, more humorous version of some of the difficulties the Romans may have encountered with their Corsican slaves is illustrated in the comic book *Asterix on Corsica.*

Lucius Cornelius Sulla settled veterans here in 81 B.C., and in 100 B.C. Gaius Marius founded the colony of Mariana at the mouth of the Golo River. Mariana, however, never managed to achieve the importance that Aléria had. Rome combined Corsica and Sardinia to become one province, but later it divided them again. Emperor Augustus made Corsica an independent province and proclaimed Aléria its capital.

Aléria experienced a second period of great prosperity under the reign of Emperor Augustus (27 B.C. to 14 A.D.) The port in the Étang de Diane was enlarged to become an important naval harbor. The city itself was fitted out with all of the significant buildings that adorned any prosperous Roman city of the time: a capitol, a forum, an amphitheater, an aqueduct, and thermal baths. The ensuing emperors, Hadrian, Caracalla and Diocletian, also contributed to the beautification and enlargement of the city.

The increasing decline and decadence of the Western Roman Empire did not pass by Aléria unnoticed. The outbreak of a malaria epidemic which spread along the east coast made a further contribution

toward depopulating the city. Christianity probably began to establish itself here after around the 3rd century A.D.; one find in Aléria which dates from this period is an oil lamp with the monogram of Christ. In the 5th century, the last inhabitants of Aléria were finally forced to give up the city after Vandals had laid a huge fire and followed it up with a rampage of plundering.

Excavations

The entrance ticket for the museum is also valid for the excavations, and can only be purchased in the museum. The excavations, which have been under the leadership of Jean and Laurence Jehasse since 1958, are still not completely finished. Today, most of the workers who sweat in the scorching Corsican sun while working on the latest excavations

Above: The almonds are ripe by late summer. Right: Remains of Roman settlement at the excavations in Aléria.

are inmates of the nearby prison Casabianda. At the moment, they're uncovering an amphitheater, which lies a couple of hundred yards or so from the part of the grounds that are open to visitors.

The sections of wall that have been excavated date from several epochs and verify the turbulent history of Alalia/Aléria. Its first foundations mark the limits of the Greek city of Alalia. Experienced in urban planning, the Romans kept altering Alalia – first under Sulla, then Augustus – so that it continued to expand, finally reaching a population of 20,000.

You enter the ancient city along its main north-south axis, the so-called **Cardo**, at the north end. The **Forum**, the central square of every Roman city, was the main arena for every aspect of public life; people's assemblies took place here, as did the administration of justice. Stumps of columns flank the square on its north and south sides; these are remains of former Roman shops. Laid out in the form of a trapezoid, the forum measures 300 feet (92 m) in length, while the short sides on the east and west are 78 (24 m) and 127 feet (39 m) wide respectively. The pedestal which catches your eye in the center of the square probably served as a base for the statue of a prominent Roman figure of the day.

Should the heat become unbearable during the sightseeing tour, you can abandon yourself to "cooling thoughts" at the **Praetorium** on the west side of the square. This important building, slightly elevated, which you reach by going up the steps and through the remaining half of a brick arch, was the administration and justice center and seat of the most important man in Aléria, the governor of the province of Corsica. And life was good; inside, administrators strolled between shade-giving plants and little pools containing plashing fountains. Like the forum, this building has a trapezoidal form. The complex, much of which is open, was bordered on three sides with roofed colonnades, built, with Roman architectural ingenuity, at a slight slant; this made it possible to collect rainwater, which flowed down this slant and into waiting cisterns.

Adjacent to the Praetorium, on its east side, is a nearly square building addition that has been almost completely destroyed and cleared away. Archaeologists presume that this was a **temple**, perhaps the **capitol**, which people reached from the forum by ascending the monumental staircase. At its center you'll notice a conspicuous ditch, the **favissa**, in which the Romans kept holy, consecrated objects. The central basins date from the 3rd century A.D.; they supplied water to the plumbing of the west wall and the bath. In the northeast corner, there were rooms which served as weapons depots or treasure chambers, and may later even have been used as a bath or cistern. It was Lucius Cornelius Sulla who had the entire Praetorium complex built; but extensive renovations and alterations continued until into the 5th century A.D.

The governor could go directly from his office through the north portico to the **bath**, or *balneum*. In the **apodyterium** he removed his garments. From that point on, he followed a prescribed bathing routine (not unlike a Swedish sauna today): first, he warmed up in the **palaestra** by doing physical exercises; he then cleaned his body with small, curved metal skin scrapers in the lukewarm bath of the **tepidarium** before finally entering the **caldarium**, a hot water or steam bath for relaxation. This procedure was followed by massages and an additional lukewarm bath before culminating in an invigorating dip in the icy **frigidarium** (coldwater bath). The thermal baths were more than just simple bathing facilities: they were a place for passing the time and recuperating – an expression of a sophisticated way of life. People spent long periods of time here, whatever their reasons: to toughen up physically, to take walks, to read, to listen to lectures, or simply to meet friends. All of these activities had a luxurious frame in this expansive complex with its colorful columns, capitals, decorative mosaics, marble paneling, and fresco-covered walls. Remains of blue and white mosaics have also been found in Aléria. Also of interest is the partially uncovered floor heating system, the **hypocaust**, little channels under the floor, supported by small columns, through which warm air circulated.

Adjacent to this to the west, archaeologists have discovered an industrial area of sorts, littered with oyster and mussel shells which were once processed and conserved here. On the eastern, narrow side of the forum is the podium of a small **temple**, 53.3 by 34.6 feet (16.3 x 10.6 m), which dates back to the time of Sulla. An inscription found here proves that the temple was consecrated to the cult of Rome and later to the Emperor Augustus.

Adjacent to the north are the foundation walls of a small building, semicircular on one side – the remains of an early Christian **basilica** were found here. Continuing farther to the north you see the traces of a house, called **Domus with dolium**. Presumably, there were work rooms here; as parts of a large earthenware jar (dolium) have been found here, as well as a grain and a salt mill. To the east, you can still see the remains of a sewage ditch. A significant finding of the archaeologists is a piece of the north portico with the following inscription: "The 15 cities required to pay cork tax to the leader of the colony of Aléria, their ruler." This is an informative indication of the economic conditions on Corsica in the 3rd century A.D.

The Jérôme Carcopino Museum in Fort Matra

The museum is located in the well-renovated Genoese Fort Matra, which

Right: Greek rhyton from the 5th century B.C. (Musée Jérôme Carcopino, Aléria).

dates from the year 1572. The fort was originally built as a garrison for more efficient surveillance of the east coast, which is the reason for its exposed position atop the hill. The museum is named after the great Corsican archaeologist Jérôme Carcopino, who participated in the excavations of Aléria and effectively reformed all of Corsican archaeology.

Extending over the second floor, the museum is reached by the stairway in the inner courtyard. The first exhibition here was held in 1963; but the museum, with its nine rooms, officially opened its doors in 1969. At that time, however, the policy was to display everything that had been found if at all possible. Since 1992, the exhibition has been better arranged; fewer objects are displayed, but they are exhibited in a much clearer fashion, and presented in a logical and chronological order. Today, the museum offers interested visitors four large rooms, so you have time to make a thorough tour. Most of the objects displayed – and certainly the most interesting ones – are from the days of the Greeks. Despite extensive excavation work, archaeologists have not been able to locate many large or significant finds from the Roman Aléria – the Vandals evidently did a thorough job of demolishing the city in the 5th century A.D.

In the **1st room**, the objects on display have to do with to the contact between Aléria and Italy or Aléria and Rome. Grouped around a pillar in the center of the room are the only three display cases in the museum with finds from the period of Aléria's Roman occupation. Most of these Roman objects come from graves of the late Roman Empire; they include numerous marble and ceramic fragments, small bronze, bone and silver figures, jewelry, an amphora with a cork stopper, a salt grinder and oil lamps, including one with a Christ monogram in memory of the coming of Christianity to Corsica. Aléria's importance as a trading and ex-

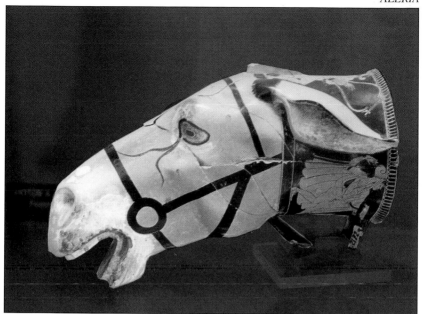

port center, particularly in connection with Italy, is evident from the cases along the walls; especially appealing to the eye are various painted ceramics from Campania, Latium and Apulia. Peering out of case 7, next to the entrance, is a mischievous bronze satyr; he was probably used to decorate a door handle.

The real highlights from Corsica's Roman epoch can be admired in the **2nd room**. In display case 2, there is a particularly beautiful red-figure Etruscan wine jug, which was found in a grave from the year 340 B.C. Depicted on it are Dionysos and Ariadne flanked by two young female bacchants. Another unusual Etruscan ceramic work from Chiusi-Volterra (4th century B.C.) is surprising because of its shape: it's a vase in the shape of a duck.

For the layman, the **3rd room** offers interesting insights into the admirable work of the archaeologists who date countless tiny shards and laboriously reassemble them, a task which requires a great deal of imagination and patience.

On the wall is an illustration of the excavation site in cross-section, showing the various layers of finds. In addition, this room displays a variety of Greek vases. Most of the objects are from graves of officials from the 5th century B.C., which contained Attic ceramics and Etruscan bronzes. Depicted on most of the vases and other containers are convivial bouts of wine-drinking and erotic scenes.

The numerous wine jugs are executed in the red-figure style, which replaced, the black-figure silhouette style at the end of the 6th century B.C. In red-figure painting, the red figures are actually drawn in negative space: the vase is painted black, and the figures left blank until later, when they are decorated with black lines.

In the **4th room**, the items on display are also grouped together under the heading of Aléria and Greece. Among them are some excellently preserved jugs, as well as some which were pieced together by patient archaeologists. The most beautiful items are from the oldest chamber

grave of the necropolis (475-450 B.C.): two fabulous drinking vessels (*rhyton*) in the shape of animals' heads are fascinating because of their naturalistic depiction. The painted part of the dog's head shows three figures, one of whom is playing the lyre, another a flute. The mule's head, too, is decorated with musicians: two singing ones and one dancing figure holding a kylix and wearing a Phrygian cap. Both works are ascribed to the painter of Brygos.

FIUMORBO

The region of **Fiumorbo** (murky water), south of the Tavignano River and west of the little town of Ghisonaccia, acquired its name from the river Fium' Orbo. The source of the river is in the Monte Renoso massif, and it is joined by a few torrents on its way to the sea. This

Above: The East Coast – a vacationer's paradise. Right: Large-scale wine production takes place on the Plaine Orientale.

hilly region is considered to be one of the most remote mountainous areas of Corsica, and it's not unusual to see the shutters of houses in the small communities closed for good. Even the inhabitants who remain can be hard to spot: most of them are shepherds who, depending on the season and climate, go back and forth between the coast and the chestnut-covered hills of Fiumorbo.

From Ghisonaccia, you can swing out on a short detour of approximately 19 miles (30 km). Just a mile (1.5 km) south of town on D 244, the road branches off to the west; in **Abbazia**, follow the D 145 and then 45 to **Pietrapola**. As early as Roman times, people were appreciative of the curative powers of the thermal springs of Pietrapola – especially for rheumatism. The small spa rooms were renovated in the 1960s; today, you generally see only locals splashing around in the sulfurous water of 95-100°F (35-38°C).

On the other side of the town, take the D 45 towards **Prunelli-di-Fiumorbo.**

From an altitude of 1,896 feet (580 m), you can take in a wonderful view of the east coast and the lagoons (*étangs*), extending all the way to Aléria.

On the way back to the east coast, you can take another little excursion within easy reach to what is probably the oldest Christian church on Corsica (6th-7th centuries). Take the D 345 towards Abbazia and the east coast. Turn left at the intersection with the D 244; after some three-quarters of a mile (1.2 km), across the bridge, a road branches off to the left. Follow it for about 650 yards (600 m) on up to an abandoned house. Below the house is the church **San Giovanni Battista**. It has archaic stonework, a square choir and a single entrance on the south side. The tour ends in Ghisonaccia.

Ghisonaccia

With a population of 3,000, the town of **Ghisonaccia**, at the mouth of the Fium' Orbo River, is the economic center of the Fiumorbo region. A typical road-side village, it's the coastal "annex" of the inland town of Ghisoni, which has expanded. Located near a beautiful sand beach, Ghisonaccia offers everything a vacationer could desire: banks, post office, supermarkets, restaurants, hotels, camps grounds and holiday resorts.

The fertile *Plaine Orientale* has been used for farming since Antiquity. After the destruction of Roman Aléria in the 5th century A.D., the estuary areas became increasingly swampy, thus creating an excellent habitat for the small, but dangerous, anopheles mosquito, the carrier of malaria. In addition, the relatively unprotected plain of the east coast was at the mercy of frequent pirate attacks, so the inhabitants often had no other choice but to flee to the more protected areas in the hinterland.

Time and again, various occupying forces repeatedly attempted to settle this fertile strip of land (see La Canonica, p. 70). Yet it wasn't until 1943 that people were able safely to live along the east coast; through extensive use of DDT, the

Americans finally managed to eliminate the dangerous anopheles mosquito.

The east coast lowlands, up to 7.4 miles/12 km wide, is the only area on Corsica where monoculture is carried out on a large-scale basis. Largely responsible for this were the Algerian French who, according to the independence treaties of Evian (1962), were forced to leave Algeria. The French government gave land on Corsica to a few thousand of these people, as a way of compensating for their losses in the former colony.

What's mainly cultivated here are grapes for the simple v*in de table* (table wine); unlike the rest of Corsica, the grapes here are harvested by machines. Because of the problems that grew out of strict monoculture, including a wine surplus, farmers in the region started to grow citrus fruits as well, and since the 1980s, Corsica has been the largest kiwi supplier in the whole of France. The fish and oys-

Above: The lagoons of the east coast offer the ideal conditions for oyster cultivation.

ter breeding business in the étangs of Urbino and Diane constitute an additional, important economic factor. With depths of nearly 33 feet (10 m), these inlets are considerably deeper than the lagoons of Biguglia and Palu.

OYSTER FARMING

Unlike the fun and fairly easy process of eating these delicacies, oyster farming is time-consuming and physically taxing work; regardless of the weather, the breeders have to go out and check their oyster beds. Today, what they usually have to face when they get there are increasing threats to their business: water pollution, an excess salt content in the ocean, new oyster diseases, storms, and sudden drops in temperature. Oysters are truly sensitive creatures. They prefer water with a low salt content and a relatively constant temperature of around 70°F (21°C). Most of the Corsican étangs fulfill such conditions, and the oysters enjoy a comfortable habitat.

Members of the mussel family, oysters rest in the étangs, as well as in the breakers of the open sea, with the convex half of their shell against the ocean floor; the upper, flat half closes the shell like a lid. Oysters are not individualists; they love living in large groups, especially in the – nowadays rare – oyster beds.

As hermaphrodites, oysters have the perhaps dubious ability to change their sex from male to female alternately; they fertilize their eggs within their shell, and then discharge them into the water. The swimming larva develop into young oysters that get a foothold on the sea floor; from then on until they die (max. 25 years), they take in and expel water, filtering out tiny plankton algae for nourishment. Much to the displeasure of Corsican oyster farmers, however, they not only take in floating organisms, they also, these days, take in a number of different toxic chemical substances and bacteria.

The Romans on Corsica knew nothing of these problems. They took advantage of the extremely favorable conditions of the **Étang de Diane** and the **Étang d'Urbino** (1,875 acres / 750 ha), located 5.5 miles (9 km) farther south, to reduce the "fattening-up period" from 3 - 4 years to 1 year. Today, both of these privately run étangs produce a good 600 tons of oysters annually, thus covering 80% of Corsica's slurping needs.

What you find on most Corsican tables is the large, meaty oyster variety *Huitre Creuse*, which you can recognize by their elongated shape and the irregular riffles of their shell. The *Huitre Plate* is considered to be the more delicate of the two. With its flat, smoother and rounder shell, this species prefers sand bars. They are far less common than their more "crinkly" relatives, taste better, and are accordingly more expensive – not too expensive, however, for the court of the Sun King, Louis XIV, who is said to have loved them.

CENTRAL EAST COAST
Accommodation
ALÉRIA: *MODERATE*: **L'Atrachjata**, tel. 95570393. **Les Orangers**, quiet hotel near the beach and town center, tel. 95570031. **L'Empereur**, R.N. 198, tel. 95570213. **Riva Bella**, holiday resort for nature lovers with bungalows and camping facilities, sand beach, tel. 95388110/95388597. **GHISONACCIA**: *MODERATE*: **Franceschini**, tel. 95560639/95561512. **Motel Sud**, tel. 95560054/ 95562591. **Marina d'Oru**, tel. 95565758, holiday resort with 800 beds. *BUDGET*: **De la Poste**, tel. 95560041. **PIETRAPOLA-LES-BAINS**: *MODERATE*: **Etablissement Thermal**, tel. 95567003, swimming pool.

Campgrounds
ALÉRIA: **Marina d'Aléria**, tel. 95570142, large, well-tended facility with washing machines, restaurant, supermarket, bungalows, on the beach. **BRAVONE**: **Bravone Plage**, tel. 95388408, open from June 15 to September 15. **GHISONACCIA**: **Arinella-Bianca**, tel. 95560478, supermarket, bungalows. **La Marine de Carpone**, tel. 95560242. **Marina d'Erba Rossa**, swimming pool, tennis, tel. 95562514. **SOLARO**: **Les Eucalyptus**, tel. 95574473/ 95574024. **Cote des Nacres**, tel. 95574065/ 95574009.

Restaurants
Restaurant du Fort, U. Ridornu, M. et Mme. Cabanie, Aléria, great for light lunches, tel. 95570931. **Le Bounty**, Plage de Padulone, Aléria, good restaurant right on the beach with fresh seafood, tel. 95570050. **Tour Bravone**, near Marine de Bravone, elevated site with terrace; ice cream, German cakes, pizza in the evening.

Museum
Archaeological Museum Jérôme Carcopino, Aléria, tel. 95570092, opening times: summer: daily 8 am-noon and 2-6:30 pm, winter: daily except Su and holidays, 8-11:30 am and 2-4:30 pm.

Sports
DIVING: **Club Nautique a Tramuntana**, Immeuble "Crocciu," Z.I. de Migliacciaru, Ghisonaccia, tel. 95561263.
WATER SPORTS: **C.N.O.S.A.P.**, V.I.V.E. de Casabianca, Domaine d'Aléria, tel. 95570679.

Taxi
GHISONACCIA: **Citer Corse Auto Rent**, Alzitone, tel. 95560981. **Hertz**, R.N. 198, tel. 95560832.

Tourist Information
ALÉRIA: Mayor's Office, tel. 95570073/ 95570332. **GHISONACCIA**: Mayor's Office, tel. 95561510.

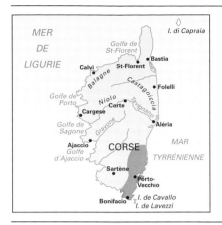

MOUNTAINS AND SWIMMING COVES IN THE SOUTHEAST

SOLENZARA / BAVELLA
HIKING TRAILS
FROM ZONZA TO THE COAST
PORTO-VECCHIO
BONIFACIO

SOLENZARA

The coast changes in appearance after you pass Solenzara: the plains of Aléria end here, and the road south now runs somewhat above the coastline; the views become more beautiful, and sandy bays tempt perspiring drivers to break for a refreshing dip in the sea.

The stretch from Solenzara to the bay of Fautea, about 12.5 miles (20 km) farther south, is especially bountiful with fish, and is called *Côte des Nacres* – **Mother-of-Pearl Coast**. It is an El Dorado for divers, and snorkelers will discover a type of wing shell with a particular shimmer nestled in the mud and sand; in French, this shell is called *plume de mer* or *nacre*. One recommended section of beach is that around **Fautea Bay**, which sports a photogenic Genoese tower. From here it is another 12.5 miles or so (20 km) through farmlands and fields to the tourist mecca of Porto-Vecchio.

In **Solenzara**, a village built along the highway on the Solenzara River – a melodious, almost melancholy name – there is everything that a tourist could

Preceding pages: Laricio pines before the Bavella Massif. Left: Hiking around the Bavella is fun – even with children.

desire: souvenir stores, shops, drugstores, restaurants, bars, cafés, hotels and a recently built, attractive yacht marina with a small sand beach. Somewhat farther north, directly on the Solenzara River estuary, there is a charming campground on the sea, where big, sweet-smelling eucalyptus trees provide refreshing shade on hot summer days. These trees were planted during the Second Empire (1850-1871) in order to dry out the swamp and to rob the anopheles mosquito of its habitat – a praiseworthy attempt, although it didn't succeed in wiping out malaria on the island.

Once you've had your fill of sun and swimming along the east coast, head inland into the southern mountainous region of Corsica. Drive from Solenzara along the Solenzara River (D 268); the first 9 miles (15 km) lead through magnificent landscape, and in many places, large swimming holes, often the size of real swimming pools, will entice you to take a refreshing swim in fresh water – especially in the dry summer months. Even while you're lost in admiration of the landscape, or examining the enormous granite rocks strewn through the river bed, you should bear in mind that the road is narrow and winding, and other drivers may also be looking off the road in search of secluded swimming spots.

97

BAVELLA

From Solenzara to the **Col de Bavella** (*Bocca di Bavedda*), you ascend from sea level to an altitude of 3,995 feet (1,218 m) within a distance of merely 18.5 miles (30 km). If you're coming from Solenzara, you'll reach the village of **Bavella** about a quarter of a mile (500 m) before the pass. Bavella is an important stop for hikers on the GR 20, the *Sentier de Grande Randonnée*, but other ramblers also use the spot to stock up on provisions or as an emergency stop for the night. There is a *Gîte d'Etape* (a modest lodge with sleeping bunks); a few old sheep farms, which the shepherds from Conca use as their summer huts; several bars; and even a pizzeria for a well-deserved lunch break.

A bit farther on, at the Bavella Pass, you can admire the oversized statue of **Notre-Dame-des-Neiges**, where pious

Above: In many mountain villages, only the elderly are left.

pilgrims have been congregating every year on August 5 since 1954; or the old laricio pine trees, gnarled and twisted by the wind. Here you have a breathtaking view of the famous **Aiguilles de Bavella** (the Needles of Bavella), rocky peaks which appear especially dramatic in the heightened shadows of the late afternoon sun. The natives have given these cliffs the more prosaic name of *Cornes d'Asino* (Donkey Ears); the highest "donkey ear" is **Punta Alta**, also called **Tour VI**, which measures 6,084 feet (1,855 m) in height. To the north, beyond the Aiguilles, you can faintly make out the largest mountain massif in southern Corsica: Monte Incudine, more than 6,560 feet (2,000 m) high.

Right next to the statue is the GR 20 long-distance trail, marked in red and white; for those coming from the north, Bavella is the last stop before the tour ends in Conca.

HIKING TRAILS IN THE BAVELLA MASSIF
Trou de la Bombe

Because it presents no particularly difficult stretches, this gorgeous hiking trail can even be attempted by families with children. You should allow three to four hours for a round trip. In spite of the easy forest trails, you shouldn't underestimate the terrain. There are so many forest roads and paths, all intersecting and joined by new ones every year, that it can be difficult to keep your sense of direction, especially when the fog rolls in. Therefore, it's a good idea to invest in the hiking trail map 4253 ET, put out by the IGN (Institut Géographique National), before you start.

From the parking lot by the Col de Bavella, you follow an unmarked path up the slope across from the Aiguilles de Bavella and the statue. After a few yards, you'll see a red-and-yellow trail marker. The trail continues to run slightly uphill

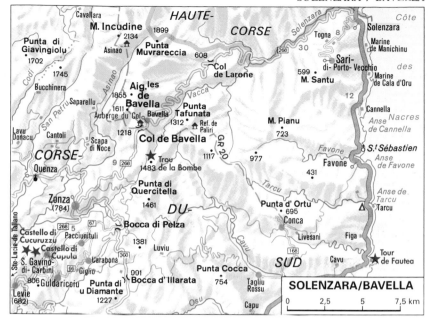

and due south. After about 40 minutes, it makes a sudden bend to run due east; at this point, however, it intersects with a forest trail which continues on due south, so make sure to keep an eye out for the red markings.

The path keeps rising to come to the **Bocca di Velaco**. Shortly before it descends a little again to reach the Velaco Pass, there's a kind of plateau from which you can survey the sweep of the mountain panorama around you. The mighty mountain directly across from you is the **Punta Velaco**, 4,864 feet (1,483 m) high; behind it on the left is the flat mountain crest of the **Promontoire** (4,658 feet/1,420 m); and at the far left you can see your destination: the rock cavity **Trou de la Bombe**.

After a few hundred yards you reach the pass. Be careful again: you have to look for little stone men which point to various destinations. In order to get to theTrou de la Bombe, take either of the northeastern paths; both will lead you there. The lower path is easier to hike on,

making a wide arc around the last spurs of rock; the upper path is a little more difficult. If you have some rock-climbing experience, you can climb directly up to the hole. Shortly before you get there, there is a nice spot for a picnic. It is best to go back the way you came.

Foce Finosa and Paliri Hut

Even without a compass and detailed map, this route is easy to follow because it runs along the well-marked GR 20 trail, the comprehensive cross-island hike. In general, the GR 20 is an alpine and strenuous hike, but you couldn't call this section difficult at all.

Starting point is, once again, the parking lot at the Bavella Pass. From here, you go a few hundred yards (400 m) along the road towards Solenzara. Between the first restaurant and a freshwater spring, where you can fill up your canteens, there is a wide path to the right (southeast). After another 750 yards or so (700 m), this path ends, and you get onto

the path marked in red-and-white (GR 20), which initially heads downhill. Make sure you keep following the red-and-white markings throughout this hike, because there are several forest trails which intersect with the GR 20 and lead off in other directions. After about an hour and a half, without having been confronted with any major ascents or descents (the total difference in altitude amounts to some 590 feet/180 m), you come to the pass of **Foce Finosa** (3,956 feet/1,206 m) On a clear day, you can see all the way to the rocky towers of the northern section of the Bavella group. Continue along to the Paliri hut, still along the GR 20, which at first heads downhill in steep curves, then gradually begins to rise again before you reach the hut. It takes about an hour to get to **Paliri** (at 3,460 feet/1,055 m), a self-catering hut. Shortly before you reach the hut, you can fill up your canteen at a spring which has been paved and curbed.

The GR 20 – which, along this stretch, follows an old herdsmen's path – used to be an important link between Col de Bavella (summer quarters) and the east coast (winter quarters).

Hikers should not only look out for the trail markers, but remember to keep turning their gaze to take in the rugged rock needles now and then. Perhaps you'll get lucky and spot one of the few Corsican mouflons, almost extinct. Once plentiful, these wild sheep are now found only in the mountains of Asco, Venaco and Bavella. There are only an estimated 200-600 of them left.

FROM ZONZA TO THE SOUTHEAST COAST

Heading south from the Bavella Pass, it is only 5.5 miles (9 km) to **Zonza**, the nearest big village. In Zonza, located on a slope 2,572 feet (784 m) high, hikers and mountain climbers can not only fortify

Above: Many hiking trails follow the old goat paths. Right: The Torrean Castello de Cucuruzzu, 2nd millennium B.C.

body and soul by feasting in the various bars and restaurants, but also pick up more information about hiking trails and the regional park; the **Bureau d'Information du Parc Régional** (Information Office of the Regional Park) is open every day (except Sundays) to help out visitors. You can find it on the arterial road (D 268) to Bavella, on the left. From Zonza, you have a choice of two routes leading back to the east coast and Porto-Vecchio.

A charming stretch leads south from Zonza to Levie on the D 268. Past Levie, take a right onto a small road and follow it 2.5 miles (4 km) to a big parking lot. From here you can view the archaeological excavations of two Torrean settlements, Cucuruzzu and Capula. You can rent a Walkman with a commentary at the excavation site before setting off on the 1.5-hour tour through a fairy-tale wooded landscape set with giant granite rocks. The site is on a granite plateau (*Pianu de Levie*) at an average altitude of 2,300 feet (700 m), with a magnificent view of the Rizzanèse Valley. The plateau was inhabited from the 7th millennium B.C. until into the Middle Ages. Objects found here, evidence of 8,000 years of human activity, are displayed in the museum in Levie.

After a shady walk you come to the **Castello de Cucuruzzu**, which has been dated back to the Bronze Age (mid-2nd millennium B.C.); it was abandoned for good in the 3rd century B.C. The site is in outstanding condition, because it lay virtually untouched under the maquis until it was discovered in 1959. Round, and facing east, the fortress was wonderfully integrated into the natural granite rock; and the thick cyclopean wall was an effective barrier against enemies. In the building itself, which was probably a religious site or a meeting place, there are various side chambers, including rooms for guards, and the main chamber, or cella. The impressive vault of the cella, 10-13 feet (3-4 m) in diameter, is built in the shape of a dome beehive, a construction found throughout the entire Mediterranean re-

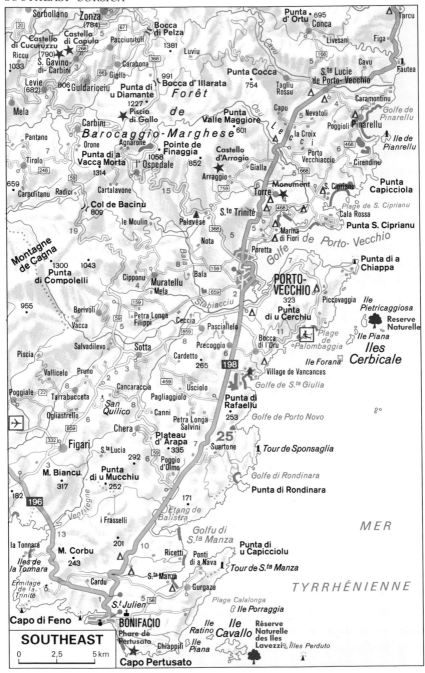

SOUTHEAST

0   2,5   5 km

gion. This is the only extant intact vault of this kind on Corsica. The entire religious monument was located some 33 feet (10 m) above the Torrean village. The inhabitants were farmers and bred cattle; millstones found here indicate that they also cultivated grain.

After another 20 minutes' walk, you reach another Torrean site which was used and inhabited up into the Middle Ages: **Castello di Capula**. Excavations are still going on around this area. Although it is basically similar to the Cucuruzzu site, Capula bears more evidence of more recent, medieval settlement than of its Bronze Age origins. Capula was the fortress of Count Giudice della Rocca, also called della Cinarca. Even though not much remains of the complex today, the fortress wall is interesting for the manner of its construction: square, evenly cut stones are cemented to the natural rocks with lime mortar – a nice example of how, in the past, a natural site was used and integrated into a new building.

As you follow the path around the site toward the exit, you can see the ruins of a 13th-century Romanesque chapel to the left. A bit farther on, shortly before the exit, there is a modern construction: the **Chapel St-Laurent** was built in 1917 on the remains of a Romanesque church. The church got its peculiar, old patina from the medieval stones which were integrated into the construction.

Sainte-Lucie-de-Tallano, farther to the west on the D 268, forms a circular crown to a rocky hilltop above the Rizzanèse, surrounded by vineyards and olive groves. In the village square, you can see a *casa torra*, a very old, fortified type of tower house.

In order to get back to the east coast or Porto-Vecchio, drive back to **Levie** and take an interesting route with great views: the D 59 through Carbini, over the **Bacinu Pass** (2,654 feet/809 m), and up to **Sotta**. Tourists rarely stray this far, so

be all the more careful to avoid collisions with local drivers. Many Corsicans seem to be unsure of whether you're supposed to drive on the right or on the left!

When driving through the little village of **Carbini**, don't neglect to visit the perfectly restored, early Romanesque church of **San Giovanni** with its giant bell tower, both from the 11th century. It was here that the *Giovannali* movement, a group founded by the Franciscans in the 14th century, began. Its members, numbering more than one hundred, rebelled against the Corsican nobility and fought for justice in the name of all of the poor. The bishop of Aléria, however, didn't put up with this kind of involvement for long, and ordered the Giovannali persecuted and killed as heretics. The movement fell apart, and a few of its surviving members made their way through the eastern part of the island, plundering and maurading, having degenerated into a kind of anarchist group ready to fight against any kind of authority.

Another alternative route, leading from mountainous Zonza back toward the sea, is the D 368, which runs directly from Zonza to Porto-Vecchio. Sharply winding, but well-built, this road goes mostly through wooden areas. In the autumn season, you can often spot Corsican hunters on the trail of real wild boars (not merely runaway domesticated pigs). The road goes over the **Bocca di Pelza** (2,867 feet/874 m) and the **Bocca d'Illarata** (3,250 feet/991 m). About 2.5 miles (4 km) after the second pass, you'll see a parking lot on the left with a snack stand; you can park your car here and take a walk to the **Piscia di Gallo** waterfall.

A path, marked in red, leads you between the pine trees and pigs. Be careful: the pigs look friendly, but they can also bite, especially if they have piglets or if you don't immediately voluntarily get out some of your sandwich. It's happened before that a sow jumped into the trunk of a horrified tourist's car, not re-

With its giant granite rocks, covered with ferns, its cork oaks, and laricio pine trees, twisted and blasted by the wind, this forest looks like the setting for a fairy tale.

You have a grand view of the Gulf of Porto-Vecchio from the hamlet of **Ospedale**. Even the Romans loved to take cures in the healthy mountain air at an altitude of around 3,000 feet (900 m). The name Ospedale refers to an old Roman hospital. From Ospedale, a pleasant hiking trail leads all the way to Porto-Vecchio, a walk of around three hours.

Coming from Zonza, you can spot, just before the edge of town on the right-hand side, a unique private swimming pool that's been cut directly into granite rock, with a magnificent view of the sea – what a life!

PORTO-VECCHIO

The two largest cities on the island, Ajaccio and Bastia, have an urban flair, but the third-largest city, **Porto-Vecchio** (*Porti-Vechiu*, 9,300 inhabitants), has the charm of a romantic Corsican village. During the summer months, however, the population multiplies, and the normally sleepy town appears to be bursting at the seams. At cocktail time, it's difficult to find an empty seat at one of the inviting cafés that line the **Place de la République**, particularly at a table that affords a view of the colorful hustle and bustle of town life.

Perched atop a cliff 230 feet high (70 m), the town is surrounded by a partially intact wall with a Genoese gate; at night, this wall is bathed in an impressive haze of orange-red light.

Even the Greeks from Syracuse knew about the excellently protected bay – they built the *Portus Syracusanus* here in 383 B.C. But the actual city wasn't founded until much later, in 1539, when the Bank of San Giorgio built a fortified town for Genoa in order to complete the line of

emerging until it had examined every bag and suitcase to its satisfaction. The trail leads along the side of a steep slope; below, to the right, is the brook Oso, which then tumbles down 164 feet (50 m) in a waterfall the locals have dubbed *Piscia di Gallo* – rooster piss. It takes between one and two hours to get there and back, depending on whether or not you want to climb all the way down into the slippery gorge; the footing is especially bad if it's been raining.

The drive to Porto-Vecchio continues on the D 368. You soon come to the retaining wall of Lake Ospedale, a reservoir which stores some 100 million cubic feet (3 million cu. m) of water to supply the Stabbiacco Valley and the region surrounding Porto-Vecchio. Driving through the 11,250 acres (4,500 ha) of the Forest of Ospedale, you'll pass picnic areas with great views along the way.

Above: Cork oaks are peeled every 8 to 12 years. Right: Traditional methods of gathering salt in Porto-Vecchio.

defenses they had erected along the entire coast of Corsica.

The only naturally protected harbor along the entire east coast was the **Gulf of Porto-Vecchio**. In spite of this, the settlement grew slowly, because the swampy river deltas here were also the home of the dangerous anopheles mosquito.

The Corsican freedom fighter Sampiero Corso came to Porto-Vecchio with his troops after an unsuccessful attack against the Genoese city of Ajaccio. On July 30, 1564, he managed to take the city. The Genoese asked for help from their ally, the Spanish king Philip II, who immediately sent a fleet under the command of the Genoese Stefano Doria (a nephew of the famous admiral Andrea Doria). Just a few months after Sampiero Corso's victory, the Genoese managed to win back the poorly defended city on November 26, 1564.

But Porto-Vecchio never developed into an important Genoese settlement. After another malaria epidemic (1581),

the natives destroyed their city as they fled it, in order to prevent the Saracens from settling here. The Genoese fortifications remained standing; even today, they still almost completely surround the city and can be seen from the swanky yacht marina.

Today, as in the past, the port is used for the export of regional agricultural products, including cork, citrus fruit, wine and olives. In addition, cattle breeding used to be important. Not until malaria was finally eradicated after World War II, however, did the city truly come into its own as a center for trade, administration and tourism, and the city limits were extended to the north along the national highway. Today, there is a shopping center in this area with big supermarkets.

Porto-Vecchio is also called the City of Salt, and with good reason. In the southern part of the city and the gulf, extensive salt works, built early in the 20th century, gleam in the sunlight. The Corsicans obtain their salt here by the traditional

method of evaporating sea water in shallow basins.

One draw that attracts the hordes of visitors who descend on the town every year is the large headland which juts out into the sea to the south of the Gulf of Porto-Vecchio. More than a mile (2 km) south of the city, a small road branches off to the left onto this promontory and leads all the way around it in an 11.5-mile (18.5 km) round trip, leading back, finally, to the N 198. This route is also ideal for bicyclists in search of a good day trip.

At the outermost point, **Punta di a Chiappa**, tourists in search of an "all-over" tan can take advantage of the nude beach. The prettiest places to swim, however, are on the southern side of the point. The **Plage de Palombaggia**, perhaps the prettiest beach on the whole Corsican coast, stands out with its fine sand, the red granite rocks which appear to glow

Above: The Plage de Palombaggia is held to be the loveliest beach on Corsica.

fiery red in the evening light, and its clear turquoise water. In addition, you'll find refreshing shade in the pine woods beside the beach. Having your car broken into, however, could spoil your fun, so make sure not to leave any valuables in the car, because you can't see the parking lot from the beach! Offshore, you can see the **Iles Cerbicales**, but no one is actually allowed on the islands of this nature preserve. Along the road is a long line of vacation homes. Farther south is the picturesque bay of **Santa Giulia**, where the first Club Med was built.

Excursions in the Area

From Porto-Vecchio there are two excursions worth taking which can be done in one – admittedly lengthy – afternoon, leading to two sites of Torrean culture dating from the Bronze Age: Torre and the Castello d'Arraggio.

Highway N 198 heads northward out of Porto-Vecchio to **Torre**. Turn onto the second small road to the right after 5 miles (8 km), past the left-hand turnoff of the D 759 toward Arraggio. After a few hundred yards, park the car on the side of the road and follow the steep uphill path to a farm. After you cross the private courtyard, archaic stone steps will lead you up to the monument which gave an entire culture its name.

Originally, all of the Torrean religious constructions had domed towers (*torre*) built over them, similar to the *nuraghi* constructions on Sardinia. These towers had openings at the top to serve as chimneys; here in Torre, ashes and charred remains were found inside, as well. Archaeologists have therefore come to the conclusion that the building was used for some sort of religious purpose; perhaps it was a burial site. Once you've crawled inside, you can see how the structure is divided into a main corridor and two side corridors. Across from the entrance there is another narrow opening which was also used as a chimney. This monument was definitely not a dwelling. The huts of the Torreans were probably at the foot of the cliff.

After checking out the interior, you can dare to take the quick and safe climb onto the roof. From up there, especially in the waning hours of daylight, you have an unforgettable view of the sea and the bay of **San Cipriano**.

Back on the N 198, drive a bit farther south and turn onto the D 759 to Arraggio. In the small village, you'll see a faded sign, hung on one of the few houses at a spot where the road curves to the right, indicating the way to the **fortress of Arraggio**; Corsicans know it as the *Castellu d'Araghju*. Park your car somewhere nearby and set out on the half-hour trek leading steeply up the mountain. At first, you go past a garden on the left with tantalizing fig trees, then you have to take sharp turns to the right up the slope. Once you've reached an altitude of 807 feet (245 m), breathless but happy, you can enter the remains of the Torrean fort: its wall, up to 16 feet (5 m) tall, gave the archaic fortress a diameter of 394 feet (120 m).

The first Torreans probably landed in the Gulf of Porto-Vecchio in around 1600 B.C. The forts were always built on exposed sites commanding a broad view of the surrounding landscape; Arraggio was one of the first forts built and is a good example of a typical one. Excavation work here started in 1967 under the direction of the archaeologist Roger Grosjean. Arraggio, like Torre, was originally built exclusively for religious purposes. From later additions, however, we can see that rooms were also set up for sentries, as well as chambers for religious and tribal leaders. Later on, the Torreans built a cyclopean wall for defense. It is remarkable that as early as the Bronze Age people could move giant rocks, often weighing tons, and assemble them into a wall without using any mortar. The view stretches far over the Gulf of Porto-Vecchio.

Driving to the southern tip of Corsica, to Bonifacio, along the national highway N 198, you'll keep noticing the profusion of cork oaks on both sides of the road. The region around Porto-Vecchio has the largest cork oak forest on Corsica (20,000 acres/8,000 ha). Cork continues to play a vital role in the Corsican economy today. It is used as insulation, as a raw material for bonding agents, such as glue, and for corks for bottles.

The trees are still peeled by hand. A tree can be peeled for the first time after 15 to 20 years. The first peeling is called "masculine cork"; it is, however, of inferior quality and is used for such purposes as a raw material for bonding agents. The subsequent peelings, the so-called "feminine cork," are better in quality. The bark, however, has to grow back for another 8 to 12 years before it is ready to be peeled. After a peeling, the naked tree trunk glows red: a favorite image of photographers.

BONIFACIO

Bonifacio (*Bonifaziu*) is often called "Corsica's most beautiful city" as well as the "southernmost city in France." Both may be true, otherwise the very first settlers on Corsica would not have selected this wonderful location for their first dwellings.

The earliest human findings on the island, dating back to the New Stone Age, were found on the outskirts of Bonifacio, below the Araguina-Sennola cliff. The skeleton they excavated here, from 6570 B.C., is called the "Lady of Bonifacio" – not without a certain degree of pride.

The impressive location of the town was mentioned by the German historian Ferdinand Gregorovius while traveling across the island in 1852: "If you imagine a colossal, pale rock pyramid, horizontally layered, turned upside down and

Above: Preparing for a day's fishing. Right: Bonifacio is enthroned on chalk cliffs high over the sea.

placed by the sea, its base pointing upwards, with, on this base, high in the air, a fortress, towers and a whole city; then you will have a picture of this Corsican Gibraltar."

Even Odysseus, Homer's hero, was attracted to the almost 230-foot-high (70 m) Miocene chalk plateau, surrounded on three sides by the sea, and the natural harbor which cuts almost a mile (1,600 m) inland. In his wanderings, he happened upon the natural harbor of Bonifacio, where he was pelted with rocks by the gigantic Laestrygons. He only barely escaped with his life. But perhaps the hostile aggressors were in fact only Torreans, trying to protect their new home from intruders?

Little is known about Greek and Roman settlements in the area. A few miles from the city, near Cape Sperone, archaeologists have excavated a Roman villa (Piantarella) and dated it from the 1st century A.D.

In 830, the Tuscan margrave Boniface founded the present city and gave it his

name. In the ensuing years, "Corsica's Gibraltar" was the object of bitter battles; its location, optimal from a strategic point of view, attracted besiegers like flies. The conflicts between the maritime republics of Pisa and Genoa made themselves felt in Bonifacio; Genoa finally won the upper hand at the end of the 12th century, drove out the local inhabitants, and settled faithful Ligurians here. Encouraged by various privileges (a certain degree of political autonomy, its own coinage), Bonifacio became the city on Corsica that was the most loyal to Genoa. Due to the town's isolated location, the locals around Bonifacio still speak Corsican with a strong Ligurian accent, even today.

Two other sieges, in 1420 and 1553, figured prominently in the island's history. In 1420, King Alfonso V of Aragon blockaded the city for five months with his fleet and Catalan army. Pope Boniface VIII had already given the island to Alfonso's father, Jacob II, as a fiefdom in 1297, and more than 100 years later his son wanted enforce his claim to the island. The inhabitants would have died of hunger during the long siege if it hadn't been for the "refreshing mercy of the women." Gregorovius reported: "... for the pious women of Bonifacio gave their milk freely to relatives, brothers, children, close friends, and cousins to drink. And during that siege, there was not one person in Bonifacio who did not suckle at a woman's breast."

The famous **Steps of the King of Aragon** (which are 187 in number) date from this period as well. According to local legend, the king's troops cut them into the chalk rock in a single night in order to take the unyielding city. In reality, the natives of Bonifacio achieved this feat in several nights, creating a link to the sea (the harbor was sealed off), thus enabling them to send to Genoa for help. Genoa actually did send help, and in 1421 the Spanish king had to give up and sail to Italy – not exactly involuntarily, however, because he was to become the King of Naples that same year.

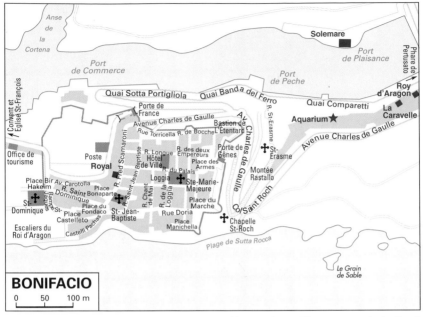

BONIFACIO
0   50   100 m

The Lower City

After a big plague epidemic in 1528 wiped out almost two-thirds of the population, the city soon received another shock: in 1553, the troops of the French king Henri II and his ally, the Turkish corsair Dragut, laid siege to the city. They shelled the city for eighteen days and nights, but Bonifacio could only be forced to surrender by means of an insidious ruse. Dragut and his men went on to devastate the town, and only the precipitous arrival of Sampiero Corso kept them from destroying it altogether.

The Lower City

Right by the entrance to the city, there's a large, guarded parking lot, where you can leave your car for a fee; it's best to do this, and go on to explore the city on foot.

The lower city stretches along the pretty marina and fishing port for about 1

Right: A path leads along chalk cliffs from Bonifacio to the southern tip of the island.

mile (1.5 km). The promenade is lined with street cafés, good fish restaurants, hotels and souvenir shops. Approximately in the middle of the promenade there's an aquarium, located in a cave, which displays the marine flora and fauna of Corsica in 13 tanks.

Here, on the wharf, you'll be approached time and again by the modern-day "Corsican pirates," who offer 45-minute boat trips around Bonifacio and to the various caves – but in fact, these excursions can be a lot of fun, if the mood takes you.

Even if you don't want to spend most of your vacation in souvenir shops, you should look in at one shop in the lower city: at the end of the wharf, shortly before the steep stairs, there is a store on the left which sells exclusively products made of cork. You will be surprised at all of the things that can be made out of this natural material, besides the well-known bottle corks: seductive brassieres, skirts, fashionable shoes, satchels, pencils, mats and much, much more...

Before you start the climb up to the upper city in the heat, you can visit the small church on the right, **St-Erasme**, dedicated to the patron saint of sailors. In the apse, which still has masonry from the 13th century, stands the processional statue of St. Erasmus; the rest of the church dates from the 19th century. In the barrel vault of the ceiling hangs a unique lamp made from a model ship. Two annual processions start at the church: one on June 2 in honor of St. Erasmus, and one on July 20 to celebrate the patron saint of crayfish fishermen, St. Sylvertius.

While climbing the steps of the **Montée Rastello**, you have the option of visiting one of the *Tailleries de Corail* on the right or left, where you can watch coral cutters at work; the "red gold" can also be purchased here in the form of jewelry or other small items. Coral is not a plant; rather, it derives from groups of invertebrate animals, or anthozoa (*coelenterates*). They usually live in colonies formed by very tiny polyps. The animals form a skeleton of lime or horn-like substances; they shed their skeletons, however, not in one single layer, but in ribs and rings of lime; and so the skeleton gradually grows into the well-known, beloved, irregular shapes.

The colorful coral which is used to make jewelry is called precious coral; on Corsica, red coral is predominant. The least expensive and simplest jewelry is a chain of irregular coral tips strung together on a Perlon cord, after their skins have been pulled off. A turbo drill has to be used for complicated pieces because the material is so hard.

Unfortunately, this precious item is becoming increasingly rare, because an 8-inch (20 cm) branch of coral takes almost 50 years to grow back. In the 18th century, residents were able to mine more than 20 tons of coral a year from the sea on the east coast of Corsica; today, they can mine only 5 tons.

At the top of the stairs is the **Col St-Roch** with a nice view of the sea. On a clear day, you can see Sardinia on the

horizon, only 7.5 miles (12 km) away. Located here is the **St-Roch chapel**. It was built on the spot where the last victim of the plague died in 1528.

To get to the upper city, or, as the natives would proudly call it, *Bonifaziu Propriu*, you pass through the **Porte des Gênes**, which was for a long time the only entrance to the city.

The Upper City

Because of the lack of space on top of the plateau, which averages only about 650 feet (200 m) in width, the buildings of the old city are crowded together. Characteristic of the architecture here are slim, tall houses with dizzyingly steep stairs (to prevent the animals from climbing up into the living quarters) lining the narrow alleys. On a dark, cloudy day when the wind is howling through the

Above: Buttresses along the Rue du Palais also serve to collect rainwater. Right: The Marine Cemetery.

streets, you could feel like you're in a suspense thriller.

You come to the small **Place des Armes** first. Once a spot for military drills, this square also held silos where considerable amounts of wheat could be stored in case of a siege. From here you can come to the **Rue des deux Empereurs** (Street of Two Emperors). As you turn onto the street you can see, on the wall of a house on your left, a plaque commemorating the fact that Charles V found lodging here, at the home of Count Philippe Cattaciolo, from October 3 to 6, 1541, when he was retreating from his disastrous Algerian campaign.

Almost directly opposite at No. 7, another sign refers to a second important personage who visited this place: Napoleon Bonaparte stayed in this house from January 22 to March 3, 1793, following his retreat from his unsuccessful Sardinian expedition. It wasn't until years later that he would be crowned Emperor of France.

From here, you can stroll through one of the narrow alleys to the parallel street, **Rue du Palais**. Noticeable here are the numerous arched buttresses which connect the houses to one another and to the cathedral, or Ste.-Marie-Majeur. This ingenious system caught rain water and conducted it into the underground cistern under the cathedral's loggia, with a capacity of 22,955 cubic feet (650 cubic m), ensuring that, even in a siege, the town's inhabitants would have plenty of water. This cistern has since been converted into a conference room.

The loggia is used as the vestibule (narthex) of the church. Under Genoese rule, the four elders, elected by the city council to serve for three months, met here to decide on city matters, and justice was administered here, as well. Next to the loggia towers the nicely renovated **governor's palace**, which once served the city hall and today houses a museum of Christian art.

The facade of **Ste.-Marie-Majeur**, originally the cathedral church, dates back to the days of Pisan rule (13th century). Prosper Mérimée classified the beautiful, elegant tower with its decorations in high relief as a historical monument in November, 1900.

Blinded by the sun, you need to get used to the darkness of the interior before you can see the extraordinary wealth of decoration, unusual on Corsica: it includes several Italian altars (17th and 18th centuries), beautiful baptismal fonts with tabernacles dating from the early Italian Renaissance, and a Roman sarcophagus from the 3rd century.

Follow Rue de la Loggia to **Rue Doria**, named after the famous family of Admiral Andrea Doria. At the intersection of **Rue St-Jean Baptiste**, a sign points the way to a speciality bakery on this street, which is almost more interesting than the small church (1785) on the corner.

At this bakery, hungry visitors can stock up on traditional local baked goods: *fugasi* cakes with orange blossom liqueur or *vea secatta*, funeral bread with nuts and raisins. This shop is by no means the province of tourists alone; you can see plenty of people from Bonifacio also standing in line.

Across the **Place du Fondaco** and along the **Rue St-Dominique**, which is striking for the rows of attractive coats-of-arms which each house sports over its entrance doors, and you come to the **Place Bir Hakeim**. The heroic monument to the Foreign Legion, originally from Saida in Algeria, was dedicated on June 23, 1963, when Foreign Legion units moved to their new quarters in Bonifacio. In 1983 the Legion left, much to the detriment of the eating establishments around the harbor. Today, the big barracks are used as sleeping quarters for the French army.

You can see the tourist information office from the square; it's through this office that you enter the Gothic **church of St-Dominique**. This is the only Gothic house of worship on Corsica; it was built

by the Order of Knights Templar between 1270 and 1343.

If you follow the road to the outermost point of the peninsula you'll come to a charming, small *cimetière*, the **Marine Cemetery**, and to the former **St-François monastery**. All that is left of the monastery is the **church** (13th century) and a convent building, where the city's music school is located.

From the Col St-Roch, you can set off on a pleasant walk with a view of the city, which is built adventurously, not to say dizzyingly, close to the edge of the rocky precipice. Across from the chapel is a footpath which leads through maquis shrubbery to the **Pertusato lighthouse**, which marks the southernmost point on Corsica.

Santa-Manza Bay has an attractive sand beach, which you reach by following the D 58 in a northeasterly direction for 4 miles (6 km).

Above: Typical Corsican profile – a young islander from Bonifacio.

SOUTHEAST COAST
Accommodation
SOLENZARA: *MODERATE:* **Maquis et Mer**, tel. 95574237. **La Solenzara**, tel. 95574218. *BUDGET:* **Tourisme Hotel**, tel. 95574044. **Orsoni**, tel. 95574025, **Mare e Festa**, Pavillon-Hotel, on the ocean, tel. 95574010.
FAVONE: *MODERATE:* U **Dragulinu**: tel. 95732030.
STE. LUCIE DE PORTO-VECCHIO: *MODERATE:* **Au Rêve**, Tarco, Pont de Tarco, tel. 95732093. **San Pieru**, Tarco, tel. 95732133. **Stella di Mare**, Tarco, tel. 95732052. **La Tour Genoise**, Pinarello, tel. 95714439.
Campgrounds
SOLENZARA: **La Côte des Nacres**, 1 km north of Solenzara, located right on a sand beach at a river mouth, with tennis, shops, and cinema in summer, tel. 95574065.
STE. LUCIE DE PORTO-VECCHIO: **Bon' Anno**, Favone, tel. 95732135. **Pinarellu**, Pinarello, with swimming pool and tennis courts. tel. 95714398. **California**, Pinarello, tel. 95714924. **Centre Naturiste de Villata**, nudist facilities, tel. 95716290/95716019.
TRINITÉ DE PORTO-VECCHIO: Golfo di Sogno, Route de Cala Rossa, tel. 95700898.
Car rental
SARI-SOLENZARA: Balesi Europcar, Route de Bastia, tel. 95574204.
Sports
BOAT RENTAL: **Schiavo Nautic**, Marine de Solenzara, tel. 95574001. **Astolfi Sud Corse Nautic**, Ste. Lucie de Porto-Vecchio, R.N. 198, tel. 95715211. *DIVING:* **Beodric Adventures**, Port de Plaisance, Solenzara, tel. 95720577. **Subaquatique Club Côte des Nacres**, B.P. 12, Solenzara, tel. 9557461
Tourist Information
FAVONE: tel. 95572221.
SOLENZARA: Mairie Annexe, tel. 95574151.
STE. LUCIE DE PORTO-VECCHIO: tel. 95714899.

ZONZA, QUENZA, SOTTA
Accommodation
ZONZA: *MODERATE:* **L'Incudine**, tel. 95786771. *BUDGET:* **La Terrasse**, tel. 95786769/95786603. **L'Aiglon**, tel. 95786779.
QUENZA: *MODERATE:* **Sole E Monti**, tel. 95786253/95786156.
SOTTA: *MODERATE:* **Mondoloni**, tel. 95712098.
Campgrounds
ZONZA: **Camping Municipal**, tel. 95786817/95786274. **U Fucone**, Route de Quenza, tel.

95786676 / 95786678. **QUENZA: Muntagnoli Corsi**, tel. 95786405.

PORTO-VECCHIO
Accommodation
LUXURY: **Grand Hotel de Cala Rossa**, Lecci de Porto-Vecchio, 6 mi/10 km from Porto-Vecchio, tennis, sailing, surfing, tel. 95716151. *MODERATE*: **Castell'Verde**, Baie de Santa Giulia B.P. 24, swimming pool, tennis, tel. 95707100. **Le Moby Dick**, Baie de Santa Giulia B.P.24, tennis, tel. 95707000. **Le Belvédère**, Route de Palombaggia B.P.56, swimming pool, tennis, tel. 95705413. **La Rivière**, Quartier de Bala, swimming pool, tennis, at quiet inland location, tel. 95701021. *BUDGET*: **Le Modern'**, 10, cours Napoléon, tel. 95700636. **Panorama**, 12, rue Jean-Nicoli, tel. 95700796. **La Chiappa**, nudist club; bungalows, tel. 95700031.

Campgrounds
Asciaghju, Bocca Dell'Oro, tel. 95703787. **U Pirellu**, pool, tennis, tel. 95702344. **U Stabiacciu**, Route de Palombaggia, tel. 95703717. **Arutoli**, Route de l'Ospédale, swimming pool, tel. 95701273. **La Vetta**, La Trinité, pool, tel. 95700986.

Transportation
AIRPORT: **Figari Sud Corse**, tel. 95710022. *HELICOPTER*· Helicopter flights over the whole island: **Helidan-Corse**, Quartier Mazzetta, Route de Bonifacio B.P.78, tel. 95720712. *BUS:* **Eurocorse Voyages**, Rue Pasteur, tel. 95701383, twice daily Porto-Vecchio-Bonifacio-Sartène-Ajaccio. *TAXI:* **Station Cours Napoleon**, Place de la République, tel. 95700849. *CAR RENTAL:* **Avis**, Imm. "Terazzoni," Route de Bastia, tel. 95701477. **Budget**, Port de Plaisance, tel. 95702570. **Balesi Europcar**, Route de Bastia, tel. 95701450.

Sports
BIKE AND MOTORCYCLE RENTAL: **Garage Legrand**, Route de Bonifacio, tel. 95701584. **Corse Moto Service**, U Centru, Route de Bastia, tel. 95704551. *DIVING:* Club La Palanquée, 6, Cours Napoléon and at the marina. *GOLF:* **Golf de Lezza**, Route de Bonifacio, tel. 95702978. *RIDING:* **A Staffa di Porti Vechiu**, Camping U Stabiacciu, tel. 95703717/ 95704751. *SAILING:* **Locorsa**, La Capitainerie du Port, tel. 95701237. **Multi-Services Plaisance**, Marines de Santa Giulia, tel. 95702913.

Tourist Information
Place de l'Hotel de Ville, tel. 95700958.

BONIFACIO
Accommodation
LUXURY: **Genovese**, Quartier de la Citadelle, tel. 95731234. **La Caravelle**, 37, Quai Comparetti, tel. 95730003. *MODERATE*: **Roy D'Aragon**, 13,

Quai Comparetti, Port de Plaisance, tel. 95730399. **Solemare**, La Marine, tel. 95730106. **Le Royal**, 8, Rue Fred-Scamaroni, tel. 95730051.

Campgrounds
Pertamina Village U Farniente, R.N. 198, quiet and well-equipped facility with campground, swimming pool, tennis, 2.5 mi/4 km north of the city, tel. 95730547. **L'Araguina**, Av. Sylvère-Bohn, shaded, terraced campsites, tennis courts, bus to the beaches, tel. 95730296. **Des Iles**, Route de Pinatarella, swimming pool, tennis, tel. 95731189.

Restaurants
Fish: **La Sémillante**, Quai Comparetti, tel. 95730834. **La Caravelle**, Quai Comparetti, tel. 95730647. *Pizza:* **L'Escale**, Quai Comparetti, tel. 95731979. **La Stella d'Oro**, Rue Doria, tel. 95730363.

Museum
Aquarium, at the harbor. Fauna and flora of the underwater world around Bonifacio in a natural grotto. Texts in English, Italian and German. April-Nov 10 am-8 pm, in summer 10 am-midnight.

Night life
L'Agora disco, tel. 95730044, and **La Fa Dièse** disco, tel. 95731789, both in the upper city.

Car rental
Avis Ollandini, Quai Comparetti, tel. 95730128 **Europcar**, Station Esso, tel. 95731099. **Hertz-Filippi Auto**, Quai Portiglioli, tel. 95730247.

Ferries
Compagnie Moby Lines, Gare Maritime, ferry service between Corsica (Bonifacio) and Sardinia, daily April to October, tel. 95730029.

Boat Excursions
Compagnie Thalassa-Rocca-Le Corsaire, tel. 95730117/95730308. **Compagnie Christina**, tel. 95730256/95731315. **Compagnie Mediteranée**, tel. 95730771.

Sports
BOAT RENTAL: **Swan Sail**, Centre Nautique, tel. 95730412. **Deltour Plaisance**, La Marine, tel. 95730300. *DIVING:* **Barakouda**, Avenue Sylvère Bohn, tel. 95731302. *RIDING:* **Ranch San Diego**, tel. 95730167. *SAILING SCHOOL:* **Les Glenans**, tel. 95730385. **Ecole de Piantarella**, tel. 95730489. *TENNIS:* **Bonifacio Tennis Club**, tel. 95730545.

Beaches
SUTTA-ROCCA: Stairs lead down from the chapel of Saint-Roch to the sea. Tiny sand beaches and large rocks to swim from. **SANTA MANZA**: 4 mi/6 km along the D 58 to the Gulf of Santa Manza. **CALALONGA**: 4 mi/6 km. 2 mi/3 km on the D 58, then right on the D 258 to the end of the street.

Tourist Information
Place de l'Europe, tel. 95731188.

MENHIRS AND BEACHES IN THE SOUTHWEST

SARTÈNE / CAURIA
PROPRIANO AND THE
GULF OF VALINCO
FILITOSA
OLMETO

Corsica's west and east coasts couldn't be more different in character. While tourists seeking sun, sand, and swimming have become a standard feature on the straight, unbroken eastern coast, and the bikini seems to be on its way to becoming the most common article of clothing, the rugged western coast features small, traditional villages and secluded bays for swimming.

The southwest is notable for its megalithic sites near Cauria, the city of Sartène, which is as Corsican as it gets, and the Gulf of Valinco, the southern-most of the four large gulfs along the west coast.

If you drive from Bonifacio westwards – past rocky bays and tracts of fallow land – you can glean a quick view of the **Uomo di Cagna** (3,992 feet/1,217 m) shortly before Pianottoli. This gigantic wobbly granite block in the **Montagne di Cagna**, the highest mountain range in the southwest, weighs about 25 tons and rests on a base of only 1.2 square inches (8 cm). Above the Gulf of Roccapina, there's an ideal place for a rest break: at the parking lot by the small Corsican restaurant *Oasis du Lion*, which also has a

bar. Here you can eat good, genuine Corsican food, and if the owner, Henri Giacomoni, is in a good mood, he'll pull out his accordion and play.

Even if you aren't all that hungry, you should stop here before the Col de Coralli to take in the great view of the **Gulf of Roccapina**. With a little imagination, you can make out the **Rocher du Lion**, a stone in the form of a reclining lion, next to the Genoese tower; and down below there is a tempting, and uncrowded, white sand beach, which you can only reach along a potholed, dusty road (follow the signs for "Camping Municipal"). The arduous drive is well worth it!

Farther to the north on the N 196 you'll find well cared-for vineyards, whose grapes are pressed into a mellow red wine in Sartène. The unsettled **Ortolo Valley** on the west flank of the Cagna mountains is particularly fertile. The narrow D 50, unpaved at the start, winds through this valley and offers an alternative, charming way to get to Sartène via Mola; from the **Col de Suara** (1,463 feet/446 m), you have a beautiful view of the proud Corsican stronghold and the Golfe de Valinco.

SARTÈNE

"The most Corsican of all Corsican cities" – this oft-quoted epithet of Pros-

Preceding pages: Ortolo valley and Montagne di Cagna, southeast of Sartène. Left: Fisherman mending his nets in Propriano.

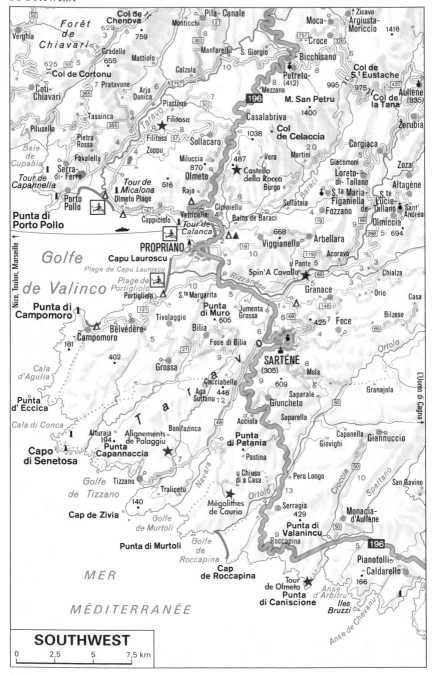

SOUTHWEST

0   2,5   5   7,5 km

per Mérimée remains one of the most fitting descriptions of **Sartène** (Sartè). High, fortress-like granite houses, shuttered windows, and crooked, medieval alleyways through which the wind howls: all of this conveys some sense of the city's mysterious, quasi-legendary history.

Nowhere else on Corsica are the signs at the city limits painted over with such tenacity, or so often used as targets by sharpshooters: Sartè remains Sartè, even if the French administration thinks they can sully it with the French name Sartène. The stubbornness of the natives of Sartè, as well as of the rest of the native Corsicans (for you see signs with French place names painted over with the Corsican equivalents all over the island), finally, in 1993, led France to start gradually writing all of the road signs on the island in both languages.

The inhabitants of Sartène haven't always have much reason to laugh through their difficult history. Even at the dawn of historic consciousness, the region of Sartenais was already densely populated. The city itself was ruled by powerful feudal lords of the extensive Della Rocca clan; the name Della Rocca appears on old maps in the name of the gulf, Gulf della Rocca (now known as the Gulf of Valinco). Even today, the names of the regions around Fozzano (Rocca) and the hinterland of Sartène (Alta-Rocca) contain reference to the noble family. The Rocca-Serras still dominate the southern part of the island even today.

At times, the population was under the control of another group of big feudal lords, the *Sgio*, who had firm control over the economy and politics. Bad times began for Sartène when pirates advanced through the easily accessible Gulf of Valinco and penetrated to the city itself. In 1565, Sampiero Corso and his troops managed to conquer the city.

The worst was yet to come; it occurred in 1583, when Algerian pirates completely plundered the city and subsequently dragged off 400 natives (one-third of the population!) to North Africa to serve as slaves. After this raid, the city's residents made sure to surround Sartène with a better-fortified city wall. Nonetheless, the region continued to be subjected to Saracen invasions until well into the 18th century.

During the Corsican war of independence (1729-1769), General Giafferi occupied the city in 1732; in spite of this, the citizens didn't recognize the Paoli government until much later (1763).

Since the 19th century, Sartène has also borne the somber epithet of "capital city of the vendetta." Somber it may be, but it's far from unjust: in the 19th century, the city's inhabitants waged bitter clan feuds and battles to the death. Powerful family clans and feudal lords warred with one another until blood flowed, and the general population was drawn into these disputes. The climax of these incredible battles arrived in the early 1830s. Borgo and Santa Anna, two quarters of the old city, waged a real guerrilla war with one another; not a day went by when you couldn't hear the sound of gunshot being fired from within the well-barricaded houses. The poor inhabitants of the Borgo quarter felt that they were at a disadvantage compared to the wealthy landowners who lived in the Santa Anna quarter, and therefore revolted against them.

In 1834, both parties signed a peace treaty in the church of Ste-Marie, which was meant to put an end to the hostilities. In fact, however, vendetta wars continued to break out time and again in Sartène, often resulting in death, until into the 20th century; and even today, the honor of one's family is no joking matter on Corsica.

Today, however, the only tangible reminder of Sartène's bloody past is the *catenacciu* (the chained one): every year on the night before Good Friday, a procession moves through the city that's

worthy of the stage. This old tradition not only attracts many Corsicans from the neighboring villages, but also a considerable number of foreigners.

Starting point of the procession is the Ste-Marie church on the Place de la Libération. At 9:30 pm, in the pitch-black night, the parade of people starts moving through the narrow streets and over the perilous stairs of the old city. The whole spectacle is illuminated only by candles, flickering in the wind, which the inhabitants of the old city put in their windows. Accompanying this is the continuous, lamenting Corsican song rising from the crowd of marchers: "Perdonno mio Dio... mio Dio perdonno" ("My Lord, forgive me").

All of this is not, however, simply a nighttime spectacle or a theater piece for the entertainment of a few foreigners, but Corsican reality. For everyone involved,

Above and right: The two faces of Sartène – forbidding house facades on the outside, friendly smiles within.

this procession is an expression of deep religious piety; it is often compared to the *Semanna Santa* in Seville.

Leading the procession in Sartène is the barefoot Grand Penitent or Penitent Rouge, swathed in a robe of blood-red silk, his head hidden by a red masked hood with two narrow slits which enable him to see. The masked man carries a cross weighing 69 pounds (31.5 kg), and he pulls an iron chain weighing 31 pounds (14 kg) behind him (hence the name *catenacciu*), which makes walking difficult. Black-clad "brothers of death," Penitents Noirs, accompany the unknown penitent. The *catenacciu* must fall down three times, just as Christ did on his way of the Cross to Golgotha. The Lesser Penitent or Penitent Blanc, wearing a white hooded robe, may help him to his feet again, as Simon of Cyrene once helped Christ.

But who is the masked bearer of the cross, who takes upon himself this kind of suffering and punishment on this unearthly night?

Only a single person knows the identity of the penitent, and this person is pledged to secrecy: the priest of Sartène. He alone knows the type and magnitude of the offense committed by the Grand Penitent; every year, a different person seeks to expiate his crime by taking on this role. It is said that only Corsicans can serve in this function.

In the 19th century, the applicants for the role of the Great Penitent were mainly inhabitants of Sartène who were involved in vendetta feuds and had fled into the maquis after committing a murder. Every year, the priest receives countless letters with requests to carry the cross and the iron chain, because many Corsicans see this as a way to cleanse their souls and purify themselves. The "bitter walk" is said, however, to be booked out for years in advance.

Only once, recount older Corsicans in Sartène, was the identity of the Grand Penitent accidentally discovered. The faithful dog of the baker of Sartène couldn't bear to be separated from his master, even on Good Friday, and it accompanied him, howling, all along the course of the procession, so at least the natives of Sartène knew the identity of that year's *catenacciu*.

When the Good Friday procession, which probably dates back to the early Middle Ages, is over, the crowd gathers again on the Place de la Libération to conclude the somber, other-worldly parade in typical French style with a village festival.

Tour of the City

Starting point for any exploration of the city is the **Place de la Libération**, once known as *Piazza Porta*, and still often called this by the natives. Shaded by palm trees, the square is inviting for visitors and locals alike; its attractive cafés are an established hangout for young and old natives of Sartène. The cafés are also great spots for a lunch break; in addition to their signature ice cream specialties, they serve salads,

123

sandwiches, or platters of cheese, sausage and ham. Particularly recommended is the **Café de la Victoire**, known for its giant sandwiches.

The square is bordered by the city hall and the impressive **Ste-Marie** church (completed in 1593), which dominates the square with its granite masonry. The main attraction in the interior is not the Baroque altar of multicolored marble (18th century), but rather the heavy wooden cross and the iron chain which the *catenacciu* has to carry through the old city during the Good Friday procession. Both pieces are immediately to the left of the entrance; in addition, there are pictures and text explaining the nighttime procession.

You can reach the old city quarter of **Santa Anna** by going through the archway of the city hall. Notable here are the narrow alleys, the steep stairs, and the high, forbidding-looking houses, some of which still have two stairways, one inside and one outside leading directly to the second or third floor. Right after entering the old city, walk down an alley to come to a 16th-century watchtower on the left; this was once integrated into the fortress wall, of which only fragments exist today.

Several alleys have been restored marvelously, and now feature shops selling Corsican artisan work. However, if you're curious enough to check out every last courtyard, nook, and cranny of the city, you'll find yourself straying from the path of medieval romanticism. Off the beaten track, the buildings are rather run-down, some almost falling down, and only the colorful laundry hanging out of the windows to dry is indication that they are still inhabited. These are the dwellings of workers from the vineyards, who usually come from North African countries such as Morocco or Algeria and earn their living working for Corsican farmers.

In the old city quarter of **Borgo**, the **Prehistoric Museum** is especially worth visiting; it is located in the former city jail, which was built in 1843.

Assembled by the archaeologist Roger Grosjean, the collection features excavated objects and finds from the time periods between 7000 B.C. to 100 A.D.In rooms 1 and 2, there's a comprehensive display of everyday objects from the Neolithic Age (6000 to 3000 B.C.): the first imported obsidian, which was used to make tools; ceramics etched with seashell motifs; and nicely worked and polished stones (grinding stones, millstones, and tools for weaving). You can also see several pieces of gold and silver jewelry from megalithic graves (3000 to 1500 B.C.).

In the following rooms 3, 4 and 5, the objects on display are around 1,000 years more recent (2600 to 1800 B.C.). Again, weapons and tools dominate here; the hoes are even made of metal, the arrowheads are made of silica and rhyolite. Also on exhibit are human bones, slightly deformed by fire, which were found in tafoni stone caves, as well as jewelry, including some made of serpentine.

In room 6, you are transported to the Bronze and Iron Ages, which correspond to the Torrean period on Corsica (1800 B.C. to 100 A.D.). Here, archaeologists have reconstructed a Torrean cult monument which was used for cremation. Imported ceramics, pearls, money and also nails are also on exhibit. After 700 B.C., during the Iron Age, ceramics with asbestos, weapons and tools made of iron, and jewelry made of bronze and glass paste appeared on the scene.

Not far from the museum is a building housing the *Département d'Étude et de Préservation des Statues-Menhirs de Corse* (Department for the Studies and Preservation of Corsican Menhirs). Two of the rooms are open to the public and

Right: Restoration work in progress on the Alignement of Stantari, Cauria.

contain reconstructed megalithic sites, genuine menhirs and copies.

If a visit to this interesting museum inspires you to go out and find some authentic megalith sites, head south out of Sartène on the N 196. About 1.5 miles (2.5 km) past the outskirts of town, the narrow, small road D 48 branches off to the right towards the sea at the 951-foot-high (290 m) Bocca Albitrina.

After 5.5 miles (9 km), look for a small, hidden and bullet-ridden sign – if it hasn't been replaced since the time of writing – bearing the legend "Cauria." Turn here, and after another 3.5 miles (5.5 km) park the car, preferably in the shade, and walk down the path, following the signs.

CAURIA

For the most part, Corsica remained a herdsmen's island up into the 20th century, and the high plateau of Cauria, south of Sartène on the D 48, has been used by herdsmen since time immemo-

rial. In Cauria you can see broad meadows dotted with grazing cows or goats, but you'll seldom spot a herdsman with them. When walking through the area, therefore, make sure you close every gate behind you!

While taking a long walk across the Cauria plateau, you go through pastures studded with awesome granite rocks and covered, in spring, with a sea of white day lily blossoms. There are three main highlights worth seeing here: the two *alignements* of Stantari and Renaggiu (*alignement* = row, in this case, row of menhirs) and the famous dolmen of Fontanaccia.

First, you come to the **Stantari *alignement*** with its 20 menhirs. These date from the period after the Torreans had already landed on Corsica, as several of them bear representations of daggers and swords (see Filitosa), which were unknown to the original Corsican megalithic peoples.

Remembrance of the dead is still deeply rooted in Corsican culture. Locals be-

lieve in that the dead are invisibly, continually present and intervene in the clan's destiny. They can bring blessings, or punish a member of the family who shirks his appointed duties. Even today, you can see stone houses for the dead, and the construction of these often costs more energy and money than that of the houses in which their living families reside.

The beginnings of the pronounced cult of the dead on Corsica go back to early megalithic culture. The ancient idea of the "living corpse" already existed even then, and people believed that spirit and body formed an inseparable whole. The basis of "religion" at that time therefore lay in keeping watch over the bodily remains, because the body was necessary to the continued existence of the soul.

According to the archaeologist Sybille von Reden, the giant menhirs could have one of two meanings: either they could

Above: The Fontanaccia dolmen. Right: Popular with sailors – the Gulf of Propriano.

represent powerful ancestors, whose energy endured in the stone; or perhaps the statues with their weapons symbolized the spirits of vanquished enemies, who now have to serve their conquerors in stone.

The menhirs in the alignments were always erected with their "faces" to the east, towards the rising sun; perhaps as an expression of the hope of resurrection. There are still many unanswered questions.

A few hundred yards away in a small chestnut oak grove is the **Renaggiu alignement**. Some researchers used to think that these 46 menhirs, lying about crisscrossed, were a menhir depot, but today it's believed that they were some sort of megalithic cemetery. Today, it's hard to see whether there was once a systematic order: there were probably two menhir rows running north-south, and some half-circles.

On the way from the parking lot to the first alignement, a marked path leads off on the right to the **Fontanaccia dolmen**,

which you really shouldn't miss. Once again, it was Prosper Mérimée who identified this megalithic tomb as a piece of Stone Age heritage on his trip through Corsica in 1840. It was already well known to the herdsmen in the area, who used it as a handy shelter in inclement weather.

The flat roofing slab alone of this huge table tomb, probably the most beautiful on Corsica, weighs 3 tons. It's interesting that the dolmen is set up in such a way that its inner rear wall is illuminated by the sun on the day of the winter solstice.

Back again on the D 48, you can drive back to Sartène by turning right. If you go left for about a mile (2 km), you'll come to a road on your right which takes you another half a mile (1 km) to the **Palaggiu alignement**. There are 258 granite menhirs in this giant group, which were set up running north-south. All of the stones are 6.5-10 feet (2-3 m) tall and bear reliefs of warriors. This site was excavated by Roger Grosjean between 1964 and 1968.

Anyone who wants a taste of sun, beach and grilled fish after so many big rocks should head for the small **Bay of Tizzano** nearby. And because fish should have something to "swim" in, you should proceed to a wine tasting at one of the vineyards along the D 48.

From Tizzano, hikers and mountain bikers can also explore the wonderful sand beaches of the secluded **Golfe de Murtoli**, to the southeast behind the Cap de Zivia.

PROPRIANO AND THE GULF OF VALINCO

The **Gulf of Valinco** is bordered on the north by Capu di Muru and the Gulf of Ajaccio; to the south, the gulf ends at the Punta di Campomoro. Three rivers empty into the sea here. The Taravo in the north and the Rizzanèse in the south have formed wide alluvial floodlands, whereas the more modest little river Baraci, at the apex of the gulf, flows directly into the sea.

Bathing and water sports are the number one activities in the town of **Propriano**, or *Prupria* (population 3,000). The Gulf of Propriano was settled as early as the Bronze Age; somewhat later, the region started trading with merchants from Carthage, Etruria and Greece.

Propriano itself was not settled until the 2nd century B.C. And even in spite of its location, sheltered from the wind, the small fishing port remained shrouded in provincial obscurity until the early 20th century. The harbor was expanded in 1906: the Corsicans added two jetties and a quay where boats could dock. Soon a lighthouse was also illuminating the way in from the dark sea. Now, people thought, Propriano could advance to become an important commercial port, a center for the export of regional products. But even all this activity couldn't manage to wake up the sleepy town. Not until

Above: On the beach at Baraci. Right: The Tour de la Calanca stands guard over the Golfe de Valinco.

visitors from the European continent started to arrive here *en masse* did Propriano grow, finally becoming one of Corsica's main seaside resorts and tourist centers.

The countless hotels in the region have two things to thank for their economic upswing: the great variety of water sports and facilities available here in the gulf, and the pretty sand beaches: **Murzettu Beach**, between the marina and the commercial port, and **Rinaddiu Beach**, close to the lighthouse Scogliu Longu, where most of the vacation facilities are.

For people who prefer more secluded spots, there are sand beaches somewhat outside of the lively city, as well. North of Propriano is **Baraci Beach**, while a few miles to the south, close to the Propriano-Tavaria club airfield, are the beaches of **Capu Laurosco** and **Portigliolo**. You can reach the latter via the D 121, and from the beach you can go to **Belvédère-Campomoro** where, as the town's name suggests, you can see the entire gulf. The fantastic sand beach is, however, no longer a secret, and in the high season it is crowded with swimmers and windsurfers. A half-hour walk (round trip) goes from here to the Genoese tower at **Punta de Campomoro**, the southernmost point of the gulf.

Propriano is a good base for vacationers; from here, you can make a number of different excursions into the hinterland.

Spin'a Cavallu (horse's back) is what the Corsicans call the famous bridge – 5.5 miles (9 km) southeast of the city on the D 268 – which was built by the Genoese in the 14th century. Although the bridge, with its pointed arch, doesn't bear any very great resemblance to the back of an animal, you could certainly, and still can, ride over this bridge on a horse or mule, as people have been doing for centuries. The bridge spans the clear water of the Rizzanèse River, another popular spot for swimming in summer.

Through this valley, the winding D 69 – a motorcyclist's dream – continues uphill to the summer resort **Aullène**. This mountain village, perched at an altitude of 2,788 feet (850 m), can also be reached on the narrow D 19, which curves through beautiful landscapes and leads through **Santa-Maria-Figaniella** (with a Romanesque church from the 12th century) to the **Valle Mala**. The unpaved D 557 continues on uphill through thick pine woods to the pass **Col de St-Eustache**, at an altitude of almost 3,280 feet (1,000 m), and then on to Aullène.

There are also beautiful beaches on the northern side of the Gulf of Valinco. The D 157 runs high above the coast, and along the sea below you will find tempting sand beaches and quiet camping spots, especially on the quiet bay by **Tour de la Calanca**. Farther to the west are the beaches of **Olmeto-Plage**, which are easier to reach. The small sea resort of **Porto Pollo** is located in a bay, protected from the wind, and boasts a pretty sand beach.

A pleasant way to pass some time is to sit and watch the flocks of colorful sails flying up and down the gulf. Windsurfers come to the Gulf of Valinco for the wind which blows in from the sea almost nonstop, all year round.

FILITOSA

Before the sun really gets hot and your thoughts have become fully occupied with planning out ways to enjoy the beautiful beaches, you should pay a visit to the open-air museum in Filitosa, nestled in the midst of nature.

In 1840, Mérimée wrote in his *Notes d'un voyage en Corse* that "deep darkness covers the early period of this island..."

Until the mid-1950s, archaeologists viewed Corsica as a sort of stepchild, apart from the mainstream of scientific research into prehistoric periods. Today, relatively new archaeological research has brought to light the interesting early history of Corsica. Within the last 40 years, intense excavations and explorations have been going on, especially in the southwest, which have led to some astonishing discoveries.

Megalithic culture (culture of huge stones) extended far beyond the Mediterranean region, from the Middle East through Brittany (Carnac) to England (Stonehenge) and Sweden. But it was on Corsica that this culture managed to survive the longest: it lasted until the end of the Bronze Age, about 1000 B.C.

The name "megalithic" comes from the Greek; it is a collective term for different cultures in the Neolithic period, which buried their dead in giant stone chamber graves, stone tombs, and later in dolmens as well.

Megalithic culture is divided into three periods: **Megalithic I**, 4000-2500 B.C., **Megalithic II**, 3000-1500 B.C., and **Megalithic III**, which is the period between 1500 and 1000/800 B.C.

Filitosa is the most important excavation site on Corsica. Here, archaeologists have found objects dating from all three periods of megalithic culture. During the last period, around 1600 B.C., the seafaring Torrean peoples invaded Corsica; they landed in the southwest and harassed the peaceful tribes of the megalithic inhabitants.

In 1946, Monsieur Charles-Antoine Cesari discovered several menhir statues on his property at the foot of the hill of Filitosa; most of them were embedded in the walls of old sheep stalls. In the early 1950s, archaeologists started excavating the site, initially under the direction of Roger Grosjean, to bring the whole complex into the light of day.

Now kept up in an exemplary manner, with a small museum where the findings from Filitosa are on exhibit, the site is administered by the sons of Charles-Antoine Cesari; they run the bar there as well,

Right: A quick shot of the central monument of Filitosa.

where you can quench your thirst or nibble on something after your tour. The specialty here is *pizza préhistorique*!

Tour of the Site

Right after the entrance is the museum; you'll have a better appreciation of this if you visit it on the way out. You encounter the first monumental menhir after a few hundred yards or so: the freestanding **Filitosa V**, one of the tallest statues on the island; it is about 10 feet (3 m) tall, 3.3 feet wide (1 m), and weighs a full two tons. Strangely enough, the upper half of the head is missing. As basrelief engravings are clearly visible, this menhir has to date from the third period of megalithic culture. The archaeologist Grosjean identified a broadsword and a dagger in a decorated sheath on the front side of the stone. On the back, you can see markings that look like the indications of ribs. Or are they meant to be a suit of armor?

It's notable that Filitosa V displays a bronze sword, although the megalithic peoples were not yet familiar with this material. Therefore archaeologists agree that the menhir must date from the mid-2nd century B.C., that is, from the period when the Torreans began to settle in the south part of the island, because they brought swords and daggers with them. This gives rise to the question of why the megalithic people chose to portray, of all things, objects of their enemies, the Torreans. Perhaps the megalithic people saw menhirs with weapons as symbolizing dead enemies who had now lost their power, so that their souls had to serve the victors.

For hundreds of years, this mighty stone served local herdsmen as a bench to rest on.

After a few yards, you reach the actual site, the **main square**, 460 feet (140 m) long and with an average width of 130 feet (40 m). To enter the site, you pass

through the **cyclopean wall**, a fortress-like ring wall.

Immediately on the right next to the entrance, you'll see the **east monument**; its true significance is still a matter of conjecture. It is a hill-like monument, a stone construction put together without the benefit of mortar. On the rear side is a big ramp, which led to a section which no longer exists. The few remains of the east monument as well as the cyclopean wall date from the early Torrean period. The ring wall indicates that the site had to be defended against hostile attacks. As the megalithic people had not yet developed such constructions, it can be assumed that the megalithic inhabitants of this village had been conquered by the Torreans, who drove them out and built a new, fortified village.

Not far from the entrance, on the left side, are the ruins of a Torrean village; excavations are still going on here. Under a huge tafoni cliff, archaeologists found modest ceramic shards, indications of the first settlement of this pretty spot: by using radiocarbon dating methods, they have dated the shards from the year 5850 B.C.

In the middle of the site you can easily spot the **central monument**. Here, archaeologists were able to make some informative discoveries. This central monument has been clearly identified as a monument of the Torrean culture. The building was originally covered with a tower dome, no longer extant, which had a small opening at its peak and was 23-26 feet (7-8 m) high (it was this tower that led Roger Grosjean to give this culture the name Torrean).

As archaeologists found traces of fire on the walls and in the niches, they assume that it wasn't a dwelling, but rather a cult location where burial rituals were held.

The fact that the Torreans embedded several megalithic menhirs face down in the walls of their cult sites was an important discovery for the researchers – it was a definite confirmation that the Torreans, with their superior weapons, ultimately

defeated the original inhabitants of Corsica.

The Torreans settled in the south around 1300-1000 B.C., driving the megalithic people to the north, where they could continue to live undisturbed and practice their cult; in the north, menhirs dating from this period have been found without any depictions of weapons.

About 800 B.C., traces of both cultures suddenly disappear from Corsica. The Torreans moved back to the neighboring island of Sardinia – probably attracted by the copper there; furthermore, the *nuraghi* structures on Sardinia display a number of similarities to the Torrean strongholds.

Fragments of menhirs, which were found in the debris, have now been set up along the top of the wall, near the spots where they were found. Almost all of

Above: Hands-on encounter with a menhir fragment. Right: Filitosa VI, a menhir fragment with a well-preserved face.

these menhir fragments are embossed with reliefs.

If you follow the path, you'll come to a road block: **Filitosa VI**, broken into various pieces. The head displays the best-preserved facial features of any of the Filitosa menhirs. You can distinctly see the bulbous nose, the eye sockets, the shape of the face, and the strange cap. Or does this distinct, separate form on the back of the head represent a modern hair style of that period?

Filitosa VI is one of the most-photographed stones on Corsica. To make the most of your film, it's advisable to visit the site in the morning or late afternoon, because the forms of the reliefs stand out best in the slanting light.

A stone's throw from here is the **west monument**, the most complicated site in Filitosa. Here you can discern the well-protected location: the main square spreads out on a plateau and was easily defensible on its western and northern sides. This monument was also used for cult cremations, but could be employed for defensive purposes, as well. The west monument is divided into two different sections, each of which is further divided into several chambers.

Don't hesitate to climb around and through this monument in order to get to know it better; the entrance is on the right next to the big rock.

A path down to the valley leads to five menhir statues, neatly lined up; these, of course, were not set up in this order by people of the Stone Age, but were helped along by more recent workers.

It's estimated that 30 to 40 men were needed to erect an average Corsican menhir (weighing one to two tons) after the megalithic people rolled them to the sites on tree trunks.

The five menhirs, all found in this area, some of them extremely weather-worn, are all at least partially sculpted. Until they were discovered, they were used as benches for herdsmen or served as building material in the walls of shepherd's huts.

At the entrance to the site, one of the nice Cesari brothers likes to point out that, among all of the old stones, you should not overlook the wonderful olive tree which shades the five menhirs. This olive tree, more than 1,000 years old, is really quite remarkable; tired visitors can enjoy a refreshing siesta under its branches.

The path leads past the museum and back to the starting point. The **museum** (*Centre de documentation archéologique*) consists of a small room with exhibits in glass cases; starting on the right by the window, it presents the finds chronologically, from the megalithic and Torrean periods all the way up to the Roman period.

To the left of the entrance is the carefully restored **Scalsa-Murta menhir statue**. Here, again, you can distinctly make out the depiction of a sword, the suit of armor and the cap on the head. The cavities on the head probably once held

horns. For the sake of comparison, a photograph hangs to the right of it showing an Egyptian Shardana image from the temple of Medinet-Habu in Thebes, Egypt.

Roger Grosjean suspected that the Torreans were one and the same as the seafaring Shardana people, who had earlier plagued Egypt with their attacks. However, this remains a matter of speculation; to this day, researchers have not been able to come up with any clear proof either for or against this hypothesis, thanks to the bewildering activities and movements of the seafaring peoples during this period.

OLMETO

North of Propriano, the federal highway N 196 winds uphill to the village of **Olmeto**, picturesquely situated along a terraced slope. Somewhat below the village is a lookout point with a magnificent view of the Gulf of Valinco and Propriano. The tall, unfriendly-looking gra-

nite houses give the impression that they are glued to the 2,857-foot-high (871 m) Punta di Buturetto.

One inhabitant of Olmeto appears in French literature. The protagonist of Prosper Mérimée's Corsican novella *Colomba*, Madame Colomba Bartoli, was a real person who died at the age of 96 in the house across from Olmeto's town hall.

The ruins of **Castello della Rocca** stand on an elevation. This was the seat of the Corsican Count Arrigo della Rocca, who, with the support of the Spanish, started, in Olmeto, the first big revolt against Genoa in the mid-14th century. In 1362, he had to flee to Spain, but he came back fourteen years later with reinforcements and drove the Genoese from the island (although he wasn't able to take the fortresses loyal to Genoa in Calvi and Bonifacio). In Biguglia, he was made a count, and ruled the island for the

next twelve years as a loyal vassal of the King of Aragon – with the wisdom of Solomon, or so they say.

The well-paved N 196 leads from Olmeto to Ajaccio through a partially wooded low mountain range with groves of oak and cork oak. At the Col de Celaccia (1,909 feet/582 m), you cross the watershed between the Baracci and Taravo rivers.

After passing the pretty health resort of **Petreto-Bicchisano**, then driving through the green Taravo Valley, you cross the Ornano, the last mountain ridge before you reach the Gulf of Ajaccio, over the **Col de St-Georges** (2,450 feet/747 m), which has spectacular views. An excursion here into the upper Ornano, to **Zicavo** (2,394 feet/730 m), is worthwhile; this is the starting point for climbing **Monte Incudine**, 7,000 feet high (2,134 m).

In addition, the **forest of Coscione**, close to Zicavo, is a nice spot to visit with its sweet chestnut, laricio pine and beech trees.

Above: Watch out for animals on mountain roads! (Col de la Vaccia, near Zicavo.)

GULF OF VALINCO
Accommodation
PROPRIANO: *LUXURY:* **Grand Hotel Miramar**, Route de la Corniche, swimming pool, sauna, tel. 95760313. *MODERATE:* **Roc e Mare**, on a cliff over the sea with its own small sand beach, 1 mi/2 km from Propriano, tel. 95760485. **Arena Bianca**, Chemin des Plages, tennis, tel. 95760601. **Bartaccia**, swimming pool, tel. 95760199. **Le Lido Beach**, Avenue Napoléon, tel. 95761774. *BUDGET:* **Le Lido**, tel. 95760637. **Bellevue**, 9, Avenue Napoléon, tel. 95760186.
YOUTH HOSTEL: **Auberge de la Jeunesse**, in the riding school building by the turnoff of the D 557 from the N 196, 800 m from the Baracci beach, tel. 95761948.
PORTO POLLO: *MODERATE:* **Les Eucalyptus**, tennis, tel. 95740152. **Arcu di Sole**, swimming pool, tennis, tel. 95760510. **Kalliste**, tel. 95740238. *BUDGET:* **Du Golfe**, tel. 95740166.
CAMPOMORO: *BUDGET:* **Le Campomoro**, tel. 95742089. **Le Ressac**, tel. 95742225.

Campgrounds
PROPRIANO: Corsica, tel. 95760832. **Tikiti**, tel. 95760832. **Colomba**, shaded, clean sites about 1/2 mi/1 km from the Baracci beach, offers sailing courses, tel. 95760642.
PORTO POLLO: U Caseddu, tel. 95740180. **Fontanella**, tel. 95740081.
OLMETO-PLAGE: Colomba, Route de Baracci, tel. 95760642. **Le Ras l'Bol**, tel. 95740425. **Abbartello**, tel. 95740493. **Chez Antoine**, Marina d'Olmeto, tel. 95760606/95760699.
BELVEDERE CAMPOMORO: Lecci e Murta, Portigliolo, tennis, tel. 95771120/ 95760267. **La Vallée**, tel. 95742120.

Restaurants
PROPRIANO: *Corsican:* **Joseph Bischof**, Rue des Pêcheurs, specialties from in-house butcher; nice German owner, married to Corsican; tel. 95763000.

Museum
Filitosa, prehistoric site and museum, tel. 95740091, early March - late October: open daily 8:30 am until 1 hour before sundown.

Transportation
BUS: **Ollandini Valinco Voyages**, 22, Rue du Général-de-Gaulle, Propriano, tel. 95760076.
BIKES/MOTORCYCLES: **Valinco Accessoires**, Rue Jean-Pandolfi, Propriano, tel. 95761184. **TTC Sarl**, Rue Général-de-Gaulle, Propriano, tel. 95761532. *RENTAL CAR:* **Budget**, Porto Pollo, tel. 95740194. **Avis**, 22, Rue du Général-de-Gaulle, Propriano, tel. 95760076. **Europcar**, 2, Rue du Général-de-Gaulle, Propriano, tel. 95760503. **Budget**, Avenue Jean-Pandolfi, Propriano, tel. 95760408.

Travel Agent
Giraschi Voyages, B.P. 32, tel. 95760062

Sports
BOAT EXCURSIONS: **Le Golfe du Valinco**, Promenades en mer, Quartier Terra Nova, Propriano, tel. 95760352/95760426. *DIVING:* **Valinco Plongée**, Route de Viggianello, tel. 95762103. **Ecole de Plongée "U Levante,"** Bar le Crocodile, tel. 95762383. *MINIGOLF:* **Hotel Arcu di Sole**, Route d'Ajaccio, Propriano, tel. 95760510. *RIDING:* **Centre Equestre de Baraci**, Viggianello, tel. 95760802. *SAILING:* **Evasion Nautique Valinco**, Port de Plaisance, Propriano, tel. 95761523/95760352. **Fen-x Marine**, Chantier Naval du Corsaire, Propriano, tel. 95762012. **Locamarine**, Port de Plaisance, Propriano, tel. 95761132/95761854. *TENNIS:* **Parc des Sports**, Quartier Saint-Joseph, Propriano, tel. 95761335. *WATERSKIING:* **Locamarine**, Arlette Gutknecht, Propriano harbor, equpiment rental, tel. 95761132.

Tourist Information
Syndicat d'Initiative, 17, Rue du Général de Gaulle, Propriano, tel. 95760149.

SARTÈNE
Accommodation
MODERATE: **Les Roches**, town center, tel. 95770761. **Rossi**, Route de Propriano, tel. 95770180. **Villa Piana**, Route de Propriano, tennis, tel. 95770704. *BUDGET:* **Fior di Riba**, at the edge of town as you go toward Propriano, tel. 95770272.

Campground
Olva les Eucalyptus, Route de la Castagna, on D69 2.5 mi/4 km from Sartène, pool & tennis, tel. 95771158. **L'Avena Arepos**, Route de Tizzano, tel. 95770218. **Arepos Roccapina**, tel. 95771930.

Museum
Musée Départemental de la Préhistoire Corse, Rue Croce, tel. 95770109. Summer: daily exc. Su, 10 am-noon, 2-6 pm; winter: weekdays 10 am-noon, 2-5 pm, closed holidays.

Transportation
BUS: **Agence Ollandini**, 4, Rue Gabriel-Peri, tel. 95771841.

Hospital
Hôpital de Sartène, Rue Croce, tel. 95770138.

Sports
ARCHERY: **ARC Club Sartenais**, M. Gongolio - HLM Funtana di Sartène - Bât.C, tel. 95770933. *RIDING:* **Centre Equestre "A Madunina,"** Lieu-dit Croccana, Route de Granace, tel. 9577 1137/95734037. *SAILING:* **Centre Nautique Lion de Roccapine**, Col de Roccapina, tel. 95734719/ 95770472.

Tourist Information
Syndicat d'Initiative, Rue Borgo, tel. 95771540.

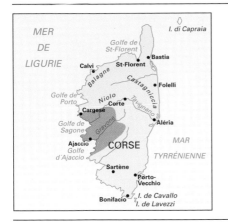

AJACCIO – IN THE FOOTSTEPS OF NAPOLEON

AJACCIO
GULF OF AJACCIO
GULF OF SAGONE
CARGÈSE

AJACCIO

The French belt out *Atshaxio*, but the Corsicans meltingly pronounce the tones *Ajadschu*. **Ajaccio** (*Ajacciu*) is the capital city of the south, beloved of many Corsicans, and, with 58,000 *Ajacciens*, far and away Corsica's largest city whatever the residents of Bastia may say to the contrary.

Here, between the narrow old city alleys, white sand beaches with well-groomed promenades lined with palm trees, and broad, elegant boulevards, you find a mixture of elegant Paris and cosmopolitan St. Tropez. It is remarkable how many extremely attractive young men and women frolic in the numerous cafés on the boulevards or on the shady squares; it appears that the high-class Ajaccio women have studied the fashion magazines fully as intensively as any woman of Paris, and have taken many of their principles and precepts to heart and given them practical application. Window-shopping, therefore, is a worthwhile occupation here; the selection of couture is in no way inferior to that in Paris, either in quality or in price.

Preceding pages: A poor catch! On the beach at Ajaccio. Left: Modern architecture confers an urban flair upon Ajaccio.

The self-confident appearance of the young women, however, does not mean that they have liberated themselves from the strict moral principles of their parents and grandparents. Even today, many women are closely guarded by their male family members.

If you stroll along the road by the seashore, lined with palms, cafés and bistros, you can sense the atmosphere of the Côte d'Azur; however, Ajaccio, even in August, is never as crowded as are the small, wealthy, and ever-popular cities of southern France.

As your ferry slowly approaches the city, famed and oft-praised for its beauty, your initial impression may be almost disappointing. What first meets the eye are the high-rise residential apartment buildings ranged along the hill of the city, which cannot exactly be counted among architecture's finest hours. Not until you enter the harbor do you see the picturesque old city. Even from the boat, you can see that the old city center is relatively small; Ajaccio didn't become the biggest city on Corsica until its newer neighborhoods were built in relatively recent decades.

Ajaccio is one of the oldest cities on the island. Reports from the Roman period mention a city named *Adiacum*, which means "to rest" or "resting spot."

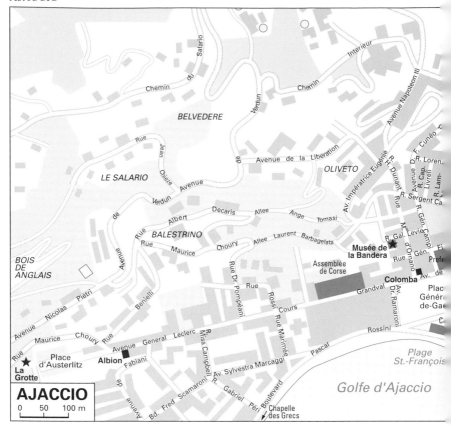

This name may have arisen because the Roman settlement, probably located in what is now the modern-day quarter of St-Jean in the northern part of the city, grew up at the site of what had once been a resting place for herdsmen and shepherds.

In the 7th century, the small market town was promoted to the seat of the bishop for the Castel-Vecchio community, but it still remained unimportant. Three hundred years later, in the 10th century, the feared Saracens swept in and destroyed the town.

After the republic of Genoa turned over the administration of the island to the Bank of San Giorgio – which wasn't a bank in modern terms, but primarily a

political organization – in 1453, the bank founded the city of Ajazzo on this spot in 1492. Only Ligurian families were allowed to settle here; for a long time, Corsicans were seen as undesirable.

Not until Sampiero Corso, in the service of the French, occupied Ajazzo, exactly 100 years after the Genoese founded the city, did Corsicans gradually begin to move in and settle here. This period also saw the construction of the citadel under the supervision of the French Marshall de Thermes.

Five years after Sampiero conquered the city, the Genoese took it back; they granted civil rights to all of the residents in 1597. The Genoese also took control of the French citadel and rebuilt it, which

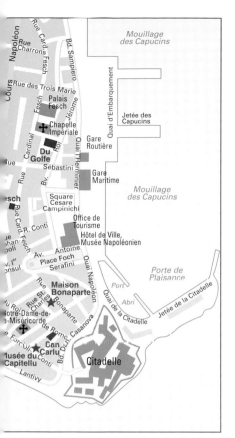

explains the Genoese coat-of-arms, a crown between two lions, over the entrance.

In 1715, Ajaccio started to administer the whole southern part of the island; almost 80 years later, in 1793, the island was officially divided into two sections, with Bastia the administrative capital of the north, Ajaccio of the southern part of the island. This resulted in a considerable increase in the city's population.

In 1769, the year the revolting Corsicans were defeated by the French at Ponte Novu, a historical event took place in Ajaccio: Napoleon was born on August 15, 1769, in Casa Buonaparte.

To this day, the magic of the emperor is still alive and well in Ajaccio. The locals continue to revere *their* emperor – and not necessarily solely to promote tourism – with songs, by naming their children after him, or with Napoleon souvenirs of every imaginable sort, made of all kinds of materials; while the imperial crown hangs, illuminated, over the Cours Napoleon every night. Even the anthem of Ajaccio, which is often sung, ends with a moving hymn to the French emperor.

The Corsican enthusiasm for Napoleon is not so easy to explain in light of the fact that the emperor actually did virtually nothing for the place where he was born. Napoleon's only concrete service to his native city was to name Ajaccio the sole capital city of Corsica in 1811. In the course of a program of reforms, the French president Giscard d'Estaing rescinded this in 1975 and divided Corsica into the two *départements* which still comprise it today.

Tour of the City

The best place to start a tour of the city, which you can easily do on foot, is the **Jetée de la Citadelle**, the jetty of the old fishing port. After climbing the steps of the jetty, you are rewarded with a panoramic view of the old city and a part of the gulf, with sleek yachts in the foreground. Directly next to the jetty, on the very tip of the point of land, is the citadel; its foundations date from the 16th century. Today, only the old fortress walls are still extant. The citadel is a military area and therefore it is not open for viewing.

A walk along the citadel walls, following the course of the Boulevard Danielle-Casanova, leads you to the **Musée du Capitellu**. In its three large rooms, this private museum presents the history of Ajaccio in the form of articles and documents pertaining to an old family of the city, going back to the 18th century. On January 9, 1909, the heroine of the Corsi-

The floor plan is in the shape of a Greek cross; the center is dominated by the tremendous dome over the crossing. Harmonious proportions confer a special charm upon the interior.

Flanking the nave to the right and left are three chapels on each side; the most impressive of these, *Notre-Dame del Pianto*, is located directly to the left of the entrance. Donated by Pietro d'Ornano, a Corsican colonel, it is decorated with beautiful stucco work, which has been ascribed to the school of Tintoretto (1518-1595).

The most precious piece in the entire church is also displayed here: a 19th-century painting entitled *La Vierge du Sacré-Coeur* by the famous French artist Eugène Delacroix (1798-1863), a Romantic painter who managed to transcend classicism in his works, and also depicted such contemporary subjects as the war of Greek liberation.

The second chapel is dedicated to *Notre-Dame-de-la-Miséricorde*, and is decorated with a crowned Virgin Mary from the 18th century; every year on March 18, this figure is borne through the city in celebrations of the feast day of the church's patron saint. The last chapel on the left honors the Virgin Mary with the Rosary. She is surrounded by 15 small painted panels from the 17th century, illustrating the mystery of the rosary. Three wooden statues depict three saints: St. Dominic, the Virgin and Child, and St. Rose of Lima.

In the middle chapel in the right side aisle, there is a beautiful 18th-century marble Madonna. The white marble high altar with its four twisting black columns was donated by Elisa Bacciocchi, Napoleon's sister and Princess of Lucca and Piombino. The altar comes from a church in Lucca – small wonder, as Elisa was sitting right there at the source.

Even in this house of worship in Ajaccio, there's something for Napoleon enthusiasts: to the right of the entrance is

can Resistance, Danielle Casanova, was born in this house. Her political activities in Paris, where she was studying dentistry, came to the attention of the National Socialist (Nazi) authorities: she was deported to Auschwitz on January 3, 1943, and died there a short time later. Today, a memorial plaque commemorates her at the Musée du Capitellu.

The nearby street Rue Forcioli-Conti leads directly to the cathedral of Ajaccio: **Notre-Dame-de-la-Miséricorde**, more familiarly called **La Madunuccia** (Little Madonna) by the locals, honoring the patron saint of Ajaccio. The plain building was built in the style of the late Venetian Renaissance (1582-1593). It was designed by the well-known architect of Pope Gregory XIII, Giacomo della Porta, who had already assisted in the construction of the church Il Gesu in Rome (1568-1584).

Above: Notre-Dame de la Miséricorde, Ajaccio's patron saint. Right: Reading the paper with café au lait on the harbor promenade.

the marble baptismal font, decorated with chubby-cheeked angels, in which the future emperor was baptized. Local legend has it that the impatient two-year-old poured the water over his head himself – a self-confident action which he modified only slightly as an adult, when he was crowned emperor: he tore the crown from the pope's hands and placed it on his own head himself.

Engraved on a marble plaque on the first pilaster on the left in the nave, you can read the emperor's last wish, which he supposedly uttered in exile on the Atlantic island of St. Helena: "*Si on proscrit de Paris mon cadavre comme on a proscrit ma personne, je souhaite qu'on m'inhume auprès de mes ancêtres dans la cathédrale d'Ajaccio, en Corse* (April 29, 1821)." (If they ban my corpse from Paris, as they have banned my person, I would like to be buried next to my ancestors in the cathedral of Ajaccio on Corsica.)

His body was not, in fact, banned from Paris: since 1840, his corpse has been lying in a giant porphyry coffin in that city's Dôme des Invalides.

If you go along the north side of the church, the Rue Saint-Charles will lead you to the house where Napoleon was born: the **Maison Bonaparte**. In front of the house, on the small **Place Letizia**, there is a bronze bust of the king of Rome, Napoleon II, who was Napoleon's only son.

The building, which seems fairly plain from its exterior, dates back to the 17th century. Carlo Bonaparte, Napoleon's father, did not buy the house until 1743. After the British occupied it from 1794-1796 (one of its residents was Hudson Lowe, who was later to serve as Napoleon's jailer on St. Helena), it wasn't until 1798 that, at the express wish of Madame Letizia, Napoleon's mother, it was completely restored and refurbished with the damages paid by the British.

The furnishings of the house which you see today, therefore, are not identical to those with which Napoleon grew up – but still, there are a number of personal

Napoleon mementos on display. In 1852, the house became the property of Napoleon III and his wife, the Empress Eugénie. In 1923, it was bequeathed to the French state, which renovated it sixty years later (1983).

In the entrance area, you immediately notice a sedan-chair, or litter. It was in this litter that the servants, on August 15, 1769, carried Napoleon's mother, seized by labor pains, as quickly as possible back from the cathedral to the house. In spite of their haste, so the story goes, she didn't quite make it to the bedroom, and therefore gave birth to her second son, Napoleon, in the *antichambre* or vestibule.

A tour of the museum, which has been open since 1967, starts on the third floor. The first of the four large rooms is devoted to the parents and the family.

Three faces of Napoleon (left to right): As a child in Ajaccio – even then, he supposedly liked to fight (19th-century watercolor); as a bottle-stopper; as a monument in Ajaccio.

Carlo Buonaparte received his law degree at the university in Pisa. After returning to his native island, the good-looking and articulate Carlo soon became the most popular lawyer in Ajaccio. When he was 18, he married the 14-year-old Letizia Ramolino, reportedly the most beautiful girl in the city. During 21 years of marriage, they had 12 children, 8 of whom survived. During the decades that followed, these eight Buonapartes or Bonapartes did their best to fulfill Jean-Jacques Rousseau's prophecy of 1762 that "this small island will one day astonish all of Europe."

Along with two family trees, personal possessions of the parents, and their portraits, this room contains a painting of another important family member: the portrait of Cardinal Fesch, stepbrother of Letizia and uncle of Napoleon. He was an active collector of art his whole life. Military campaigns in Italy gave this church official a chance to expand his collection in a rather unorthodox manner. At one time, his treasure is said to have consisted

of 17,626 art objects, of which 16,000 were paintings (mainly of Italian origin). As he neglected to make a definitive will, almost everything was sold after his death. His plan to introduce the youths of Ajaccio to art history by means of a permanent exhibition could only insufficiently be carried out. Today, the 1,000 or so paintings which remain are on exhibit in an excellent museum in the Palais Fesch.

In the **second room** you can meet the eight famous Buonaparte children. The "little" princesses and kings, as well as the emperor of France, are shown in a proper light in portrait busts and paintings. Following an old Corsican custom, Napoleon, once he gained power, didn't forget his family, but rather made sure that everyone got a kingdom or a princedom; for the baby of the family, Girolamo (also called Jérôme, because the Bonapartes took on French names only after emigrating to France), he even created a custom-made realm: the kingdom of Westphalia.

Rooms three and four contain remembrances of Napoleon's last visit to Ajaccio in 1799, and a few relics of his last days on St. Helena, such as a wreath of dried flowers from his funeral. A few engravings and documents recall the two visits of Napoleon III and his wife, the Empress Eugénie, to the island in 1860 and 1869.

On the **second floor** are the private chambers of Madame Letizia, who died in Rome as the "mother of kings" at the advanced age of 86, leaving a fortune of millions behind her. The rooms here are filled with furniture which was gradually, at Letizia's request, brought here from various countries around the world.

First, you enter the salon, then the sleeping chamber of *Madame Mère*, furnished with a dresser made of rosewood, and then the antechamber where Napoleon was born. Notable here are the secretary and the commode (late 18th century) inlaid with lapis lazuli, onyx and agate. Napoleon brought the ebony and mahogany crib you see here back from

Syria with him as a present for his mother.

The next two rooms are later additions, built between 1790 and 1796. The last room you enter is the dining room, which is a bit startling by virtue of its "faux marbre" wallpaper and fine chestnut furniture.

From the museum, you can follow the Rue Bonaparte to reach the **Place Foch**. This square, lined by Canary date palms, is a popular gathering place for young and old. Inviting stone benches in the shade tempt passers-by to sit down, rest their feet, and watch the passing people or let their eyes roam across the picturesque bay and harbor, watching the big ferries dock and depart.

Adorned with a marble statue, the pretty **Fontaine des Quatre Lions** (Fountain of Four Lions) ornaments the upper end of the square. Who was this

Above: Napoleon in Roman garb (Place Foch). Right: You have to try goat's- or sheep's-milk cheese at least once.

man, garbed in a Roman toga and sporting a laurel wreath on his head, whose statue now serves as a favorite perch for the city's pigeons? How could it be anyone else: of course, it's the city's most famous native son, Napoleon. In his right hand he is holding a globe adorned with a tiller mounted on it – the symbolism speaks for itself.

If you head down towards the water, you will see the city hall on the left; this building houses more than just the city administration. It contains, for example, the **Musée Napoléonien**, which exhibits mementos of Napoleon and his family: several family portraits, Napoleon's baptismal certificate (dated July 21, 1771, and still written in Genoese dialect!), his death mask, and other similar objects.

Right next to the city hall is the tourist information office, where you can pick up a free map of the city.

The fish market is held at the rear of the city hall, while a colorful daily market is held on the square opposite,

Square César Campinchi. The market is at its biggest and most beautiful on Sundays, when, in addition to delicious Corsican culinary specialties, Corsican music, clothes and handicrafts are also on offer.

Diagonally opposite, on the Quai l'Herminier, is the new harbor building of the **Gare Maritime**, where you can book ferry crossings to France and Italy, as well as bus tours. Directly adjacent to it is the bus station **Gare Routière**; there's regular bus service from here in all directions, to a variety of destinations throughout the island.

From Square César Campinchi, you take the Rue Conti to reach **Rue Cardinal Fesch**, a lovely shopping street. Window-shopping and strolling along here are somewhat quieter than they are on the parallel street Cours Napoleon. The facades of the houses are currently being restored and painted in beautiful pastel colors.

A few yards farther on as you head towards the Palais Fesch, you can see the small, dark passageway Guingetta on your left. You should go on in, because there is a small restaurant here, **Da Mamma**, in a lovely courtyard (open only in the evenings). Here you can eat genuine Corsican cuisine, and when the weather is nice you can even eat outside in the courtyard under a giant rubber tree. Next to it is a very good shop selling Corsican specialties and pottery, which is open until late in the evening.

If you continue to walk along Rue Fesch, you will soon reach the impressive, classical **Palais Fesch**, where you can see Cardinal Fesch's famous collection of paintings. Napoleon's uncle, who died in Rome in 1839, commissioned the construction of the building in 1827, but it wasn't completed until long after his death.

After the Louvre, the Museum Fesch has the largest collection of Italian art in France, and it's therefore one of the most important provincial museums in the French-speaking world. Since the palace was reopened in 1990 by the French Min-

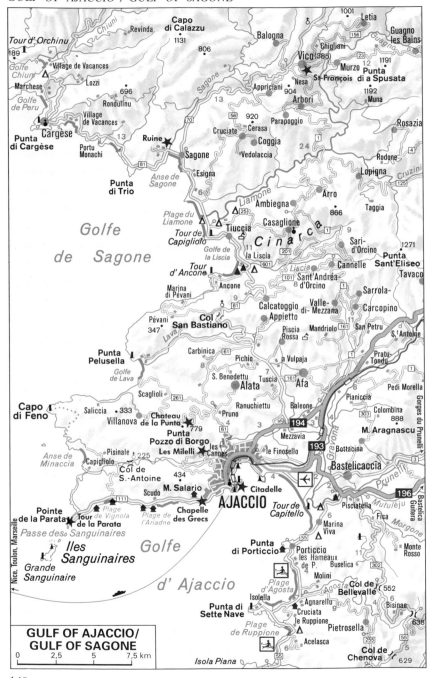

GULF OF AJACCIO/
GULF OF SAGONE

0   2,5   5   7,5 km

ister of Culture, Jack Lang, visitors can peruse, as well as Italian Old Masters from the 14th-19th centuries, works by French, Spanish, Flemish and Dutch artists. In addition, the exhibition rooms on the ground floor host various rotating shows.

The theme of the Virgin and Child is well represented on the second floor, where it's taken on by such well-known artists as Giovanni Bellini (*Virgin and Child*), Sandro Botticelli (*Virgin and Child, supported by an angel under a garland*), and Bartolomeo Veneto (*Virgin and Child*); these paintings all date from the Renaissance period of the *quattrocento* (15th century).

Among the ample collection of 16th-century works, two paintings of the Venetian school stand out in particular: *Leda and the Swan*, by Paolo Veronese, and Titian's *Man with a Glove*. On the same floor, seventeenth-century works by regional painters are also on display. The third floor is devoted to paintings from the 17th to 19th centuries. The 17th and 18th centuries are represented by a good collection of still lifes (by Spadino, Castelli, Coninck, Recco, and other painters). 19th-century Italian art is represented mainly with landscapes and portraits.

The left wing of the palace contains the library founded by Napoleon's brother, Lucien, in 1801; it has over 50,000 volumes.

In the museum you can buy a ticket for the **Chapelle Impériale**, located in the opposite right wing. Built in 1857 by order of Napoleon III, this imperial chapel served as the Bonaparte family tomb. This is the last resting place of Cardinal Fesch, Napoleon's parents, and other family members.

By following Rue des Trois Maries from the Palais Fesch, you can reach the lively **Cours Napoleon** with its countless sidewalk cafés and shops. Also located here are the main post office and the

headquarters of the prefect of southern Corsica, the Palais Lantivy.

Behind the prefecture, in the tiny Rue Général Levie, is the **Museum A Bandera**, opened in 1988. The various stages of settlement and especially the military history of Corsica and the Mediterranean region are documented in its five rooms. Models, maps, weapons, uniforms and coins, help vividly to depict the interesting history of the island up to the period of the Résistance and the liberation of the island in 1944.

From the spacious **Place Général-de-Gaulle**, called **Piazza del Diamante** by locals, you have an extensive view out over the Gulf of Ajaccio. In the summer the square is usually empty, for there is very little shade here.

As you might have come to expect by now, this square also proudly boasts its own Napoleon memorial. Created by the artist Viollet-le-Duc in 1865, it is sometimes called "the ink well" due to its strange shape: it depicts Napoleon as a Roman emperor, surrounded by his brothers.

Below the square, across from the municipal beach of St-François, are the casino and the congress building. Next to these, along the coastal promenade, are numerous cafés and bars which stay open until late into the night.

From the Place Général-de-Gaulle, you can walk up the slightly ascending but shady Cours Grandval, about half a mile long (1 km), which turns into the Cours Général Leclerc.

First, you'll see the building of the former Hotel Continental on the right, which is surrounded by a splendid flower and palm garden. Today, this building is home to the **Assemblée de Corse**, which handles important issues concerning Corsica.

At the end of the street, on **Place d'Austerlitz**, is the most impressive of all of the Napoleon monuments, created by the sculptor Seurre in 1938. This is,

however, a copy – the original is in the courtyard of the Dôme des Invalides in Paris.

Napoleon presents himself in a military pose atop a giant pyramid, proudly looking down over "his" city. If you take one of the two stairways up to the top, with lists of Napoleon's victories in battle and other sundry accomplishments engraved between them, you can stroll back down the other side along a pleasant path. Here you walk past extremely beautiful, eroded tafoni rocks and caves, where, so they say, Napoleon played as a child.

THE GULF OF AJACCIO

If you plan to stay in the southern capital city for a few days, you'll have plenty of time to take a number of interesting day excursions.

Above: In the Gulf of Ajaccio. Right: View north from the Tour de la Parata, along the rocky coast.

For example, you can make the excursion out to the western point of the Gulf of Ajaccio, Pointe de la Parata. Highway D 111 leads past the casino, along the coastal promenade and out of the city. The northern coastal highway passes through the better neighborhoods of Ajaccio, where you'll notice several tall apartment buildings (every apartment has a view of the sea). Many of the apartments in these buildings have been rented or bought by French from the mainland as retirement homes. The newer apartment buildings, christened with flowery names, blend quite well into the cliff over the sea.

On the left, just outside the city limits, is the Greek chapel, **La Chapelle des Grecs**, built in 1632. This modest little Baroque chapel is a reminder of the Hellenistic community which was driven out of Cargèse by the herdsmen of the Niolo in the 18th century. They were given this chapel in 1731; it contains a painting of the coronation of the Virgin Mary, surrounded by saints and benefactors.

Diagonally opposite is an extensive cemetery, which looks like a miniature city when seen from afar. A tour can be interesting, and not only for the old tombs and chapels – here, for instance, you'll also find the grave of the well-known pop singer Tino Rossi, who spent the last years of his life in his concealed villa off the coastal highway (close to Scudo Beach); he died in 1984.

The road ends at **Pointe de la Parata**, which is dwarfed by the well-preserved Genoese tower **Tour de la Parata** (17th century). Leaving the parking lot, you can take a rewarding, half-hour tour of the western point of the island. If you're good on your feet, take the narrow, very steep path on the right which leads to the peak – although this requires you to go on all fours at some points. Once at the top, you can catch your breath in the shade of the Genoese tower and enjoy the panoramic view of the gulfs of Ajaccio and Sagone.

Only a narrow ridge of land connects this peninsula to the main body of the is-
land; four small islands, peaks of a sunken cape, lie offshore. These are called the **Iles Sanguinaires**, the bloody islands (*sanguinaires* = bloodthirsty), because the granite on the islands glows vivid red when the sun sets. It is also conceivable, however, that the French name derives from *Sagonares Insulae*, the Latin term for the islands lying south of the Gulf of Sagone.

Ruins of a quarantine station and a lighthouse still stand on the largest island. In 1869, the French author Alphonse Daudet lived in this lighthouse for a while. He described his experiences in the story "The Lighthouse on the Sanguinaires," which was published that same year in his collection of stories *Letters from My Mill*.

On the way back to Ajaccio, white sand beaches, such as **Scudo Beach**, entice you to take a swim. You'll encounter other beautiful beaches south of here, close to the tourist town of **Porticcio**. One beach gives way to another: the **Plages de Porticcio** and **d'Agosta**, for example, which offer a variety of water sports facilities. Behind the peninsula d'Isolella is the somewhat quieter **Plage de Ruppione**.

From Ajaccio, you can also go on an excursion to the country house of the Bonaparte family, **Les Milelli** (3 miles/5 km northwest of Ajaccio on the Route d'Alata). The two floors of the house which are open to the public are filled with 19th-century Corsican furniture. In May, 1793, Madame Letizia, together with her daughters and Cardinal Fesch, left Ajaccio, fleeing from the British, and settled down here. Six years later, Napoleon set foot on "his" island for the last time on his way back from his Egyptian campaign, and spent several days here.

The D 61 also brings you to the **Château de la Punta**; if you turn left after the Bocca di Pruno, after another 3.5 miles or so (6 km) you'll see the castle, or what's left of it, on the left; it was badly damaged by a fire. It belonged to the noble family of the Pozzo di Borgo, the most influential family in Ajaccio next to the Bonapartes, and at the same time Napoleon's bitterest enemies. Count Carlo Pozzo di Borgo, born one year before Napoleon, was a delegate and chief state prosecutor of Corsica, and he even had to leave the island during the Napoleon's reign.

The Punta Castle was constructed by the Pozzo family, modelled on the Palais des Tuileries, which burned down during the Paris Commune rebellion in 1871. In fact, the actual valuable stones of the Tuileries palace were expressly shipped from Paris to the island, where they were used to complete the construction between 1886 and 1894.

The road continues up the mountain to **Punta Pozzo di Borgo** (2,547 feet/779 m); from here, you can enjoy a great view of both gulfs and the city. Back at the

Right: To reach the reservoir of Tolla, take the D3, with marvelous views along the way.

Pruno Pass, you can take the D 261 back down to the attractive sand beaches of the **Golfe de Lava** (with hotel facilities), which is part of the Gulf of Sagone.

Heading east from Ajaccio, you can also take a nice day trip to the mountains. Head to Cauro (N 196) and proceed from there on the D 27 to **Bastelica**.

At an elevation of 2,616 feet (800 m), this village is, in winter, a good point of departure for ski tours and cross-country runs on the Plateau d'Ese. Corsicans, however, know this village principally as the birthplace of the freedom fighter Sampiero Corso; and a statue of the hero, in a proud pose, has been erected here in his honor.

If you don't want to tackle the challenge of driving up the unpaved pass road D 27 to the Col de Scalella (3,908 feet/1,195 m, with a view of Monte Renoso, which is 7,691 feet/2,352 m in altitude), you can choose to return to Ajaccio via a shorter route, on the D 3. This road, with its many beautiful views, runs high above the **Prunelli Gorge** (*Gorges du Prunelli*), past charming villages (Tolla, Ocana) and the shimmering blue-green **Tolla Reservoir**.

THE GULF OF SAGONE

The Gulf of Sagone, the largest gulf on the west coast, is bordered to the south by Capo di Ferno and to the north by the Cargèse peninsula. At Pointe Capigliolo, it extends far inland, forming the Gulf of Liscia.

The gulf is surrounded by rolling hills overgrown with maquis and green oak and olive trees.

Leaving Ajaccio, follow the N 194 through Mezzavia, a shopping and industrial area, and turn onto the D 81, heading toward Tiuccia/Sagone. This well-built road gradually wends its way up the mountain, reaching its highest point at the **Col de San Bastiano** (1,517 feet/464 m). At the pass (Corsican: *Bocca*), a pink

granite stele commemorates the first air flight over the Mediterranean. Louis Capezza and Alphonse Fondère left Marseille in a hot-air balloon at 4:30 pm on November 14, 1886, and landed safely in bad weather near Apietto in the middle of the night.

From the pass, you can only see as far as the Gulf of Lava, but shortly afterwards the view opens up to include the bays of Liscia and Sagone. The road goes steeply down the mountain and arrives at the sea at the **Gulf of Liscia**. At the end of the gulf is the beach resort town of **Tiuccia**, with vacation facilities, hotels and campgrounds. Between here and Sagone (Saone), there is one vacation resort after another.

Sagone was once a small Roman settlement, and the seat of one of the five most important bishoprics on Corsica after the 6th century. In the Middle Ages the settlement grew in importance; during this period the bishop's domains extended north all the way to Calvi. Sagone was destroyed by marauding Saracens in

the 16th century. In addition, the frequent flooding of the Sagone River made life hard for the residents; as a result, the bishop moved his seat inland, to Vico, in 1572. After relinquishing Sagone completely, he left the somewhat remote bishop's seat of Vico again in 1625, and moved to Calvi.

The Genoese built a round tower in the western part of the settlement in the 16th century, because the site afforded them a clear view of both the gulf and the harbor.

Today, you can't see all that many relics of the town's former history. This up-and-coming little place lives almost exclusively off of its flourishing summer season; there are vacation apartments and houses here, as well as several hotels and campgrounds. But night owls won't find much here – Sagone has only a few cafés and bars where you can while away the night hours.

The only surviving relics of the past, other than the Genoese tower, are the ruins of **Sant'Appiano Cathedral**, built

in the 12th century. The remains of an apse, probably a construction from the 4th or 5th century, can still be seen in the baptistery. The ruins are located behind Sagone on the arterial road heading towards Cargèse (D 81). You reach them by following a short dirt road just past the bridge over the Sagone River.

Directly in Sagone, the D 70 branches off to lead into Corsican mountain country. After some 9 miles (14 km), you arrive in the village of **Vico**, which has barely 1,000 inhabitants, and sits perched atop a mountain crest at the Col St-Antoine (1,606 feet/491 m). This village is nestled between the headwaters of the river Liamone and the sources of the Sagone River, and still is considered an insider tip. Best time to visit is during the hot summer months, because the climate is generally pleasant here even in the month of August. In the small town,

Above: The monastery of St-François in Vico. Right: Cattle-breeding without force in the mountains – these cows need no fences.

which even boasts a decent hotel, people are quick to notice a car that doesn't have Corsican plates, and after you've passed through a few times, you'll start to recognize the people, and they'll begin to greet you in return.

It is hard to imagine that the bishop of Sagone moved his seat to Vico from 1572-1625. Today, the only testimony to the village's erstwhile important role is the **monastery of St-François**, about half a mile (1 km) from town. The gleaming white structure is enthroned above the upper Liamone Valley.

Gian Paolo de Lecca founded the monastery in 1481, and it was run by Franciscan monks until 1793. After the Genoese damaged it in the late 15th century, the monks rebuilt it into its present size with the help of the local populace in 1627. In 1793, supporters of the French Revolution drove the monks out of the monastery. Missionaries from the order *Oblats de Marie Immaculée* have been living in the buildings since the 19th century (1836).

Curious visitors, if they want, can be led through the grounds and church by a *Père Oblat*. If you are interested in a tour, ring the bell inside the church on the right by the entrance.

The church itself dates from the 17th century. Inside, there's a marble tabernacle above the high altar (17th century) and an impressive 15th-century wooden crucifix, the oldest crucifix on Corsica. Below it is the grave of Father Albini, a 19th-century Corsican missionary. In the quiet, idyllic inner courtyard, an old sundial divides the day into hours.

From here, as from Vico, you can see the **Punta di a Spusata** (3,898 feet/1,192 m), the "Mountain of the Bride." According to older Corsicans, the story went as follows: the elderly Lord of Cinarca was smitten with the beauty of a young, poor shepherdess, and finally married her. The new bride soon started to treat her mother with contempt and disrespect, ransacked her parents' house, and finally even stole her mother's kitchen scraper. In despair, the mother cursed her ungrateful daughter, who shortly thereafter turned into stone.

Route D 23 leads from Vico to **Guagno-les-Bains** (8 miles/12.5 km from Vico), passing through Murzo on the way. This small thermal bath spa was turning into a ghost town, but they have recently renovated the old thermal bath building, making the village once again an attractive place for tourists and natives alike.

Corsicans have been using these two sulfurous springs since the 16th century. The water in the spring to the west of the village, *L'Occhiu* (the eye), is 98°F (37°C) in temperature, and is supposed to relieve eye and respiratory diseases. Rheumatism, skin diseases and arthritis can be treated at the other spring, *Source Venturini* (average temperature 125°F/52°C).

In the course of history, several illustrious Corsicans have taken a cure here. Pasquale Paoli came here every year; and Madame Letizia also recuperated in Guagno-les-Bains after the wars of inde-

pendence, accompanied by her two oldest sons, Joseph and Napoleon, who probably weren't yet wasting their time thinking about politics at that date.

In the village of Murzo, a small unmarked and unpaved road branches off from the main road. If you take it, you will, after a charming drive of some 4 miles (6 km) through the countryside, discover the town of **Muna** to the left on a cliff.

This spot is a real contrast to the well-known coastal villages. The few people who live here get by without electricity. Some of the houses are already falling down, and some are being carefully restored by their owners, most of whom live elsewhere. At any rate, there are plenty of great subjects for photographs here, and you probably won't run into any other tourists.

Above: Rock roses are flecks of color in the maquis. Right: Abandoned houses in Muna. Far right: Icon of St. Spiridion in the Greek Orthodox church of Cargèse.

After this little excursion through the desolate mountainous region of Corsica, you return to the coast of the Gulf of Sagone by going back the way you came. From Sagone, it's another 8 miles (13 km) to the next city, Cargèse.

CARGÈSE

Visitors who aren't yet well versed in the history of the island may view the town of **Cargèse** (*Carghiese*), with its current population of 1,000, as just a typical tourist venue on the west coast with vacation facilities and hotels. Club Méd has even set up an outpost on the attractive sand beaches here. But because the beaches and tourist facilities are somewhat outside of the town, Cargèse, with its colorful small gardens and whitewashed houses (unusual for Corsica), is worth visiting even in the summer months. Many people are therefore captivated by the city, and start looking into the possibility of buying a vacation home here.

The two big churches facing each other are clearly an attraction: one is Roman Catholic, while the other is Greek Orthodox. When you encounter this unusual sight, you'll be impelled to delve further into the history of Cargèse.

It starts in the 17th century, when approximately 800 Greeks from Vitylo (today: Oitylos) on the Peloponnese had to flee under pressure from the Ottoman Empire. They negotiated with the Genoese for asylum on the island. Finally, in 1675, they were granted an unsettled tract of land 31 miles (50 km) north of Ajaccio, where, one year later, they founded *Paomia* (peacock), situated above present-day Cargèse.

The industrious Greeks got to work and soon turned the area into the most fertile and productive land in the entire area. The Greeks lived well here for almost half a century, but they aroused the envy of the poor Corsican herdsmen in the island's mountains. In 1729, at the start of the war of independence, the Greeks refused to fight against their benefactors, the Genoese; this led the Corsicans to believe that the Genoese and the Greeks were allies.

Corsican herdsmen plundered and destroyed Paomia that same year. They attacked again in the following year, and as the Greeks could not hope for any support from Genoa, they fled to Ajaccio in the dead of night, where they lived in exile for 43 years (1731-1774). The Chapelle des Grecs on the Route des Sanguinaires is testimony to the time they spent in Ajaccio.

Since 1769, the French flag has flown over Corsica. The Greeks, who had no hope of being accepted by the Corsicans, seized the opportunity to get in good with the new government. They formed a military regiment, which the French general, Count Marbeuf, immediately integrated into his troops.

In 1774, Marbeuf awarded the area around Cargèse to the Greeks as compensation for their loss of Paomia, and he had 120 houses built for them right away. Today, you can hardly find any Greek names in Cargèse at all. This is also partly due to the fact that the Greeks were forced to "Italianize" their names right after their arrival: Papadakis, for example, would be changed to Papadacci.

The first of the two existing churches was the Roman Catholic one. This Baroque-style house of worship was built in 1820 for the large number of Corsicans who moved to the area at the beginning of the 19th century.

The Greek Orthodox church was not built until much later, between 1852 and 1870. Inside, an iconostasis (1886), a wooden wall decorated with icons, separates the nave from the sanctuary. Originally from the Grotta-Ferrata monastery near Rome, it was a gift to the Greek colony.

The Greeks themselves brought four icons with them from their native land. On the 16th-century icon to the left of the iconostasis, St. John the Baptist is portrayed with angel's wings; on the right, you see the three doctors of the Greek church, Saints Basil, Gregory Nazianzus and John Chrysostom. Under the platform by the entrance there's an epitaph (in this tradition, a plaque erected in remembrance of a deceased person) depicting Christ's burial, flanked by the Virgin Mary, Joseph of Arimathea and Nicodemus; this icon dates from the 13th century. Behind the iconostasis, on the right next to the altar, is the last of the original icons from Greece: the Virgin Mary with the infant Jesus, surrounded by angels and the adoring saints Nicholas and Spiridion, the patron saints of the church.

The language of the liturgy is still ancient Greek; but you can no longer hear modern Greek in Cargèse. The faithful receive a Greek-French prayer book, designed to help them follow the mass. After all, almost 300 inhabitants of Cargèse still adhere to the Greek Orthodox faith.

AJACCIO

Accommodation

LUXURY: **Eden Roc**, Route des Sanguinaires, 5 mi/8 km from town center, but with bus connections, heated swimming pool, on the sea, thalassotherapy, tel. 95520147. **Les Mouettes**, 9, Boulevard Lucien-Bonaparte, swimming pool, on the sea, tel. 95214438. *MODERATE:* **Albion**, 15, Avenue Général-Leclerc, in the city, but quiet location, tel. 95216670. **Du Golfe**, 5, Boulevard du Roi-Jérome, on the marketplace, lively activity every morning, tel. 95214764. **Fesch**, 7, Rue du Cardinal-Fesch, B.P. 202, typically Corsican hotel in the center of town, tel. 95215052. **Castel-Vecchio**, Route d'Alata, swimming pool, tel. 95223112. **Sun Beach**, Route des Sanguinaires, swimming pool, tennis, on the sea, tel. 95215581. *BUDGET:* **Arcade**, 115, Cours Napoléon, relatively new chain hotel in low-to mid-priced range, tel. 95204309. **Bonaparte**, 2, Rue des Halles, tel. 95214419. **San Carlu**, 8, Boulevard Danielle-Casanova, tel. 95211384.

Campgrounds

Pech-Barette, above the Route Sanguinaires, 3 mi/5 km out of town, 200 m from the beach, tel. 95520117. **Les Mimosas**, Route d'Alata, tel. 95209985.

Restaurants

CORSICAN: **Au Bec Fin**, 3, Boulevard Roi-Jérome, tel. 95213052, **Da Mamma**, Passage Guinguetta, tel. 95213944. **A Pignata**, 1, Rue des Halles, tel. 95219536. **Aux Palmiers**, 3, Place Foch, tel. 95213860.

Museums

Musée Fesch, 50, Rue Fesch, tel. 95214817, opening hours: summer: daily 9 am-noon and 3-7 pm, in July and August also open Fridays 9 pm-midnight. Winter: daily except Sundays 9:30 am-12:15 pm and 2:15-6 pm.

Maison Bonaparte, Rue Saint-Charles, tel. 95214389, opening hours: summer: 9 am-noon and 2-6 pm. Winter: 10 am-noon and 2-5 pm. Closed Sunday afternoon and Monday morning.

Musée du Capitellu, 18, Boulevard Danielle-Casanova, tel. 95215057, opening hours: summer: 10 am-noon and 2-6 pm, closed Sunday afternoon and Monday morning. In winter, telephone to arrange appointment.

Musée "A Bandera," 1, Rue Général-Levie, tel. 95510734, opening hours: summer: Tu-Sa 9-noon and 3-7 pm. Winter: Tu-Sa 9 am-noon and 2-6 pm.

Entertainment

CORSICAN GUITAR MUSIC: **Au Son des Guitares**, 7, rue Roi de Rome, tel. 95511122, every night after 10 pm. **Pavillon Bleu**, Avenue Général-Leclerc, tel. 95214722.

NIGHTCLUBS: **Le Roi Jérome**, Avenue du Pre-

mier Consul, tel. 95213966. **Le Week-End**, Route des Sanguinaires, tel. 95520139, **Le Dolce Vita**, Route des Sanguinaires, tel. 95213520.
CINEMA: The following cinemas are located on the Cours Napoléon: **Empire**, tel. 95212100. **Laetitia**, tel. 95210724. **Bonaparte** and **Le Club**.

Sports

DIVING: **Club les Calanches**, Hotel des Calanches, Route des Sanguinaires, tel. 95520234. **Club Plongée Amirauté Cip**, Port Amirauté, tel. 95202679. *RIDING:* **Les Ecuries du Prunelli Poney Club d'Ajaccio**, Route de Sartène, Campo dell'Oro, tel. 95230310. *SAILING:* **Ajaccio Marine**, Port de l'Amirauté, tel. 95203131. **Locazur Sacops**, Quai de la Citadelle, tel. 95215520. *TENNIS:* **Tennis Club d'Ajaccio**, Le Casone, tel. 95512627.

Transportation

BY AIR: **Air France/Air Inter**, 3, Boulevard Roi-Jérome, Aéroport de Campo dell'Oro, tel. 95294545. Airport information: tel. 95210707. *HARBOR:* tel. 95212801, **S.N.C.M.**, Quai l'Herminier, tel. 95296699/95296688. **Corsica Ferries**, Port de Commerce, tel. 95510639. *BY TRAIN:* **Station/SNCF**, Boulevard Sampiero, tel. 95231103. Trains to Bastia via Corte and to Calvi, 4 times a day. *BUS:* **Autocars Santoni**, excursions, Z.I. du Vazzio, tel. 95226444. **Autocars Ollandini**, excursions, 1, Route d'Alata, tel. 95239240. **Eurocorse Voyages**, 2 x a day: Ajaccio-Corte-Bastia and Ajaccio-Propriano-Sartène-Porto-Vecchio-Bonifacio, Gare Routière, tel. 95210630. **S.A.I.B.**, 2 x a day, except Sunday, Ajaccio-Porto-Ota, Gare Routière, tel. 95224199. *TAXI:* Station Place du Diamant, tel. 95210087. Station Avenue Pascal Paoli, tel. 95232570. *CAR RENTAL:* **Avis Ollandini**, Aéroport/Campo dell'Oro, tel. 9523214, Place Général-de-Gaulle, tel. 95239250. **Budget**, Aéroport/Campo dell'Oro, tel. 95204533, Résidence "Diamant", 1, Boulevard Lantivy, tel. 95211718. **Europcar**, Aéroport/Campo dell'Oro, tel. 95231873, 16, Cours Grandval, tel. 95210549.

Tourist Information

L'Office du Tourisme, Hotel de Ville, Place Foch, B.P.21, tel. 95214087/95215339.

PORTICCIO
Accommodation

LUXURY: **Le Maquis**, tennis, swimming pool, tel. 95250555. **Sofitel Thalassa**, Golfe d'Ajaccio, with thalassotherapy, tel. 95294040.
MODERATE: **Frantour Marina Viva**, swimming pool, tennis, tel. 95250315. **Les Flots Bleus**, Molini Agosta Plage/B.P.3, tel. 95254957.

Campgrounds

Benista, Pisciatello, tennis, tel. 95251930. **Mare e Macchia**, Route de Terra-Bella, swimming pool, on the sea, tel. 95251058.

Sports

DIVING: **Club Subaquatique Agosta**, Molini, tel. 95254026. **Corse Plongée**, Route de Molini, tel. 95255008.
RIDING: **Centre Equestres de Porticcio**, tel. 95251105/95251133.
SAILING: **Yachting Club**, Les Marines 1, tel. 95250562. **Loca Nautic**, tel. 95217023/95251785.

Tourist Information

Syndicat d'Initiative, Plage des Marines, tel. 95250702.

GULF OF SAGONE
Accommodation

CALCATOGGIO: *MODERATE:* **Le Grand Bleu**, on the sea, swimming pool, diving, tennis, tel. 95522035.
BUDGET: **La Madrague**, Orcino Plage, tel. 95522102.
CARGÈSE: *MODERATE:* **Les Lentisques**, Plage du Péro, tel. 95264234/95264661. **Beau Rivage**, Plage de Chiuni, tel. 95264391.
BUDGET: **Cyrnos**, Rue de la République, tel. 95264003.
SAGONE: *MODERATE:* **Cyrnos**, tel. 95280001. **U Libbiu**, swimming pool, tel. 95280606.
TIUCCIA: *MODERATE:* **Cinarca**, swimming pool, tel. 95522139/95517100.

Campgrounds

CALCATOGGIO: Le Calcatoggio, tel. 95522831. **CARGÈSE:** **Torraccia**, tennis, tel. 95264239/95204021.
SAGONE: Sagone Camping, tel. 95280415. **TIUCCIA:** **U Sommalu**, tel. 95522421.

Sports

DIVING: **Centre Subaquatique**, Hotel Cyrnos, tel. 95280001. *SAILING:* **Pieri Location**, Route du Puntiglione, Cargèse, tel. 95264420.
TENNIS: **U Camarale**, Route de Vico, Sagone, tel. 95280142.

Tourist information

CARGÈSE: Rue du Docteur-Dragacci, tel. 95264131.

HINTERLAND OF SAGONE
Accommodation

VICO: *MODERATE:* **U Paradisu**, Route du Couvent, swimming pool, tel. 95266162.

Restaurant

MURZO: Auberge "U Fragnu," Antoine Nivaggioli, tel. 95266384. Reopened in 1995, only locals eat here.

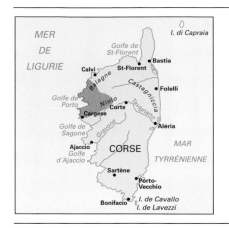

PORTO – BLUE SEA AND RED ROCKS

THE GULF OF PORTO
PORTO / LA SCANDOLA
LES CALANCHE / HIKES
FROM PORTO TO CALVI

THE GULF OF PORTO

The **Gulf of Porto**, located in the region of the Parc Naturel Régional de la Corse (Corsica's nature park), is considered one of the highlights of a stay on the island. If you happen to see it on one of the frequent sunny days, you'll find that reality here comes closest to the kind of paradise promised in brochures and advertisements.

The Gulf of Porto can be reached from the south by way of Cargèse on the D 81, and from the north on the same road, which is extremely winding along this stretch, going through the Balagne Déserte. A good road, the D 84, also connects the inland mountain region to the deep blue gulf, passing through the forest of Aitone and the Niolo Highlands on the way.

The gulf, which cuts almost 7 miles (11 km) inland, is bordered to the south by Capo Rosso and to the north by the red headland of Capu Seninu, 2,024 feet (619 m) high; directly adjoining it to the north is the small Gulf of Girolata.

The gulf is famous for its marine life, which is still mostly intact; but in fact, the whole region is known for its unique fauna. For instance, it's the nesting-ground for the only osprey (also called fish hawk) couples which still live on French territory.

PORTO

Porto, the biggest city around and a tourist magnet, lies at the apex of the gulf. Here, you won't find a town center that gradually grew up over the centuries – Porto was deliberately designed as a vacation resort, and everywhere you sense that the planners took great care to avoid such architectural eyesores as are found in tourist ghettos à la Mallorca or Gran Canaria. Here, there are none of those irritating high-rises for package tourists – the vacation domiciles are made of red granite and homogeneously integrated into the environment. There are restaurants, cafés, hotels and camping spots, as well as a few private homes, which are inhabited year-round.

In the tremendous hustle and bustle which goes on here in the summer months, it's easy to forget that Porto is not actually an independent city in its own right, but belongs to Ota, 3 miles (5 km) further inland. In the winter, however, this is immediately noticeable, because Porto drains of people in this sea-

Preceding pages: The mountain village of Evisa, a popular spot for day trips. Left: Purple granite – a hallmark of the Calanche.

son as if a plug had been pulled after the summer inhabitants have moved back to their year-round homes, for the most part in Ota, to recover from the tourist season and gear up for the next one.

Porto has two sections. If you come by car you arrive directly at the small harbor, the **Marine de Porto**. The spacious square here was built only a few years ago. It's no accident, by the way, that so many benches were installed here: for from here, you can see the most fantastic sunsets you'll find anywhere on Corsica. The waiters at the surrounding restaurants have stopped even taking notice when, in the evening, half of their guests suddenly stand up without a word and, leaving their Corsican specialties to get cold, storm the square, armed with cameras, in order to photograph the marvelous sunset and the glowing, blood-red rocks around the water.

Above: The magnificent sunset in Porto – an hour for romantics. Right: In the Gulf of Porto.

It takes about ten minutes on foot to get from the harbor to the beach, a walk which leads you across the elegant, arched pedestrian bridge over Porto River. Its last stretch before it runs into the sea has been dug out and expanded, so that now, boats can anchor better here than in the harbor, because the somewhat calmer river delta is protected from wind and surf. Even in the high season, the long beach, lined with eucalyptus trees, is never full. Maybe the rough gravel stones and high surf scare away most tourists who want to swim.

If you don't mind taking a long drive before going swimming (circa 12.5 miles/20 km), you can drive from Porto to Piana, through the Calanche. In Piana, a small road, the D 824, branches off to the **Plage d'Arone**, a picturesque bay with a charming sand beach and a small café.

Undisputed landmark of Porto is the **Genoese Tower**, standing loftily on an exposed cliff. In 1994 they restored the crumbling walls and set up a small mu-

seum inside devoted to the history of the tower.

Don't, by any means, neglect to take the three-hour boat tour from Porto to the nature reserve La Scandola. On the return trip, the boat anchors for a half hour in Girolata on the Gulf of Girolata.

LA SCANDOLA

To the north, the peninsula **La Scandola** forms one edge of the **Gulf of Girolata**, thus also marking the end of the Gulf of Porto.

This nature reserve, founded in 1975, was granted World Heritage listing by UNESCO on December 15, 1983. Two goals are being pursued in France's first nature reserve, which simultaneously protects the sea (2,500 acres/1,000 ha) and land (2,298 acres/919 ha): first, to protect the natural environment, and second, to maintain a zone of untouched nature to facilitate scientific study of the growth and development of the flora and fauna of this region.

The regulations in La Scandola are strict: on land, there are no camping, fires, or even hunting allowed. It is also strictly forbidden to take plants as souvenirs or to get too close to animals while photographing them. You can only reach this enchanting peninsula by boat or on foot – the most comfortable way is by sailboat or by motorboat. Due to the strict nature conservancy rules, stays are limited to a maximum of 24 hours. You should also refrain from fishing and diving here.

In addition to granite and slate, you can also find volcanic rock on Corsica, especially in the northwest of the island. The peninsulas La Scandola and Senina have the most spectacular volcanic rock, approximately 250 million years old. At one point, the captain of your ship will point out the "organ pipes," lava which has solidified into regular, even block forms, which you can easily see from the boat.

In the nature reserve there are only a few species of birds; the sparse maquis vegetation, dry climate, and scarcity of insects here do not create a very enticing habitat for most birds.

Marine birds are more frequent, such as different types of cormorant, which nest in small groups in the tafoni holes. Other birds who live here are the buzzard, peregrine falcon, and the osprey, which has become quite rare in Europe, and which make quite a sight when they majestically fly over the cliffs. In the early 1990s, rangers counted 19 pairs in the nature park.

Worldwide, there are still a considerable number of osprey, but unfortunately their numbers in Europe have been extremely reduced. Because this big bird of prey hunts fish, people – fishermen, that is – hunted them vigilantly; in addition, water pollution means that ospreys have a smaller food supply available to them today than was once the case.

Ospreys builds their big nests, easily seen from the boat, on the highest points of the rocky cliff; here, they are relatively safe from most enemies, including man. They start building their nests in March and finish in August, and hatch out one to three chicks in one nest.

Some of the ospreys spend the winter in their Corsican homeland, despite the frequency of cold storms; others fly as early as late autumn to warmer and wetter climes.

La Scandola also provides an interesting insight into the underwater world and its plants and animals. Wonderful corals and colorful fish can be observed through the glass-bottomed tour boats. If you want even closer contact with the denizens of the sea, you can book guided diving tours. Interested parties should inquire at either the booking office for the La Scandola boat tours in Porto, or at the Maison de la Mer in Galéria, which is also an information office for the La Scandola nature reserve.

The sea is not all that draws travelers to Porto – the fascinating mountain region, which you can see from town, is also worth the trip.

LES CALANCHE

An excursion through the **Calanche** near **Piana** is especially nice in the late afternoon, when the sun sinks into the sea and bathes the bizarre, pink-colored granite cliffs in a dazzling light. The word calanche is etymologically derived from the Corsican word *calanca* (harbor of refuge), because the hidden bays here offered refuge to many ships during heavy storms.

In 1883, the French author Guy de Maupassant, in his novel *A Life*, memorably described how his two protagonists encountered Calanche: "They set out at sunrise. Soon they stopped in their tracks. A forest lay before them – a real forest of purple granite: surprising shapes – molded by time, by the biting wind and the fogs of the sea. More than 900 feet high, thin, round, twisted, bent, misshapen, unexpected, bizarre, these astonishing cliffs appear to be trees, plants, animals, memorials, people, monks in habits, horned devils, huge birds – a race of monsters, a menagerie of nightmares which a god gone mad had turned into stone at a whim... then suddenly, as they left the chaos, they discovered a new gulf, surrounded by a bleeding wall of red granite, and the scarlet cliffs were reflected in the blue sea."

These impressive cliffs are still fascinating today, with their tafoni structures, a frequent appearance in the granite of Corsica. Tafoni, or in the singular, tafone, comes from *pietra tafunata*, or perforated stone (the Corsican word *tafonare* means to perforate). These are cliffs riddled with holes or cavities; sometimes they are shaped like the curtains of a baldachin, or hollow brick blocks. These formations are found mostly at lower and medium altitudes (3,300-4,900 feet/ 1,000-1,500 m).

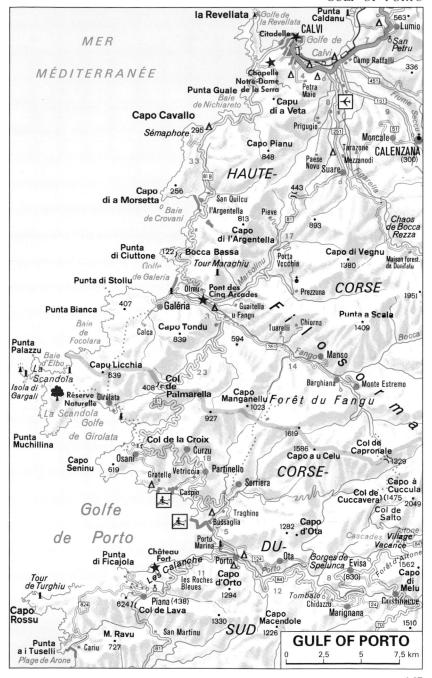

GULF OF PORTO

0   2,5   5   7,5 km

The question of how they were formed is still debatable. The German geomorphologist W. Klaer believes the formation of the tafoni cliffs to be a chemical process: when there are strong fluctuations in temperature, such as after rainfall or when night dew is followed by the powerful rays of the sun, ferrous oxide hydrates are released on the rock surface. These hydrates form hard crusts, and beneath the crust, water running off erodes irregular cavities into the rock over the course of time. When the crusts finally peel off in the form of scales, what remains looks like the skeleton of a hollow brick block. The red color of the granite is also a result of the high percentage of ferrous oxide.

Tafoni formations are very old; Klaer was able to prove that some of them go back to the last interglacial period (150,000-190,000 years ago), maybe even back to the last Tertiary period. If

Above: Tafoni is the name for these bizarre, weathered formations of granite rock.

you keep your eyes open while hiking, you can even see recent tafoni separations.

HIKES AROUND PORTO

The Calanche is a paradise for hikers and climbers. There is something for everyone here, whether you're up for a real mountain hike or just out for a long walk.

Hikes to Château Fort

In order to get to the starting point for this walk, which takes about an hour (round trip), you take the D 81 from Porto heading to Piana. Shortly before reaching the actual Calanche, there is a large cliff in a curve to the left that looks like a dog's head, which is why it has been dubbed **Tête de Chien**. To the right of the head is a well-marked trail, which leads to the outermost cliffs (not dangerous). It ends on a plateau 1,086 feet (332 m) above the sea; on the tip of the plateau is a stocky rock in the shape of a tower, which the Corsicans named Château Fort (fortress). To get back, you have to take the same trail. Be careful during rainy weather, because parts of the trail are steep and rocky and it can be dangerous.

Shortly after the dog's head, as you go toward Piana, there is a stone house at the side of the road. If you look closer, you'll see that it is a charming bar with a terrace and a souvenir shop. Strangely enough it is called **Les Roches Bleues** – The *Blue* Rocks – although the rocks are red here. The riddle isn't solved until spring, when the stonecrop plant covers the rocks with its blue blossoms. There is a good view of the Gulf of Porto from the lovely terrace; here and there you can spot the forms of brightly-clad rock climbers dotted over the red tafoni rocks as if glued onto them.

You can take several hiking tours from Roches Bleues. An approximately 45-minute hike starts directly opposite the bar and is marked with a blue dot in a white square. At first it is a short, steep climb, then there is a shady descent through the woods, around a curve and back to the starting point.

A three-hour-tour also starts opposite from Les Roches Bleues. It takes you through the woods in a long arc and after a hairpin curve, you come out on the road again, 1.2 miles (2 km) from your starting point.

A beautiful one-hour, high-altitude tour starts some 1000 feet (300 m) south of the bar. A small shoulder for parking and a statue of the Virgin Mary in the rock (*Oratoire de la Vierge*) are easy to spot. Right next to this is the old mule trail, which starts with a short piece of grueling, steep climbing. The hike is easier afterwards, and affords breathtaking views of the Gulf of Porto and the bizarre rock formations. About halfway along the hike, a naturally formed "heart" in the rock comes into view; here, people in

love are supposed to make a wish. The trail ends at a soccer field, which you cross lengthwise; then you find yourself back on the road, which either leads back to the bar, or, if you take the other direction, to Piana.

Hikes to Capo d'Ortu

The "local mountain" of Porto is the **Capo d'Ortu**, some 4,250 feet high (1,300 m). The hike starts at the soccer field mentioned above, at an altitude of around 1,635 feet (500 m). You should calculate six hours of hiking for the complete trip; that is to day, this is a day trip. Cross the soccer field and take the trail at the upper left-hand (northeast) corner; it soon leads to a bridge over Piazza Monica Brook. After that, the trail is well-marked, at first in orange-green, and later only with orange. The trail takes you along gradually ascending sharp bends for about an hour through the woods up to Bocca di Piazza Monica (3,316 feet/956 m). From here, you can take one of two trails to climb the mountain; of these, the trail on the left – the north trail – is the easier one. Follow the trail up to an altitude of 3,839 feet (1,174 m). The rest of the ascent (another 30 minutes) is marked solely with little stone men and is only recommended for experienced mountain climbers.

After all of these sporting activities, you can look forward to a hearty meal and refreshing drinks in the nearby charming town of Piana.

Not far from Porto on the D 84 is the picturesque **Gorges de Spelunca**. The road winds through steep curves for 15 miles (24 km) up to Evisa, taking you up another 2,744 feet (830 m); at almost every curve, you have a new view, and a new dramatic photo opportunity, of the wild Spelunca Gorge, which has cut its way through porphyry rock. The Aitone and Tavulella Rivers meet here to form the Porto River, a raging torrent in

winter, which empties into the sea a few miles from here.

If you come from Porto, you will soon come to the village of **Ota** on the left side of the cliffs, surrounded by high rocky peaks. **Capo d'Ota**, about 2,943 feet (900 m) high, hovers right over the village, culminates in a distinctive peak: it looks as if someone had placed a wobbly, round rock on top of the mountain. In the village of Ota they say that the natives have anchored the back of the rock with chains for added protection, in fear that the rock might fall on their heads. And if you believe that...

The stretch from Porto to Evisa is rife with curves and precipices. At an altitude of 2,714 feet (830 m), **Evisa** is a pretty health resort on a cliff terrace, set against a picturesque mountain background. The village, nestled in a chestnut grove, is also a stopover on the trail *Tra Mare e Monti* ("between mountains and the sea," see p. 238), and therefore has several hostels and simple hotels. A popular destination for an excursion in summer is the nearby **Forêt d'Aitone** (over Aitone Gorge); some of its venerable laricio pine trees are more than 165 feet high (50 m).

Hikes thorough the Spelunca Gorge

The best way to hike through the Spelunca Gorge is from the top (Evisa) to bottom (towards Ota), as the walk involves mastering a difference of 1,962 feet (600 m) in altitude within three hours. This may sound strenuous, but the walk is well worth it, presenting you with a wild, romantic gorge surrounded by steep, towering mountains. There is even something here for the culturally-minded: the old mule trail was laid by Romans, and thus at times you are hiking on flagstones from the days of the Romans. About halfway along the hike, you reach an ideal spot for a picnic – the medieval Genoese bridge, **Pont de Zaglia**,

Above: High above the Spelunca Gorge. Right: Swimming holes invite hikers to take a refreshing break.

where the Aitone and Tavulella rivers converge.

The hike starts directly next to Evisa's cemetery, which, if you are coming from Porto, is located right at the edge of the village; you can easily spot the consistently well-marked trail (orange) on the left-hand, precipitous side. From here, it is virtually impossible to lose your way. After a three-hour march, you arrive at the old Genoese **Pianella Bridge** and the D 124; to the right, this leads to Ota, and to the left, back to the D 84 (Porto - Evisa).

Tired hikers will find pretty pools for swimming where they can refresh themselves during the last part of the hike and at the very end, near the D 124.

THE WEST COAST ROAD FROM PORTO TO CALVI

The coastal road from Porto to Calvi is exactly 50 miles (81 km) long. Drivers should not underestimate the winding road, however, and leave themselves plenty of time. You will need up to three hours for this stretch during the high season, when a lot of camping vehicles are on the road; even though the road has been recently expanded, there isn't enough room for two wide campers to get past each other in many spots.

There's compensation for the passengers, if not as much for the drivers, on this long stretch: the views from the road out over the Gulf of Porto really are a dream.

If you want to take a quick jump into the temptingly blue waters of the gulf, there are two possibilities. About 3 miles (4.5 km) past Porto, the small road D 724 leads to **Plage de Bussaglia**. There are also overnight accommodations and a camping spot here. In the village of Partinello, 5 miles (8 km) further down the road, the D 324 branches off to the **Plage de Caspio**.

The villages of **Partinello** and **Curzu** are very secluded. They do have a modest tourist infrastructure, however, as they are located on the *Tra Mare e Monti* hiking trail, so there is a small shop here, a café and even a modest lodge, a so-called *Gîte d'Etape*, where hikers can stay overnight.

At the foot of Capu Seninu (2,024 feet/619 m) is the 889-foot-high (272 m) **Col de la Croix** (Cross Pass). From here, you have your first view of the Gulf of Girolata.

Girolata is the only village on Corsica that can only be reached by boat or on foot. You can wander down to the village from the pass in one to two hours.In days gone by, the tiny bay was guarded by the Genoese fort of the Doria family; it still stands here today as a ruin. Sailboats cruise into the bay in the summer, and the crews enjoy the heavenly tranquillity that reigns on sea and on land – especially in the evening. The picturesque fishing village depends on the crayfish catch for its livelihood, as well as on tourism; in summer, tour boats from Calvi and Porto anchor here several times a day. Then this sleepy town wakes up for an hour, activating its disproportionately large number of cafés; only to slip back, after the boats have gone, into its customary dreamy *dolce vita*.

You also have a good view of the Gulf of Girolata from the **Palmarella Pass** (1,334 feet/408 m).

From here, a narrow road leads down to **Filosorma**. Below, almost at sea level, the Fango River flows along. The Fango Valley can also be easily explored on a bicycle, because Route D 351 comes to a dead end after 6.5 miles (10.5 km). The view from here takes in the highest mountain peaks on Corsica: the Paglia Orba Massif and the Bonifatu Massif, both usually covered with snow until June.

You have the best view of Paglia Orba (8,257 feet/2,525 m) and the perforated

Right: From the hiking trail Tra Mare e Monti, there are magnificent views over the bay of Girolata.

Capu Tafunatu (7,636 feet/2,335 m) from the **Pont des Cinq Arcades** (Bridge of Five Arches).

A short excursion (2.5 miles/4 km) from here leads to **Galéria**, which in the last few years has developed from a sleepy fishing village into a small vacation resort. In spite of the many vacationers, you can still, even during the crowded summer months, find peace and quiet on the long pebble beach near the 17th-century Genoese fortress tower. The Fango flows into the sea here; however, during the hot summer months it is fairly dried out. At its mouth, a small freshwater pond has formed – a wonderful change from the salty seawater. Hikers on the *Tra Mare e Monti* also like to rest here for a day.

From the Bridge of Five Arches, drivers have the choice of the shorter and faster connection to Calvi (D 81), which runs through the inland, or the more time-consuming, but indubitably more charming coastal road (D 81 B).

The coastal road to Calvi goes through an area which is called **Balagne Déserte** (barren or desolate Balagne). This is a karst region – in contrast to the fertile Balagne south of Ile-Rousse – which is almost completely covered with maquis, and in particular the low vegetation of the garigue. Even the meager covering of earth is washed away in places, so that only bare rock is visible.

In the spring, however, this area is also covered with a lush carpet of blossoms; its barren character isn't evident until late summer and autumn, when everything dries up here and fires, which break out almost annually, do their part. In spite of this, the route along here is fascinating, as it winds, for the most part, right along the rough coast.

A few miles past Galéria, you pass a settlement consisting of only a few houses, **Argentella**, on Crovani Bay. Here, what you'll notice are large ruins along the road, where a silver mine once

was housed. This small town became famous – or infamous – in 1960, when the French government put forth plans to use the former ore mines for underground atomic tests. The French Minister of Energy tried to pacify the Corsicans, who were incensed at this proposal, with promises of the supposed benefits the project would bring them: the harbor and airport in Calvi would be expanded, bad roads would be improved, and they were guaranteed 100 new jobs. But the Corsicans feared, and rightly so, that the water would be contaminated, and they received the support of the influential ocean explorer Jacques Cousteau. As a result, the French government ultimately dropped the project.

Some 2 miles (3 km) beyond Argentella on the right is a giant, deserted castle which can be seen from the road – the ruins of **Château de la Torre Mozza**. Even if the château's defiant character makes it resemble a fortress, it had a romantic purpose: Prince Pierre Bonaparte, the cousin of Louis Bonaparte (Napoleon III), set up a comfortable love nest for himself here. Pierre was Prince-President of the Second Republic, but his political career failed. So he settled on Corsica in 1852, following the motto "back to nature and love."

From the next hill you have a nice view of the **Revellata Peninsula** and **Capu di a Veta** (229 feet/70 m), the "local mountain" of Calvi. About 2.5 miles (4 km) from Calvi, a narrow road on the right steeply climbs up to the *Chapelle Notre-Dame de la Serra*.

Unfortunately, the drive up is not exactly pleasant – depending on wind and weather conditions – because here everyone can clearly see the unvarnished side of Corsica's garbage problem. Plastic bags and other discarded items, often with a less than pleasing aroma, keep flying up in your windshield as you proceed. The guilty party here is the garbage dump, which cannot be seen or smelled from Calvi: they only burn the mountain of garbage, which grows especially rapidly in the summer months, when the

wind is blowing from a favorable direction and the stench can blow out over the sea.

Another garbage problem is likewise solved in the heart of Corsica's beautiful environment: at regular intervals, you can spot junked cars which have been pushed off cliffs. These aren't, as you might assume, the remains of spectacular car crashes; rather, they're planned, as this is a common way for owners to "dispose" of cars. Someone even once took the trouble to count the wrecks: there were more than 16,000. That means one junked car for every 15 inhabitants. Cleaning this up would be a Sisyphean task.

In fairness, one should mention here that Corsica is considered to be a model for the whole Mediterranean region in terms of sewage disposal: the sewage of the coastal communities passes through a

Above: This "traditional" manner of disposing of your wrecked car is now also prohibited on Corsica.

sewage treatment plant before it is piped into the sea.

There is a small parking lot 1.3 miles (2 km) from the turnoff; from here, it is only a short walk to the **Notre Dame Chapel**. It was built in the 19th century on the ruins of a sanctuary from the 15th century, which was destroyed during the siege in 1794. The house of worship is always closed, and there is a white statue of Mary in the rock next to it. The chapel draws more curious "onlookers" than art historians, because from the peak of the 706-foot-high (216 m) hill, you have a wonderful view of Calvi, the isolated citadel, the sweeping Gulf of Calvi, and the island's mountains, including the Bonifatu Massif; on a day with good visibility, you can even see the Monte Cinto Massif.

From up here you can also see a trail that leads from the chapel to the center of Calvi. This look-out point is a good point of departure for a visit to this harbor city, whose immense fortress was once loyal to Genoa.

PORTO
Accommodation
MODERATE: **Le Bélvedère**, La Marine, near the beach, tel. 95261201. **Kallisté**, sea view from many rooms, tel. 95261030/ 95212760. **Cala di Sole**, swimming pool, tennis, tel. 95261244. **Le Marina**, swimming pool, tel. 95261034. **Le Mediteranée**, pool, tennis, tel. 95261027. *BUDGET:* **Bella Vista**, tel. 95261108. **Bon Acceuil**, tel. 95261210. **Beau Séjour**, Quartier Vaita, tel. 95261211.

Campgrounds
Les Oliviers, 1 mi/1.5 km from the sea, with restaurant, near the Porto river, tel. 95261449. **Sole e Vista**, 1 mi/1.5 km from the sea, tel. 95261571. **Le Porto**, behind the Gendarmerie, lovely new place 1/2 mi/1 km from the beach with bar and small shop, tel. 95261367. **Funtana a l'Ora**, on the river, tel. 95261548.

Restaurants
CORSICAN: **Chez François**, Chemin de la Tour, tel. 95261096. **Restaurant** in the **Hotel Le Cyrnée**, La Marine, tel. 95261240. **Le Bélvedère**, La Marine, attractive terrace with view of the fishing harbor, tel. 95261201.

Transportation
CAR RENTAL: **Europcar**, Capo d'Orto, tel. 95261114. **Bartoli Porto Location**, tel. 95261013. *BUS:* **Autocars SAIB**, Porto-Calvi, twice a day, Ota-Porto-Ajaccio, twice a day, tel. 95224199. *TAXI:* **Félix Ceccaldi** in Ota, tel. 95261292.

Sports
BOAT RENTAL: **Les Bateaux du Soleil**, near the beach, Dino Pompei, tel. 95261755/ 95261764. *BIKES / MOTORCYCLE:* **Porto Location**, tel. 95261013. *DIVING:* **Centre de Plongée du Golfe de Porto**, tel. 95261029. *MINI-GOLF:* La Marine, tel. 95261755. *RIDING:* **Centre de Randonnées Équestres de Letia**, tel. 95266994. **Centre Équestre de Montagne**, Evisa, tel. 95262166.

Boat Excursions
Réserve Naturelle Maritime de Scandola-Girolata-Calanches de Piana, Cie Des Promenades en Mer, Porto Marine, tel. 95261516/95261234 (Hotel Monte Rosso).

Entertainment
Discotheques **Fanfan** and **Cesar Palace** at the edge of town (Porto).

Tourist Information
Syndicat d'Initiative, La Marine, tel. 95261055.

GULF OF PORTO
Accommodation
PIANA: *LUXURY:* **Capo Rosso**, Route des Calanches, swimming pool, tel. 95278240. *MODERATE:* **Les Roches Rouges**, tel. 95278181.

BUDGET: **Continental**, tel. 95278202. **Mare e Monti**, a hostel (*Gîte d'Etape*), tel. 95278214.
PARTINELLO: *MODERATE:* **Le Clos des Ribes**, tel. 95273036.
SERRIERA: *MODERATE:* **L'Eden Park**, Plage de Bussaglia, swimming pool, tennis, tel. 95261060. **L'Aiglon**, Plage de Bussaglia, tel. 95261065. **Stella Marina**, Plage de Bussaglia, swimming pool and restaurant, tel. 95261118.

Campgrounds
OSANI: Camping e Gradelle, right on the isolated Gradelle beach, access from the Col de la Croix, fine for tents, small open-air restaurant and mini-store, tel. 95273201.
PIANA: Plage d'Arone, tel. 95206454.
SERRIERA: Le Bussaglia, Route de Calvi, on the beach, tel. 95261572.

HINTERLAND OF PORTO
Accommodation
OTA: *MODERATE:* **Chez Félix**, *Gîte d'Etape* and restaurant, tel. 95261292/95261460. **Des Chasseurs**, *Gîte d'Etape* and restaurant, Corsican cooking, tel. 95261137.
EVISA: *MODERATE:* **L'Aitone**, member of the chain Logis de France, well-tended hotel on the way out of town toward Col de Vergio, swimming pool, bar and restaurant, tel. 95262004. **La Châtaignerie**, tel. 95262447/95262445. **Scoppa Rossa**, tel. 95262022/ 95262308. *BUDGET:* **Du Centre**, tel. 95262092. **Gîte d'Etape**, simple hostel with kitchen for residents, M. Ceccaldi, tel. 95262188.

Campground
L'Acciola, at the edge of town by the turn-off to Vico and Sagone, terraced chestnut grove, with restaurant, tel. 95262301/ 95262029.

GALÉRIA
Accommodation
MODERATE: **Cinque Arcate**, Fango, tel. 95620254/ 95652040. **Filosorma**, Route Bord de Mer, tel. 95620002/95620092. **Stagnolo**, in the Ideal Camping facility, tel. 95620146.
BUDGET: **A Farera**, Fango, tel. 95620187/ 95650155. **Stella Marina**, Route de la Plage, restaurant with terrace, marvelous view of the gulf, tel. 95620003. **L'Auberge**, near the church, small but comfortable, tel. 95620015. **L'Azelli**, *Gîte d'Etape*, at the entrance to town, low-priced, tel. 95620046.

Campgrounds
Ideal Camping, 300 m from the sea, with bar and restaurant, tel. 95620146. **Les Deux Torrents**, tennis, on the river, tel. 95620067.

Tourist Information
Syndicat d'Initiative, tel. 95620227.

THE BALAGNE, THE GARDEN OF CORSICA

CALVI
BALAGNE
HIKES IN THE BALAGNE

CALVI

Calvi, the principal city in the fertile Balagne in northern Corsica, is an old vacation resort with lots of tradition. The very name Calvi summons up visions of carefree vacation fun, and the spot is every bit popular as the vacation paradise of the South, Porto-Vecchio.

The city of 4,800 inhabitants, which lies on the western side of the Gulf of Calvi, offers just about everything for a jam-packed, active vacation. First of all, there is the 3.7-mile-long (6 km) fine sand beach, one reason that so many visitors come here every year in July and August that Calvi's population is increased almost tenfold. The spreading branches of the pine trees along the beach provide refreshing shade here. And for two weeks every summer, jazz takes over the historical citadel city – this music festival is an indication that Calvi's people are trying to offer vacationers more than just sun and surf.

You can explore the charming coast around here with the Balagne line of the *Micheline*, the Corsican train system. And if you're looking for an active vaca-

Preceding pages: Storm clouds over Calvi. Left: It takes a lot of climbing to get to the portal of St.-Jean-Baptiste in Calvi.

tion, you're in the right spot in Calvi, too. People who love water sports can choose between diving, sailing, windsurfing and water-skiing.

The mountains, which often remain snow-capped until May, appear to be tantalizingly close from the cafés on the harbor promenade, and it isn't far to the high wooded mountain valley of Cirque de Bonifatu. Calvi's culturally rich backwoods, the Balagne, is covered with hiking trails of all kinds.

In addition, you should also take the time to get to know more about the city's eventful history – the best way to undertake this is to stroll through the crooked tiny alleys of the citadel, soaking up the atmosphere and exploring.

The naturally protected bay of Calvi was probably already used by Greek and Phoenician sailors; the city was first founded, however, by the Romans in the 1st century A.D. They called the settlement *Sinus Caesiae* or *Sinus Casalus*. As in Aléria, Christianity started to spread here after the 3rd century A.D.; this has been verified by the discovery of an early Christian basilica.

The marauding Saracens did not spare Calvi when they plundered their way through all of Corsica between the 9th and 11th centuries. Shortly thereafter, the Pisans occupied the city and were re-

sponsible for its economic upswing between the 11th and 13th centuries. There were constant disagreements with Corsican noble families during this time, who tyrannized the population from a nearby, fortified spur of cliff. As a result, the inhabitants of Calvi turned to the powerful Genoese for help in 1278; the Genoese reacted immediately, and made Calvi into their most important fortress. Up until the 18th century, the city was a stronghold of Genoese power in the western Mediterranean.

The population profited from the same privileges which were also awarded to Bonifacio, and Calvi received the status of an autonomous city. Under Genoese rule, the citadel was expanded.

Proof of how well the citadel was built was furnished in the mid-16th century, when it was twice (1553 and 1555) able to withstand the onslaughts of the Corsi-

Above: Every summer, Calvi's jazz festival attracts plenty of visitors. Right: A lovely back...

can freedom fighter Sampiero Corso and his ally, the Turkish pirate Dragut. Dating from this period is the inhabitants' motto, which can be read today chiseled over the entrance to the citadel: *Civitas Calvi semper fidelis* (Calvi, the ever-faithful city).

Pasquale Paoli did not succeed in taking Calvi even after Genoa ceded the island to France in 1768 during the Corsican fight for freedom. During this period of heavy battles, the inhabitants of the city even gave shelter to Paoli's opponents, including Napoleon and his mother, who were forced to flee Ajaccio in 1793.

From June 16 to August 5, 1794, 6,000 English and Paolist troops laid siege to the citadel and shelled it day and night. It was in this battle, in which Calvi ultimately capitulated, that Admiral Nelson was hit by a stone splinter and lost his right eye. Two years later, in 1796, the English also left Corsica, and Calvi became the last city on Corsica to go over to the French.

The Citadel

The citadel, which originally could only be reached by a suspension bridge, is an independent small city, situated high on a granite cliff projecting out into the sea

To get to the entrance, you have to cross the **Place Christophe Colombe**, which also serves as a parking lot and a place to play boules. A monumental memorial stands here in remembrance of both world wars. It was created by the French sculptor Emmanuel Frémiet (nephew and student of François Rude). A new **Columbus Memorial** decorates the citadel wall which borders one side of the square.

Once you're through the arched gates and in the citadel, turn immediately to the right to get to the information office of the upper city.

An initial walk along the outer citadel ring offers beautiful views from the three bulwarks Teghiale, Malfetano and Spinchone.

The tour of the inner citadel starts at the former palace of the Genoese governor, which is now the **Sampiero Corso Barracks** – the Foreign Legion is stationed there. Their large, main barracks are located on the outskirts of Calvi.

Calvi is the only city today on Corsica where the Legionaries, with their shaved heads, white caps and red aiguillettes are part of the city scenery – and that since 1967! The Legionnaire units were transferred to Corsica at the end of the Algerian war (1962) because Corsica offers ideal conditions for tough training and conditioning: diving, parachute jumping and survival training in the impenetrable maquis. In 1983, the Legionaries were pulled out of the other citadels on the island. The unit in Calvi, 1,600 strong, is called *deuxième REP* (*Regiment Etranger de Parachutistes*), the only airborne unit of parachute troops in the Foreign Legion.

The Foreign Legion, founded in 1831 by the French king Louis-Philippe, is part of the French army. At first, it was used

to secure France's colonies in northern Africa. Even today, the legion is only sent into action in cases where the problem areas are located outside of Europe.

To this day, the legionnaires continue to have a somewhat dubious reputation, because applicants can also register under an assumed name. They are assured absolute anonymity; in return, they have to commit to five years of active, hard duty, and be in excellent physical condition.

The relationship between the Corsicans and the legionnaires has been strained after several incidents with island inhabitants (in 1976, for example, two herdsmen were murdered by a deserter). Every evening there are tight controls in the harbor bars, in order to make sure that the legionnaires do not get out of hand.

Diagonally across from the Place des Armes, 217 feet (80 m) above the sea, is

Above: St. Francis in the church of St.-Jean-Baptiste.

St-Jean-Baptiste, which, seen from the outside, is a rather simple house of worship. The Genoese built a church in the form of a Greek cross on the same spot in the 13th century, but it was badly damaged in 1567 when the powder magazine exploded. Three years later, the church was rebuilt as a summer seat for the bishops of Sagone. Several years later, the bishops moved to Calvi, and the church was elevated to the status of cathedral.

If you let your gaze wander over the interior, flooded with light, you'll be impressed with the rich decorations, proof of the prosperity of the citizens of Calvi. Immediately to the right is a **holy water stoup** made of alabaster (1441), decorated with angels' heads and coats-of-arms of wealthy citizens (lions, fortresses, seated leopards). On the left, behind a grating, there's another marble water basin (1494) and a Renaissance-style **baptismal font**, donated in 1569 by the wealthy Calvese merchant Vincentello.

Looking up, you can see, behind gratings, the **boxes** where the noble ladies of Calvi sat to avoid having to sit with the common people during mass.

By the right pillar is a **pulpit** made of carved ebony, decorated with carved images of John the Baptist and the four symbols of the Evangelists. You can also make out the date 1757, which was the year the citizens of Calvi donated this pulpit.

Above the lateral altar on the right is a black ebony crucifix with the revered "Black Jesus," *Christ Noir*, about which locals recount the following story. In 1553, when Sampiero Corso and his allies, the Turks, were besieging the city, the inhabitants of Calvi were at their wits' end. Finally, they resolved to march around the city walls carrying the crucifix; and lo and behold, the Turks miraculously gave up the siege immediately. Since then, the crucifix has also been

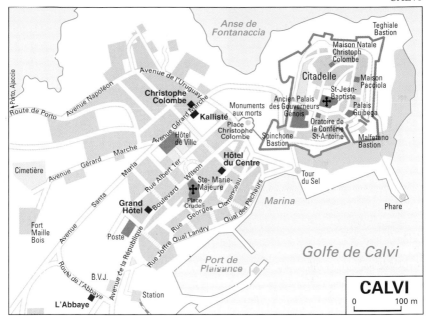

Anse de Fontanaccia

Teghiale Bastion

Maison Natale Christoph Colombe

Route de Porto, Ajaccio

Avenue de l'Uruguay

Avenue Napoléon

Route de Porto

Christophe Colombe

Avenue Gérard Marche

Kallisté

Hôtel de Ville

Monuments aux morts

Place Christophe Colombe

Citadelle

Ancien Palais des Gouverneurs Génois

St-Jean-Baptiste

Maison Pacciola

Palais Guibega

Oratoire de la Conférie St-Antoine

Malfetano Bastion

Spinchone Bastion

Hôtel du Centre

Cimetière

Avenue Gérard

Marche

Maria

Rue Albert 1er

Wilson

Ste-Marie-Majeure

Boulevard

Place Crudeli

Rue Georges Clemenceau

Quai des Pêcheurs

Tour du Sel

Marina

Phare

Santa

Grand Hôtel

Fort Maille Bois

Avenue

Poste

Rue Joffre Quai Landry

Rue de la République

Rue

Route de l'Abbaye

B.V.J.

Station

Golfe de Calvi

Port de Plaisance

CALVI

0   100 m

L'Abbaye

known as the **Christ des Miracles** (the miraculous Christ).

The choir is decorated with a beautiful, 17th-century **marble altar** from northern Italy; above it, there is a masterful wooden triptych by the painter Barbagelata (1458). Its side panels depict the Annunciation and scenes from the lives of Mary and Jesus. The central panel has been lost; replacing it today is a statue of John the Baptist.

On the left, in a niche, is another art work revered by the citizens of Calvi: **La Vierge du Rosaire** (The Virgin Mary with Rosary). Originally from Seville, this 15th-century statue is taken down during Holy Week, dressed festively and carried through the city in a ceremonial procession.

"Genoa and the ever-loyal Calvi quarrel over only one point," wrote the cultural historian Ferdinand Gregorovius in his historical sketches of Corsica in 1852. Calvi claims to be the birthplace of the discoverer of America, Christopher Columbus.

Columbus himself did say that he was Genoese – but that doesn't prove that he was actually born in the city of Genoa, because, as we know, Calvi belonged to the sea republic of Genoa in the 15th century, too. Needless to say, most Corsicans are convinced that Columbus came from Calvi.

The way to the intrepid ocean explorer's alleged house heads uphill for a bit by the cathedral. An alley branches off to the left; after a few stairs, which lead down again, you turn right and find yourself in front of the deplorable remains of the house where Columbus's parents allegedly lived. If a **memorial plaque** didn't remind you that Christophe Colombe was supposedly born in this house in 1441, you could easily overlook it.

Not only do scholars fight over the birthplace of the famous explorer, but his date of birth is just as unclear. Columbus was said to be about 70 years old when he died in Valladolid in 1506, meaning he was born in 1436.

183

According to Genoa, however, the discoverer of American wasn't born until 1451 – wherever he was born.

One argument which seems to uphold the idea that Columbus was born on Corsica is that several documents written by Columbus himself contain elements of the Corsican language. But wasn't 15th-century Corsican, especially in Calvi, almost identical to Genoese?

Whatever theory one chooses to espouse, one thing seems fairly certain: the mystery of the birthplace of the discoverer of the New World will continue to occupy some Western historians for years to come.

Walking through the cobblestone alleys of the citadel, you come to the **Maison Pacciola**. An inscription informs you that Napoleon and his mother Letizia stayed here in 1793. Because they opposed Paoli, they both had to flee Ajaccio

Above: In Calvi, Foreign Legionnaires are a part of the landscape. Right: If you can, you can – even in the middle of the marina.

and go to France. Stopping over in Calvi, they found shelter in the citadel – where Paoli was not particularly well-liked – with Napoleon's godfather, Laurent Guibega.

Not far from here is the 15th-century **Palais Guibega**, which served as a summer residence for the bishops from Sagone.

In Rue St. Antoine, below Place du Donjon and the barracks, you will find the **Oratoire de la Confrérie St-Antoine** (Oratory of St. Anthony). This was once the seat of the order of the same name, which settled on Corsica in the 14th century and was active in spiritual as well as social guidance.

In the oratory, which dates from the 15th century, there is a museum of Christian art from the Balagne, with works from the 16th-19th centuries. Take a look at the relief made of slate over the door lintel of the entrance. St. Anthony is depicted with his small pig between John the Baptist and a kneeling St. Francis. The interior is divided into three aisles; the windows open onto Calvi Bay. Immediately to the right of the entrance is a wooden triptych of the Lombard school (late 15th century or early 16th century), with a crucifixion scene as the centerpiece; on the left is the archangel Gabriel and on the right is an image of the Annunciation. In addition, you can peruse a collection of richly-decorated liturgical robes from the 17th and 18th centuries, gilded and painted coats-of-arms of the city, and a collection of ritual objects of engraved, gilded silver (holy water, incense and host chalices from the 17th to the 19th centuries).

To the left of the altar, protected in a glass cabinet, is a beautiful ivory figure of Christ. It is attributed to the Florentine sculptor Jacopo d'Antonio Tatti (who died in 1570 in Venice), better known to most people as Sansovino. Although the figure is small, the artist succeeded in giving it realistic anatomical proportions

and an expression of suffering (with tiny tears in the eyes). On the left wall, two frescoes depict the Crucifixion: the older fresco, dating from the 15th century, is barely discernible, whereas in the other fresco from the 16th century, you can clearly pick out Christ between St. Anthony, the Virgin Mary, St. Sebastian and St. Roch.

The lower city with its small pedestrian streets entices you to stroll and shop. At the harbor, which is a fishing, trade and transport harbor all in one, vacationers have a hard time making the right choice between the numerous boulevard cafés and restaurants on the **Quai Landry**. A stroll beside the yacht marina is always exciting, as the really big French and Italian luxury liners often tie up here. Here on the harbor promenade, you can book boat trips to the **Grotte des Veaux Marins** (Seal's Grotto) on the cape of Revellata, or to **La Scandola**.

The church of **Ste-Marie-Majeure**, located on the charming **Place Crudeli**,

goes back to the year 1774. The cupola and bell tower were not added, however, until the 19th century. In the dusky interior, there are two paintings well worth viewing: *The Assumption of the Virgin,* dating from the 16th century and the *Annunciation* (17th-century Florentine school), both from the ubiquitous Fesch collection.

Place Crudeli turns into a lively outdoor restaurant in the evenings. You should reserve a table in advance if you're in the market for a romantic evening meal.

THROUGH THE BALAGNE

From Calvi and Ile-Rousse, you can go on some nice excursions into the hill country of **Balagne fertile**, the fertile Balagne. This part of the Balagne, which stretches from Calvi through Ile-Rousse to the Lozari Delta and is bordered on the south by Monte Tolo (4,356 feet/1,332 m) and Monte Grosso (6,334 feet/1,937 m), has been called "The Garden of Cor-

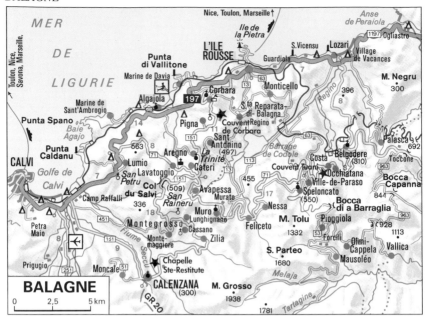

sica" since time immemorial. Orange, citron and almond trees thrive in this fertile soil; of course, vineyards and olive groves also contribute to the prosperity of the locals.

Unfortunately, the fires that break out almost annually destroy large agricultural areas. The catastrophic fires of 1957, when almost all of the olive groves burned down, and the fires of 1985, traces of which can still be seen today, paralyzed the agricultural industry, leaving the way open for tourism to become the island's number-one source of revenue.

Characteristic of this hilly region are the nicely renovated medieval villages, which are picturesquely enthroned on the hilltops.

Even in prehistoric times, the fertile region of the Balagne was already settled; numerous finds of tools from this period

Right: The Balagne village of Belgodère isn't called "beautiful place to stay" for nothing.

have substantiated this. By the days of Antiquity, the region was bustling with activity: the Phoenicians, Greeks and Etruscans traded here. Finally, the Romans were drawn here, too, and they made the land arable. Traces of them have been found in the erstwhile Roman settlements of Calvi, Ile-Rousse, Algajola, Speloncato and Calenzana.

The Saracens, feared everywhere, were especially drawn to this bountiful area, and they occupied it for a time. Peace did not return until the advent of Pisan rule (11th-13th centuries). The Pisans built several Romanesque churches, which is why Corsicans also call this region "The Holy Balagne."

The Genoese expanded the economic power of the Balagne, Cap Corse and the city of Bastia, and it was under their rule that the important citadels were constructed in Calvi and Algajola.

As a counterweight, Pasquale Paoli built the city Ile-Rousse in the 18th century, in order to fight better against the Genoese – especially against Calvi.

From Calvi, the N 197 is the quickest way to Ile-Rousse.

Lumio, which, seen from Calvi, is so nicely illuminated at night, shows some signs of its former prosperity: an imposing church (17th/18th centuries) stands here, built in a Northern Italian Baroque style.

After another 3 miles (5 km), you come to the small beach resort **Algajola**, with its fine sand beach and small harbor. Founded by the Phoenicians, the city experienced its period of greatest prosperity in the 17th century, with the olive and oyster industry, when it was a small Genoese garrison. After being plundered by the Saracens in 1643, the residents built a fortress wall in 1664 to protect the city against further attacks; the wall still stands today.

At the start of the Corsican independence wars (1729), the Corsicans occupied Algajola. Shortly thereafter, the town became unimportant again because Paoli founded the city of Ile-Rousse very close by.

Up until the present day, Algajola has maintained its medieval charm with its narrow streets, small squares, the church St-Georges and the citadel (not open to the public).

The actual tourist area lies 1.8 miles (3 km) farther west: **Marine de St-Ambroggio**, with a large marina (200 berths), vacation apartments, hotels, cafés and restaurants.

Following the coast, it is another 5 miles (8 km) on the N 197 to an important center of tourism in Balagne: **Ile-Rousse** (*Isula Rossa*). The city of 2,300 inhabitants gets its name, "Red Island," from the offshore island **Ile de la Pietra**, whose red granite glows so nicely at sunset.

Designed on the drawing board in 1758, the city was initially called Paoliville, named after its founder Pasquale Paoli, who created in it a purely Corsican port that was wholly independent of Genoa. The French, however, renamed the city Ile-Rousse after they annexed the island.

The city is built on an orderly grid of straight streets at right angles to each other. At the heart of it all is the atmospheric **Place Paoli** with a marble bust of the freedom fighter. This square, with inviting sidewalk cafés under shady plane trees, is a favorite gathering place for young and old alike.

On the west side of the square, steps lead up to the austere parish church, built in the classical style; the elegant **Palais Piccioni** on the south side is home to the venerable high-class hotel *Napoléon Bonaparte*; to the north, the open market – which offers fresh produce directly from the growers – leads the way into the old town.

Despite its long history of some two centuries, the city doesn't have any great historical buildings to offer. The remains of a **Genoese tower** at the end of Rue Notre Dame bear an inscription referring to the foundation of the free city of Paoliville.

With its fine white sand and clear water, the **municipal beach**, separated from Place Paoli only by a street and the Balagne train tracks of the Corsican train line, tempts you to take a swim.

But you can reach a real dream beach on the N 197, which runs along the coast. After traveling a mere 4.4 miles (7 km), you can see the turquoise-colored water and the wide sand beach of **Lozari**, which is never overcrowded, not even in high season. You can't see the parking lot very well from the beach, so be careful of car break-ins. The best rule of thumb: don't leave anything valuable in the car. Better yet, don't leave anything at all in the car.

The Balagne excursion now leads inland, towards Belgodère. **Belgodère** ("beautiful location") has 330 inhabitants and sits atop a 1,014-foot-high (310 m) hill; it is one of the larger villages in Balagne. Open only for actual services, the church of **St-Thomas** (1269) has a 16th-century panel painting in the choir with a scene depicting Mary and the infant Jesus, as well as a carved Baroque retable.

In the Middle Ages, this village was part of the fiefdom of the Malaspinas, descendants of an old Pisan family. This family built a fortress on the top of a hill, but only ruins remain today; still, the short climb is worthwhile, because from up here you can see the entire Regino Valley and the Codole Reservoir, created in the 1980s.

The Parisian painter Suzanne Valadon lived in this region with her son Utrillo in 1912/13, and the lovely landscape inspired her to paint her bright, colorful paintings.

A few miles farther to the west, you pass the former Franciscan monastery **Tuani**, which was taken over by Dominicans and has been private property since 1964.

Speloncato lies about 6 miles (10 km) from Belgodère. This picturesque little town, on a mountain spur in front of Monte Tolo, got its name from a 26-foot-long (8 m) and circa 20-foot-wide (6 m) natural rock tunnel (in Corsican, *spelunca*, which can also mean "grotto" or "cave"). One side of the tunnel, also called *Pietra Tafonata* (Corsican for "perforated stone"), points the way to the central **Place de la Libération** and the church of Ste-Marie.

Every year on April 8 and September 8, you can experience a strange natural spectacle in Speloncato. After the sun has already disappeared behind the mountains, around 6:00 pm, its rays appear a short time later through the opening of the Pietra Tafonata, and illuminate the Place de la Libération again for a few seconds.

The mountain road goes on past the hamlet of Feliceto and leads to **Muro**. The large Baroque church with its impos-

Right: In Sant' Antonino, you can sample the products of the organic farmer Monique.

ing white facade forms a flagrant contrast to the surrounding, small, dark dwellings. Inside, there are several examples of late Baroque art. On Ash Wednesday in 1778, the choir of the church collapsed under the heavy weight of snow, killing 59 people. A short time later, the village residents rebuilt the choir.

Muro becomes a popular site of pil grimage every year during Lent; people are commemorating a miracle. In 1730, the face on a crucifix here, which is now carefully preserved, is said to have started to bleed while encircled by a glowing halo.

After another 2.5 miles (4 km), you reach an intersection by Cateri. From here you can see Aregno and **Sant' Antonino**, the "Eagle's Nest," situated on a round mountain top. It can be reached by following first the D 151, then the D 413, which branches off to the right. You can see the impressive lay of the village as you drive up; it appears to be glued onto the round hilltop at an altitude of 1,635 feet (500 m).

Park the car in the large parking lot at the church, because Sant' Antonino can only be visited on foot or on that typical Corsican vehicle, the donkey. The climb through the narrow medieval alleys and passageways, through courtyards of gra nite houses and past small shops, makes you perspire, especially at midday. Once you reach the top, you are rewarded with a view of the northern Balagne, all the way to Algajola and – to the southeast – all the way to the mountains, which re main covered with snow into early sum mer.

The family of the Counts Savelli, from Corbara, founded the town in the 9th cen tury. The general population of the Ba lagne was allowed to use the well-pro tected facility as a refuge during the Sa racen invasions.

Today, there are still about 60 year round inhabitants of Sant' Antonino. In the summer, the number increases many times over, when the well-renovated houses, which are rented out as vacation apartments, fill with guests.

At the entrance to the village, next to the parking lot, you can take a break with the organic farmer Monique Antonini (from Sant' Antonino, as her name indicates), and refresh yourself with lemonade. In autumn, you can order the excellent specialty "mélange," fresh-squeezed lemon juice mixed with grape juice. Monique also has various wines, as well as nutmeg, homemade jams and, of course, lemons.

Every morning, the postman stops at Monique's house and gives her the mail for the entire village, which is then either picked up in person or carried up by Monique herself; you really can't blame the postman for wanting to spare himself the climb.

After you've filled up on vitamins and organic products at Monique's, you can continue on your way with renewed energy.

Aregno, on the D 151, is especially worth seeing for its Romanesque Pisan church, the **Église de la Trinité**, which is about half a mile (1 km) south of the village at the cemetery. The character and construction of this 12th-century village church are strongly reminiscent of the San Michele church in Murato, which dates from the same period (see p. 68). Notable here is the beautiful polychrome masonry of blocks of light and dark granite, which lightens up the severe form of the building itself.

The symbolism of the primitive sculptures is interesting. Over the main entrance, there's an arch with 15 keystones, which has a small figure in high relief at each end. These two symbolic figures resemble the ones on the west facade of San Michele in Murato: they represent the medieval division of power between church and state. The sculpture with the stave-like object in its hand is an allegory for law (the object is a scroll of laws).

Right: Pigna is the acknowledged center of Corsican crafts.

The figure in the long robe symbolizes the clergy (church robe).

The consoles in the upper tympanum depict human masks, bear heads and twigs. Rather than a console in the upper section of the arcade, there's a double window, divided in the middle by a thin column. Above this is a low bas-relief depicting two snakes entwined around each other, heads down; while at the very top, over the gable, there sits a peculiar, freestanding sculpture: the so-called "thorn puller."

In the Bible, thorns and thistles are symbols of earthly toil and God's punishment for sinners: when the farmland is cursed, thorns and prickly underbrush grow there (Genesis 3:17 ff.). The thorn in the sculpture's foot illustrates the punishment for anyone who has gone down the path of sin. Here in Aregno, the "thorn puller" is sitting to pull the thorn out of his foot: a reminder to anyone who sees him to recant his or her sins before entering the church.

Farther north above the D 151 you can see **Pigna**, which lies – like Sant' Antonino – on a mountain ridge, and radiates considerable charm. Moorish in appearance, the village is surrounded by olive groves, which were badly damaged by fire in the summer of 1985.

Today, Pigna is a center for Corsican handicrafts. If you're not looking for plastic Napoleons or souvenirs "made in Taiwan," then you are in the right place, for here you find small shops in crooked alleys where Corsican handicrafts are produced using natural materials and according to old traditions: lambskin vests, carvings of chestnut wood, pottery, silk scarves, paintings and all sorts of foods, including wine, honey, liqueurs, or chestnut cake.

This organization goes back to the artists' association CORSICADA (*Communauté d'Organisation Rurale pour le Service, l'Information et la Création dans l'Artisanat d'Art*), founded in 1964

by Tony Casalonga. It supports young artists who work in remote villages. The organization enables them to make a living from traditional handicrafts without being forced to move to the mainland. In Pigna, the **Casa di l'Artigiani** (House of Artisans) exhibits the works of artisans who do not live and work in the village itself.

Farther on, the D 151 leads to the **Dominican Monastery of Corbara**. Monsignor Nicola Savelli originally built this house at the foot of the lookout mountain Monte Sant' Angelo (1,838 feet, 562 m) to serve as an orphanage in 1430. In 1456, the building was converted into a monastery. It was badly damaged during the French Revolution, and after 1857 Dominican monks rebuilt it and gave it the form you see today.

The huge fire in 1985 did not spare the monastery, and the church was hardest hit; it has since been completely rebuilt and renovated. The monastery of Corbara is a so-called *ritirio*, used as a facility for laymen who want to retreat and spend a few weeks of their vacations in introspective meditation.

1.5 miles (2.5 km) to the north is the village of **Corbara**. Here, in what was once the capital city of Balagne, Pasquale Paoli announced the foundation of Paoli-ville, later called Ile-Rousse.

Corbara also has links to the history of Morocco through the almost unbelievable adventures of the historical personage Marthe Franceschini. Pirates sold her parents as slaves to Tunisia, where Marthe was born. As luck would have it, the family was able to flee at one point, but they were then captured on the way home by Moroccan pirates. The sultan permitted the parents to return home after spending 8 years in Morocco, but he kept their daughter in his seraglio, and finally married her. When Marthe died of the plague in 1799, she was the Sultana of Morocco.

A worthwhile excursion from Calvi or Cateri (on the D 151) leads you to **Calenzana**. This town, at the foot of Monte Grosso (6,337 feet/1,938 m), is sur-

rounded by olive and almond trees; it's best-known as the starting point of the cross-island hiking trail GR 20. Hikers can stock up on food here. Local specialties are the tasty maquis honey and *cus-giulelle*, a kind of dry cake which is refined with white wine from Calenzana.

The Baroque church **St-Blaise** (17th and 18th centuries) towers over the church square; it was built from plans of the famous Milan architect Domenico Baina. Directly next to it is an elegant bell tower (1870-1875), also built in the Baroque style. Adjacent to the campanile is a cemetery with 500 German graves (**Campu Santu di i Tedeschi**).

During the Corsican war of independence, which started in 1729, the Genoese hired 9,000 German mercenaries from the Austrian Emperor Charles VI to reinforce their troops. 800 of these troops, under the command of von Wach-

tendonck, were supposed to force the rebellious village of Calenzana to surrender. Outnumbered by the armed soldiers, the inhabitants could only hope to obtain a victory by means of a trick: they let their bee colonies loose on the army. Panicked, the soldiers fled to the nearest brook; but the villagers were already waiting for them there, and they massacred almost two-thirds of the soldiers.

You come to the small chapel **Ste-Restitute** after driving east for another half mile or so (1 km) on the D 151. The church door is locked, so leave your passport at the tobacco shop on the church square in exchange for the key to the chapel. The chapel is devoted to the Corsican martyr Ste-Restitute, who was beheaded under Emperor Diocletian in the 4th century A.D. Two processions take place annually in her honor. Only parts of the walls of the 11th-century Romanesque church are still standing. The largest part of the present-day chapel dates from the 16th century; the choir was redone in the Baroque style.

Above: In the Casa di l'Artigiani, Pigna.
Right: Calenzana is the northwestern point of departure for hikers on the GR 20.

HIKING TOURS
IN THE BALAGNE

An extensive network of hiking trails leads through the fertile Balagne. For the most part, the trails are well-marked and suited for hikes of every level of difficulty, from easy to quite challenging, from short walks on mule trails without much incline to climbing to the top of the lookout peak of Monte Tolu (4,356 feet/1,332 m).

From Algajola to Ile-Rousse

The following day trip can be terminated at any time in one of the villages along the way, and you can take a bus back. The recommended map is the IGN 4149 OT 1:25,000 map.

The route goes through Algajola, Aregno, St-Antonio, Corbara Monastery, Corbara and Ile-Rousse. If your feet are tired, you can also negotiate the return trip from Ile-Rousse to Algajola with the Balagne train.

From Algajola, you take a small street heading south, which crosses the train tracks and leads to the cemetery. Take a left at the cemetery and continue to follow the small street, which crosses the N 197 and runs into a path after a few minutes. After about 10 minutes, you reach a road to Aregno, which has very little traffic. Follow the road for about a quarter of an hour; along the way you pass the old Chapel Annunziata on the right.

When you reach a watercourse, you can either take a shepherd's trail (leading inland, on the left), which ends shortly before Aregno at a paved road (the D 551), or you can stay on the idyllic small street.

After walking for 1 to 1.5 hours, you arrive at Aregno, where you can refresh yourself at a bar on the village square.

The route leads out of Aregno towards the cemetery above the town, where the remarkable Romanesque-Pisan church of the Trinité is located. Directly left of the cemetery wall is a steep, inclining path

which takes you up to the Eagle's Nest of Sant' Antonino in about an hour, from an altitude of 785 feet (240 m) to 1,472 feet (450 m). The path is well-marked (in orange) for its entire length, and you can see the town on the clifftop ahead of you for most of the way.

The next starting point is the big parking lot by the church of Sant' Antonino, which is below the village. On the left side you can see several grave chapels along the slope: head for them. Once there, you can easily see the path; it leads down along a cliff (be careful if it's been raining, as it can get quite slippery), until you see the gleaming white monastery of Corbara. Along the entire path, hikers have sweeping panoramic views of the Balagne and the coast.

Just behind the monastery, the path leads to a small road again (D 151). Here you have the option of making a detour to

Above: The Pisan Romanesque sculptures (12th century) of the church of Aregno merit a detour.

the left to explore the handicraft village of Pigna, or hiking on to Corbara along the road to the right.

At the edge of the village of Pigna, a path leads back to Corbara. From there, you can cross the fields on various mule and livestock trails to the N 197, where you still have to hike a mile or so (1-2 km) back to Ile-Rousse. From Ile-Rousse, the Balagne trains run along the coast through Algajola to Calvi several times a day.

Monte Tolu (4,356 feet/1,332 m)

Climbing Monte Tolu is – literally as well as figuratively – the high point of anyone's stay in the Balagne. From the peak of this lookout mountain you can see the entire hilly coastal region, with the charming cities of Calvi and Ile-Rousse. To the south you can see the northern spur of the high mountains, Monte Padro, and on a clear day you can even see Monte Cinto's peak, the highest on the island, which is usually covered with snow.

At first, you drive to the picturesque mountain village of Speloncato, described above, which lies at the foot of Monte Tolu. Go across the market square here and turn left between two restaurants onto the D 63, going toward Pioggiola and Olmi-Cappela.

The road goes up the mountain to **Bocca di a Barraglia**, at an altitude of 3,594 feet (1,099 m). There is an open space here at the pass where you can leave your car while you take the three-hour hike.

To the south, there's a ridge covered with antennas. From the path, you can see that there's another path leading along this ridge; this is what you want to follow. This route remains easily visible for its whole length, and stays on the ridge the whole time, although it doesn't always ascend, but also dips downhill in several places.

CALVI
Accommodation

LUXURY: **La Villa**, Chemin de N.-Dame de la Serra, pool, tennis, tel. 95651010. *MODERATE*: **L'Abbaye**, Route de l'Abbaye, in an old (16th-century) monastery near town center behind the train station, tel. 95650427. **Le Grand Hotel**, 3, Boulevard Wilson, tel. 95650974. **Kallisté**, 1, Avenue du Commandant-Marche, tel. 95650981. **La Revellata**, Route de Porto, tel. 95650189. **Christoph Colombe**, Place Christoph-Colombe, tel. 95650604. *BUDGET*: **Hotel du Centre**, 14, Rue Alsace-Lorraine, in the old city, low-priced, tel. 95650201. **B.V.J. Corsotel**, quality youth hostel with no age limit, Avenue de la République, tel. 956514.

Campgrounds

Bella Vista, Route de Pietramaggiore, 1/2 mi/1 km from the beach, tel. 95651176/95607252. **Dolce Vita**, Route N 197, right on the beach, restaurant and shop, tel. 95650599. **Le Mouflon**, tel. 95650353. **Les Castors**, Route de Pietramaggiore, tel. 95651330. **Paduella**, Route de Bastia, tel. 95650616/ 95651320.

Restaurants

CORSICAN: **La Ciuciarella**, Quai Landry, on the harborfront promenade. **U Fornu**, Impasse du Boulevard Wilson, tel. 95652760. **Le Royal**, 15, Rue Clémenceau, small family restaurant with friendly service, tel. 95651654. *PIZZERIA*: **Le Marly**, Avenue de la République, tel. 95650634.

Entertainment

Jazz Festival, highly recommended, every year at the end of June-early July, information: tel. 95651667/ 95650050. **La Camargue**, Discotheque (high entrance price), casino, restaurant and bar in one, on the N 197 toward Ile Rousse.

Transportation

BY AIR: Aéroport Sainte-Catherine, tel. 95652009/ 95650354. *HARBOR*: tel. 95651777. **S.N.C.M.**, Quai Landry, tel. 95650138. *TRAIN*: Station, Avenue de la République, tel. 95650061. *TAXI*: **Station Taxis**, Place de la Porteuse-d'Eau, tel. 95650310. *CAR RENTAL*: **Avis Ollandini**, 6, Avenue de la République, tel. 95650674, airport, tel. 95650605. **Hertz-Filippi Auto**, 2, Rue Joffre, tel. 95650664, airport, tel. 95650296. **Europcar**, Résidence "Danielli," Avenue de la République, tel. 95651035, airport, tel. 95651019.

Travel Agents

Calvi Corse Touristique, Immeuble Vieux Chalet, tel. 95651135. **Corse Voyages**, Immeuble les Remparts, Boulevard Wilson, tel. 95650047.

Sports

DIVING: **Club Plongée de la Citadelle**, B.P. 104, tel. 95653367. *MINIGOLF*: Avenue Christoph Colombe, tel. 95650140. *SAILING*: **Calvi Charter**

International, Port de Plaisance, tel. 95653343. **Calvi Nautique Club**, Port de Plaisance, tel. 9565 1065. *TENNIS*: Court reservations, tel. 95652113.

Tourist Information

Port de Plaisance, tel. 95651667.

ILE ROUSSE
Accommodation

LUXURY: **Napoleon Bonaparte**, Place Paoli, best hotel in Balagne, swimming pool, tennis, lovely restaurant right by the pool, tel. 95600609. *MODERATE*: **La Pietra**, tel. 95600145. **Santa Maria**, Route du Port, B.P. 19, swimming pool, tel. 95601349. *BUDGET*: **Le Grillon**, 10, Avenue Paul-Doumer, tel. 95600049.

Campgrounds

L'Orniccio, tel. 95601732/95600583. **Les Oliviers**, tel. 95601992/95602564. **Balanea**, Route d'Algajola, tel. 95601177. **Campéole**, lovely place about 300 m from the beach, also rents wooden bungalows, tel. 95602020.

Car Rental

Europcar, tel. 95601326, Esso Station, tel. 95601226. **Hertz-Filippi Auto**, Imm. "Le Relais," Avenue Paul-Doumer, tel. 95601263.

Tourist Information

Place Paoli, tel. 95600435.

BALAGNE
Accommodation

ALGAJOLA: *MODERATE*: **L'Ondine**, 7, Rue A.- Marina, swimming pool, tel. 95607002. **Pascal Paoli**, tennis, swimming pool, tel. 95607156. *BUDGET*: **Saint-Joseph**, tel. 95607212.
BELGODERE: *MODERATE*: **Les Mouettes**, swimming pool, tel. 95600323/95603931.
CALENZANA: *BUDGET*: **Auberge de la Forêt**, in the Forêt de Bonifatu, tel. 95650998/95651187. **Monte Grosso**, 48, Rue du Fond, tel. 95627015.
LUMIO: *BUDGET*: **Bellevue**, Avenue des Lauriers, tel. 95607207.
PIOGGIOLA: *BUDGET*: **Auberge Aghjola**, swimming pool, tel. 95619048.
SPELONCATO: *MODERATE*: **Spelunca**, tel. 9561038.

Campgrounds

ALGAJOLA: **De La Plage**, tennis, tel. 95607176/95607150. **AREGNO**: **Cantarettu City**, Aregno Plage, tennis, tel. 95607089/ 95607880. **CALENZANA**: **Paradella**, Route de Bonifatu-Square, tel. 9565009/.
LOZARI: **Le Clos des Chênes**, Route de Belgodère, swimming pool, tennis, tel. 95601513.
LUMIO: **Panoramic**, Route de Lavatoggia, swimming pool, tel. 95607313.

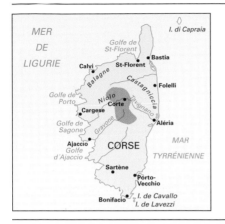

CORTE AND THE NORTHERN MOUNTAINS

CORTE
HIKES AROUND CORTE
NIOLO
HIKES IN THE NIOLO
FOREST OF VIZZAVONA

THE SECRET CAPITAL: CORTE

Corte (*Corti*), with a population of 5,700, is not only the heart of Corsica from a geographic standpoint, but also from a historical and nationalistic point of view.

The city is surrounded by the highest mountains on the island and lies in a basin created by the Tavignano River. East of town are the foothills of the Castagniccia; to the west and south are the fringes of the central granite mountains (Rotondo Massif). This basin has remained an important agricultural region to the present day, producing wine, olives, chestnuts, cheese and wood. There is, however, little industry.

Located at an altitude of 1,308 feet (400 m), the town of Corte extends around an isolated, towering rocky hill, atop which the city's hallmark, its citadel, is perched. At the foot of this fortress cliff, enthroned more than 325 feet (100 m) above the valley, the crystal-clear mountain waters of the Restonica empty into the Tavignano, which flows out of a

Preceding pages: Corte's citadel – built on the cliffs like an eagle's aerie. Left: Time seems to have stood still in the streets of Corte's old city.

wild gorge here. All of this is surrounded by a backdrop of impressive mountain scenery.

To the natives, however, all of this natural beauty pales in comparison to the city's political and historical significance. Corte, also called the secret capital city of the island, was the former stronghold of the Corsican resistance, the center of Corsican patriotism and the independence movement.

Corte makes a more urban impression than would seem to be indicated by its relatively small number of inhabitants. Although much smaller than the "big cities" of Bastia and Ajaccio, Corte can boast of having been the nation's capital city during the all-too-brief period of Corsican independence (1755-1769).

Today, the mountain town still lives off of its erstwhile reputation, a reputation which still burns bright in the hearts of Corsican nationalists; Corte, therefore, has remained the spiritual center of the Corsican independence movement. This is evident when you look at the displays of the shops along Cours Paoli, which are clearly targeting natives and not tourists; it's also notable that Corte has the only university on the island.

This institution of higher learning has its own special history. Bastia and Ajaccio also wanted to be the seat of the

university and thus the center of Corsica's intellectual elite, but tradition and patriotism finally won out in the choice of location.

Pasquale Paoli founded a university here as early as 1765, but the victorious French closed it almost immediately, in 1769, because they suspected that the Corsican students were a new hotbed of resistance. As patriotic Corsicans did not want to be reeducated as French, in 1970 several Corsican students decided to demonstrate for the establishment of a university on their island. Until then, anyone who wanted a university education had to move to Aix-en-Provence, Nice or Paris.

As the French government did nothing at first, as has so often been the case where Corsican issues are concerned, the students themselves organized a so-called summer university in Corte in 1971. Subjects included Corsican cul-

Above: Corte – university town and starting point for mountain hikes.

ture, language, traditions and history. Still, the French government didn't react until 1975, when it finally established a university center here, a branch of the University of Nice. The first seminar, however, wasn't actually held until 1981.

The university in Corte has been independent since 1982. At first, it was tentatively planned for 600 young Corsicans, but it already boasts more than 2,000 students studying every imaginable subject, including economics, law, humanities and science, as well as medicine. Only about 35% of Corsicans who want to study are able to do so at the **Pascal Paoli University**. One of the university's strengths are departments specifically dealing with the Corsican language, native culture and traditions.

Due to its location as a "traffic hub" at the mountainous heart of the island, Corte was an attractive site even to early Roman colonists. They named their settlement, which was easily accessibly from the sea, *Cenestum*. It remained inhabited up into the 11th century.

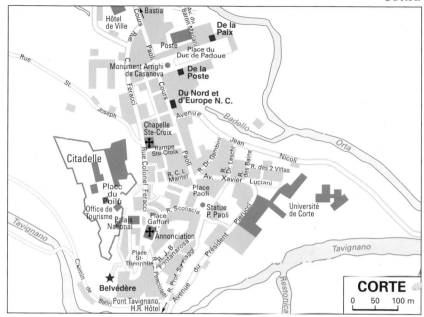

In the early 15th century, the Corsican adventurer Vincentello d'Istria conquered the fortress of Corte for the Spanish king of Aragon; he converted it into a fort in 1419. 20 years later, the Genoese drove him out of the strategically important inland stronghold, which remained firmly in Genoese hands again after 1459.

In 1553, the feared Corsican freedom fighter Sampiero Corso from Bastelica and his men stood before the gates of the citadel. The inhabitants of Corte voluntarily gave him the keys to the city, but a short time later (1559), the island was given back to Genoa in the treaty of Cateau-Cambrésis. Thus Corte was once again under the rule of the mighty maritime republic – a state of affairs which continued for the next 200 years.

Under the leadership of the doctor Jean-Pierre Gaffori, who had been born here, a Corsican liberation army succeeded in taking the citadel in 1746; soon thereafter, they had to defend it against Genoa with their very blood. Corte had become the most important inland base on Corsica, because anyone who had control of the "heart" of the island could easily advance into all of the other regions. The Corsicans, women as well as men, managed to defend the citadel with extreme patriotic zeal. Their leader, Gaffori, was treacherously murdered near Corte in 1753, but soon thereafter the famous Pasquale Paoli was appointed his successor. He named Corte the capital city of the nation of Corsica, and it soon developed into the economic and spiritual center of the island.

Paoli's government blessed the island with fourteen years of independence (1755-1769), which have remained unique in Corsican history. But Corsica again became French in 1769. Many locals remain firmly convinced that Corte will be named the island's capital city if Corsica is ever again granted its independence.

Its bustling university life has helped Corte to maintain its lively character. Unlike other mountain towns, where the

younger generations tend to leave and the populations consist primarily of older people, you can find a well-balanced mixture of young and old in this town's inviting sidewalk cafés, talking over cups of coffee or sipping pastis.

City Tour

With its many shops and cafés, Cours Paoli is the city's main traffic artery as well as its main thoroughfare. Coming from Bastia and heading slightly uphill, it first leads past the **Hôtel de Ville** (city hall), in a park on the right, and the square **Place du Duc de Padoue** on the left. A bronze statue on this square is a memorial to General Arrighi de Casanova, who was born in Corte in 1778 and later became the Duke of Padua (Northern Italy).

Cours Paoli, always busy, leads directly to the **Place Paoli**, lined with res-

Above: A cool drink in the shade – café survival techniques for hot summer days.

taurants and cafés. It forms a link between the upper and lower cities, and naturally the "father of the fatherland," Pasquale Paoli, is present – in the form of a bronze statue – to keep an eye on the goings-on in the square. This memorial was completed in 1864 by the artist Victor Huguenin. From here, a steep flight of stairs leads up to the picturesque upper city.

You first arrive at the small, peaceful **Place Gaffori**, named after the freedom fighter from Corte who was also praised as the "protector of the nation."

Across from the church is the former house of the Gaffori family; you can tell which one it is by the bullet holes, still visible, left by the Genoese in 1750. Gaffori's brave wife Faustine is also honored in Corte, and over a glass of red wine you can hear of her heroic deed. When Corsica was fighting against the maritime republic of Genoa, the Genoese took advantage of Gaffori's absence to try and capture his family and hold them as hostages. But they didn't reckon with the bravery of the Corsican women. Faustine, with a gun in her hand, barricaded herself and a few of her friends in her house, and they fought the Genoese for days. The enemy peppered the house with bullets. Terrified, Faustine's friends advised her to surrender, but the courageous woman dragged a powder keg into the downstairs room, grabbed a burning torch, and swore that she would blow up the house and all its inhabitants if her friends ceased firing at the enemy. And so all of them held off the Genoese attack once again, until Gaffori rushed to the scene with several other Corsicans and freed his wife.

The scene with Faustine and the powder keg is illustrated in a relief on the pedestal of the **Gaffori Statue**, which stands on the square of the same name. A second relief depicts an earlier incident, when the Corsicans, under Gaffori's leadership, stormed the citadel occupied by the Genoese. The Genoese commander anticipated the citadel's fall and ordered his men to tie Gaffori's son, who had already been captured, to the wall of the citadel so that his father would hold his fire. And indeed, the Corsicans ceased firing immediately. After a moment of profound silence, so the story goes, Gaffori suddenly gave the order to fire again. The Corsicans did so, and managed to storm the citadel; miraculously, Gaffori's son remained unharmed.

Across the way is the **Église de l'Annonciation**, which dates back to the year 1450. Both the facade and the interior were renovated in the 17th century. The interior is interesting; usually, only the side entrance is open. Once your eyes have adjusted to the dimness, you can see a wooden crucifix from the 17th century and a nicely carved wooden pulpit from a former Franciscan monastery. But the church's main attraction is the chapel dedicated to **St-Théophile**, added on later. Baptized under the name Blaise de

Signori in Corte in 1676, the saint was active as a Franciscan monk until his death in 1740, and was canonized in 1930. In 1979, the waxworks museum Grévin in Paris executed a wax figure of Saint Theophilus lying on his deathbed and exhibited the piece in the Church of the Annunciation. Today, believers worship St. Théophile as the patron saint of Corte.

Behind the church, cross Place St-Théophile, walk past the radio station Corte, take the few steps and you reach Belvédère. This lookout platform, some 325 feet (100 m) above the Tavignano River, commands a great view of the old town of Corte, the landscape in the river basin, and the confluence of the two rivers Restonica and Tavignano.

If you keep as close as possible to the fortress walls on the way back, you'll reach **Place du Poilu** within a few minutes. Charles and Letizia Bonaparte lived in the modest house No. 1 for about a year; and Napoleon's brother Joseph Bonaparte was born here in 1768. According to Gregorovius, the house was supposedly worthy of "the birth of a Napoleon."

Opposite this is a tall, fortress-like edifice: the **Palais National**. Built as the seat of the Genoese administration, it served Paoli as a seat of government from 1755-1769. In 1765, it housed the first Corsican university. Today, the building belongs to the Pasquale Paoli University once again; it serves as the Center for Corsican Studies.

Across from here is the entrance to the **citadel**, which was used for more than 20 years (1962-1983) by the French Foreign Legion, and has only recently been opened to the public. As the only inland fortress built on Corsica, it has been a much-desired and fiercely contested object in the course of its history.

Immediately to the right of the entrance is a room which contains information on the Corsican regional park, as well as an exhibition of contemporary regional art.

To reach the oldest part of the citadel, the tower (also called the "Eagle's Nest"), built in 1419 by Vincentello d'Istria, you ascend a flight of 166 steps. Taking up the entire south end of the cliff, the tower is surrounded by a second, much wider ring, most of which was expanded under Louis XV in the 18th century. The large barracks, however, were the work of Louis XVI.

The citadel didn't receive its present appearance until the 19th century under the Citizen King, Louis-Philippe. On his orders, the houses and the chapel inside the fortress walls were torn down. During the Italian occupation in World War II, the military buildings served as a prison for Corsican patriots; later, the French Foreign Legion temporarily moved in here.

For the last few years, the citadel has been open to the public. Inside the prison cells, the walls bear graffiti executed by Corsicans and legionnaires. There are long-standing plans to open a museum of Corsican history in the Serrurier barracks.

You return to the lower city by following Rue Colonel Feracci and then heading down the steps on the right across the ramp Ste-Croix. Before you head down, you'll see the **Ste-Croix chapel** on your left; the first mentions of this building date from the 16th century. Its interior resembles that of the Baroque chapel St-Roch in Bastia.

HIKES AROUND CORTE

Corte is the starting point for numerous hiking tours through the high mountains. As a result, many hikers and backpackers frolic around here in the summer months, flooding the city even after the

Right: Don't try this at home – or even in the ice-cold waters of Capitello Lake.

students have disappeared for summer vacation.

Hikes in the Tavignano Valley

One nice hiking tour, where you can determine the length and duration yourself, starts right in Corte. First you climb the Rampe Ste-Croix and turn onto Rue St-Joseph, directly across from the church Ste-Croix; at the end of the street is a signpost which indicates the various trails and the times you need to complete them.

You can't miss the trail that's marked in orange. Right at the start, it abruptly branches off steeply up to the right, whereas the route you've been following continues to run straight on, ending approximately an hour later at the bottom of the valley by the river. After its steep start, the uphill path ascends more gently, crossing two small side valleys.

The farther you hike, the more often water holes entice you to rest. After hiking for about three hours, you come to a very lovely swimming spot by a suspension bridge over the Tavignano River. You can picnic here, and go back the way you came if you so choose.

From the bridge, the trail heads uphill to Lake Nino (5,700 feet/1,743 m), the source of the Tavignano River. The stretch to the Lac de Nino, however, is hard to do in only one day, and once you get to the lake, you'll find "only" natural beauties – no food, that is, or accommodation. Not until you get farther northwest, at the Col de Vergio, do you find a ski hotel with a restaurant, located at an altitude of 4,578 feet (1,400 m). On the way, before you get to the lake, you pass the Refuge de la Sega (where you can spend the night, but there's no service) and the rustic Bergerie de Tramizzale, known for its fresh goat cheese.

However, if you start out in the early morning, take a taxi from Corte to the Vergio ski lift, and start the Lake Nino-

Tavignano Valley tour at the upper section, you can make it back to Corte on a long one-day hike (8 hours), as the route from here is mostly downhill.

The Restonica Valley

Most visitors say that the **Restonica Valley** is the most beautiful valley on Corsica. Even Gregorovius praised the river's clear waters on his travels through Corsica in 1852: "Its water is as clear, as fresh and as light as ether, and it is famous far and wide throughout the country of Corsica. This incomparable spring has such a sharpness to it that it cleans and polishes iron quickly and keeps it from rusting." Famous far beyond the borders of Corsica, the valley, with its clear water, remains even today one of the most frequently-visited hiking areas on the island.

From Corte (1,295 feet/396 m), a narrow road winds 9.3 miles (15 km) through the Restonica Valley up to the Bergerie Grotelle (4,480 feet/1,370 m).

Although countless cars drive through the Restonica Valley, it isn't hard to find quiet, secluded, romantic spots. There is a restaurant in the middle of the forest and an idyllically-situated campground.

The trail leads through a charming mountain brook valley, where you can splash in big swimming holes. Further on, the landscape is transformed into a romantic mountain wilderness, surrounded by granite cliffs more than 6,540 feet (2,000 m) high: on the left are the first foothills of **Monte Rotondo** (8,574 feet/2,622 m) and on the right, somewhat lower, is the mountain crest which separates the Restonica and the Tavignano valleys. The Ice Ages formed the valley, and you can still see traces of the glaciers: a deeply indented valley in its lower reaches, it becomes a trough valley higher up, with shoulders, round peaks and the cirque lakes Melo, Capitello, Goria and Oriente, all popular destinations for hikers.

To hike to the lakes, as well as to the mountain Punta a le Porte (7,564

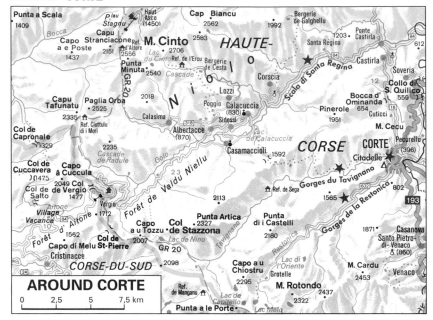

AROUND CORTE

0   2,5   5   7,5 km

feet/2,313 m), start at the **Bergerie Grotelle** (4,480 feet/1,370 m), which has a restaurant in the summer. The size of its spacious parking lot gives you an idea of what it is like here in the high season.

Most people who embark on day hikes from Corte take a short hike to Lake Melo or even Lake Capitello. Only rarely do mountain-climbers essay the highest mountain in the region, the wonderful lookout mountain Punta a le Porte (7,564 feet/2,313 m).The trail from the Bergerie Grotelle to **Lake Melo** (5,595 feet/1,711 m) can be completed in about one hour, with 1,112 feet (340 m) of vertical ascent. The rocky trail is well-marked and above all easy to see, so that you are never in danger of losing your way.

After some 30 minutes you reach a small plateau, where two paths lead to Lake Melo. The first one is the longer of the two; it branches off to the left and goes along the cliff. This route is recom

mended for hikers with a good head for heights.

The other path goes over a low cliff, where you have to climb for a short stretch with the help of well-anchored chains; even for beginners, it doesn't present any major problem. After a short time, you reach the cool green waters of Lake Melo, at an altitude of 5,595 feet (1,711 m); known to have a plentiful supply of fish (trout), the lake is surrounded by local anglers from the early morning on.

The steep route to **Lake Capitello** (6,311 feet/1,930 m) starts on the west side of Lake Melo; from a distance you can see Restonica Brook flowing downwards, indicating the route along which you're going to climb up. You start, however, far to the right of it. The trail to Lake Capitello is marked by little stone men; to master the 650-plus feet (200 m) of vertical ascent, some easy climbing is required.

After about 40 minutes of hiking, dark blue Lake Capitello appears between

Right: White-water kayaking on the Golo, the island's longest river.

high, towering cliffs; it is the deepest lake on Corsica (137 feet/42 m). Even in late summer there are still patches of snow here, as the lake is frozen eight months of the year; it is, therefore, hardly suitable for swimming.

If you want to get to the peak of **Punta a le Porte**, climb from the lake in a southerly direction, up the cliffs that border the lake on the east. From here you can see the peak for most of the climb, which takes a good two hours. After you've reached a ridge at an altitude of 6,942 feet (2,123 m), the trail meets up with the GR 20, marked in red-and-white, which you take westwards.

Here, too, the ascent to the peak is marked with small stone men. This stretch is recommended only for experienced hikers with good equipment, as it leads across a dangerous field of scree and – depending on the season – also a field of snow.

From the peak, you have a panoramic view of the high Corsican mountains all the way to the west coast.

THE NIOLO AND ITS TRADITIONS

Even today, the landscape of the **Niolo** (*Niellu*) is still remote; only a single road, the D 84, leads into this isolated region.

Natives gave this grand tract of gorges a much more poetic name: **La Scala di Santa Regina**. It wasn't until 1889 that road engineers used dynamite to build the D 84 through the granite, in order to make the Niolo more accessible. Even today, the 9-mile-long (15 km) Scala di Santa Regina, which starts in Ponte Castirla and ends in Calacuccia, is the only eastern access route into the high mountain valley. Before it, there was only a narrow mule track, which still can be seen above the road.

The Alpine orogeny in the Tertiary period made its mark on Corsica, too; when the region rose, the rivers changed their courses and created new riverbeds. The longest river on Corsica, the **Golo**, gradually dug into the mountain range to form this gorge.

Within some 12 miles (20 km), the river completes a total vertical descent of 1,640 feet (500 m). Today, two water works have made use of the resulting energy potential to generate electricity. The water also flows through an tunnel from the headwaters of the Tavignano River into the Calacuccia Reservoir.

Depending on light and weather conditions, the gorge shows a number of different faces. On sunny days, the granite appears to glow red, while in fog or when it rains, it appears dark and eerie; this is one reason that there are many tales and legends surrounding the Scala di Santa Regina and the Niolo. Locals recount the story of a dramatic battle between the powers of good and evil that took place in this area: in the early days of Christianity, St. Martin and the devil kept running into each other here. One day, St. Martin was plowing peacefully when the devil swore

Above: Forest fire in the Scala di Santa Regina. Right: Procession at the Santa Festival in Casamaccioli.

and cursed St. Martin, took his plow, and threw it towards the Golo. At that moment, the mountains broke apart and crumbled into a chaos of rocks. After this horrible event, St. Martin pleaded to the Virgin Mary for help; she put the rocks back into order in such a manner that there was an entrance into the Niolo, enabling the Golo River to flow again. St. Martin thus gave the gorge the name *Scala di Santa Regina* (Stairs of the Holy Queen).

Up until the late 19th century, there was only a herdsmen's trail leading through the gorge, which the shepherds used to drive their herds to the coast in September to take advantage of the milder climate there. As soon as the snow in the Niolo melted in late May or early June, they moved back to their native mountains.

The Niolo, the basin of the headwaters of the Golo River, lies between 2,600 and 3,270 feet (800-1,000 m) above sea level. It extends over more than 9 miles (15 km) in length, and is some 6 miles (10 km) wide. Bordering it are mighty mountains some 6,500-8,000 feet (2,000-2,500 m) high: Punta Artica, Capu a u Tozzu, Paglia Orba, Punta Minuta and Monte Cinto.

In spite of its isolation, the Niolo was already settled in the Stone Age: archaeological finds demonstrating this are exhibited in the museum in Albertacce. The Niolo has remained a land of herdsmen and farmers to this day; each family has a small sheep or goat herd and a little land where they grow grain and vegetables. Tourism didn't start to bring money into the region until a few years ago. In **Calacuccia** there are several hotels and lodges, and you can also rent private rooms. Today, the Niolo is also recognized as a health resort by virtue of its pure, clean air, and it's ideal for sports enthusiasts, whether they prefer mountain climbing, water sports, or skiing at the Col de Vergio.

Shortly after leaving the gorge you come to the highlands. First sight here is the large **Calacuccia Reservoir**. The retaining wall was inaugurated in 1968 and can hold back up to 883 million cubic feet (25 million cu. m) of water.

On the south side of the lake is the village of **Casamaccioli**, a typical sleepy mountain nest with 140 inhabitants. But once a year, from September 8th-10, the village comes alive when half of Corsica comes to its *Santa* festival. The origin of the festival is the birthday of the Virgin Mary, who is worshipped here in the form of a statue which is said to have miraculous powers. This Madonna figure, which stands in a side chapel of the parish church, once belonged to a monastery which was torn down. The natives say that the people then put the statue on a mule and let the mule go without a guide. They wanted to build a new church for the Virgin Mary on the spot where the animal first stopped. As Providence would have it, the mule took its first rest in Casamaccioli. Since then, a

festival with a procession is held every September 8 in honor of the Virgin Mary. It has developed into a giant, three-day celebration, at which local products are also sold. During these three days, the Niolo is transformed into a hive of activity. The lines of cars reach all the way around the lake, and hotel rooms are booked out way in advance.

Perhaps the most impressive event for foreign visitors is the so-called *chjama è rispondi* (call and answer) competition, which involves an old tradition of antiphonal singing. Due to the isolation of the region, the Niolo has preserved many of its old traditions, and is thus also known as the "ethnic heart of Corsica." The local population cultivates Corsican music traditions in particular. In Casamaccioli, the singers are evidently having a great time while singing to each other with improvised a cappella songs. This spectacle is also filmed by French television. The few foreigners who come to this truly genuine Corsican festival are, by the way, welcomed heartily, as long as they can keep up in the pastis-drinking department.

At the end of the lake, in the direction of the Col de Vergio, you pass **Albertacce** with its small archaeological **Museum Licninoi**. This institution is named after the original inhabitants of the Niolo, the Licninoi. Ptolemy, the 2nd-century Greek geographer, reported that the Licninoi were one of the twelve tribes that settled Corsica before the Romans did. Interesting finds from the Iron Age are exhibited here.

HIKES IN THE NIOLO

Heading west on the D 84, you come steadily closer to the Monte Cinto Massif; along the way you pass the forest area of **Valdu Niellu** (3,270-5,230 feet/1,000-1,600 m), the Corsican "Black Forest."

The area, part of the regional park, is the single largest wooded area on Corsica. It covers an area of 11,500 acres (4,600 ha) between Paglia Orba and Punta Artica. Over two-thirds of the trees are black spruce; above an altitude of 4,250 feet (1,300 m), the forest has a mixture of beech and birch trees, while in the highest regions of the mountains alders and willows predominate. The best wood on the island comes from this area, something also due to its extreme climatic conditions: it is a Mediterranean mountain climate with an annual average of 67 inches (1,700 mm) of precipitation. The average temperature in January is close to the freezing point; in August, on the other hand, it is 64°F (18°C).

Hike to Lake Nino

The hiking trail described here starts at the **Maison Forestière de Popaghja** (3,519 feet/1,076 m) and ends at the ski lodge at the **Col de Vergio** (4,578

Right: Skiing at Easter – ascent to Paglia Orba.

feet/1,400 m). The *maison forestière* has a large parking lot; it's about 6 miles (10 km) from Albertacce and 6.5 miles (10.5 km) from the Col de Vergio.

An easy forest path starts at the parking lot and heads uphill, marked with a wooden sign to Lake Nino. Altogether, you should plan on 5-6 hours for the hike to Col de Vergio, without breaks. Follow the yellow trail markings to Colga Brook. Continuing on, make sure you always stay on the right side of the brook. After about an hour, you'll have reached the edge of the forest, and you cross the brook shortly before the Bergerie Colga. Here you can already see the slope which leads to the top of the pass. There is a steep stretch over rock slate; you don't have to have a good head for heights to negotiate it, but you should be extremely careful crossing it when it is wet.

Once you reach **Bocca a Stazzona** (5,762 feet/1,762 m), you can already see Lake Nino, some 65 feet (20 m) lower down, and the moorland (*Pozzines, pozzi* = well). The glacier lake, formed about 14,000 years ago, is the second-largest lake on Corsica (15 acres/6 ha). It is the source of the Tavignano River.

The path leads down to the lake, and on the west side you meet up with the GR 20, marked in red and white. Follow this well-marked trail across the **Bocca a Reta** (6,157 feet/1,883 m) and then keep heading downhill to the **Col de St-Pierre**. Follow the easy-going forest trail for the last hour of hiking. Look for a huge pile of rocks or a sign with the inscription **Castel di Vergio**, because you can take a short-cut and head steeply uphill directly to the ski hut.

Castel di Vergio is one of three ski lodges on the island; in the summer, it offers room and board to hikers.

Hike to Paglia Orba

Plan two days for the tour described below. It's best to leave in the afternoon

and hike from the Vergio Pass to the Refuge **Ciottulu di i Mori** (6,511 feet/1,991 m) in about 4 hours. There is a modest lodge here, which only has certain food items in the summer (packaged soups). You should start your climb of Corsica's third-highest mountain, **Paglia Orba** (8,257 feet/2,525 m), early on the following morning. After returning around lunch time, you can enjoy a break before climbing down to Col de Vergio in the afternoon.

The hiking tour starts at a bend in the road (4,349 feet/1,330 m) which is called **Fer a Cheval** (horseshoe) because of its characteristic shape. It's located about 1.5 miles (2.5 km) from Castel di Vergio (toward Niolo), and there's room to park (don't leave valuables in the car!). This hike leads through a charming and diversified landscape. Part of the stretch goes by the Golo River; in the summer its pretty swimming holes come as a welcome surprise.

Up to the refuge, the trail is identical with the GR 20 and therefore you can't miss it. The climb to Paglia Orba and/or to **Capu Tafunatu** (7,635 feet/2,335 m), next to it on the left with its easily recognizable hole, is not an easy task – some climbing experience will be necessary. While you can climb Paglia Orba without roping up, it is necessary to secure yourself when climbing to the peak of Capu Tafunatu.

From the Refuge Ciottulu di i Mori, head north (don't follow the GR 20 any more, which heads east); you can see both of the mountains from the start. You don't have to choose which mountain to climb until you reach the **Col des Maures**. Both climbing trails are marked with little stone men. The trail to Paglia Orba branches off to the right, where you have to do some easy climbing right away. Be careful not to get too far off to the left. Once you finally reach the peak, you have, on a clear day, the best view of the "roof of Corsica." The peak rises almost straight up from the valley, so that you looking down from a height of almost 3,270 feet (1,000 m). On either side

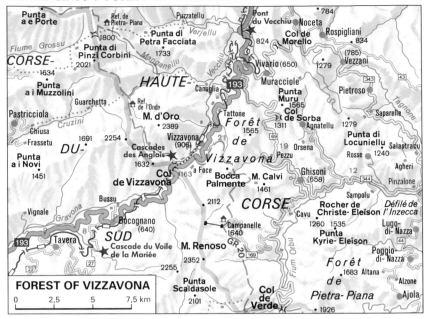

FOREST OF VIZZAVONA
0   2,5   5   7,5 km

of you are Monte Cinto and the charming Capu Tafunatu, looking almost close enough to touch.

Monte Cinto

The highest peak on the island, the 8,849-foot-high (2,706 m) Monte Cinto, is only for experienced climbers. There are two routes: along the east ridge (from Calacuccia via the Refuge de l'Erco) or up the north face (from Asco Valley); the latter is the shorter and easier route. To get to it from Ponte Leccia, take the D 47, which ends by the ski lodge **Haut-Asco**, at an altitude of 4,742 feet (1,450 m). The ascent takes about six hours, the descent about four. The ascent is marked in red and with little stone men, and it can be done without any climbing worth mentioning, but as you have to cross many stretches of unshaded, rocky terrain with lots of scree on your way down, this tour can be very strenuous.

If you want to jump right into the sea after completing a mountain hike, you can reach Porto quickly on the D 84. You pass Col de Vergio on the way, the highest pass on the island (4,830 feet/1,477 m), which is often closed in winter due to snow. At such times, the Niolo is cut off from the west coast again, just as it was in the past.

THE FOREST OF VIZZAVONA

One of the prettiest forests on Corsica stretches between the 7,812-foot-high Monte d'Oro (2,389 m) and Bocca Palmente (5,379 feet/1,645 m). The **forest of Vizzavona** covers an area of 3,815 acres (1,526 ha), lying at altitudes of between 2,600 and 5,400 feet (800-1,650 m); it is comprised mostly of laricio pine and beech trees. Visitors are especially drawn to the shady hiking trails, which extend over some 30 miles (50 km), as well as the ski area of Muratello, which is open between mid-March and late April.

As this region can also be easily reached from the "big" cities of Bastia and Corte (on the N 193 or with the Corsican trains), the forest serves as an ideal corner of nature where anyone suffering from the summer heat can easily escape to cool off – not only the sweating year-round inhabitants of Ajaccio.

Coming from the north, you keep heading uphill and through **Venaco**, a popular vacation town at the foot of Monte Cardo, towards Col de Vizzavona. **Vivario** is 654 feet (200 m) above the awe-inspiring gorge of the Vecchio River, where people like to fish for a very tasty type of salmon trout. The Verjellu River, which flows into the Vecchio not far from Vivario, is well-known as a bountiful fisherman's paradise.

Shortly past Vivario, you can opt to go on an excursion on the narrow D 69 **over the Col de Sorba** to Ghisoni. From the Sorba Pass (4,287 feet/1,311 m), you have a grand view: to the west is the Vecchio valley and the mighty Monte d'Oro, to the east the view stretches to the alluvial plains of the east coast, and if the visibility is good, you can even see the sea.

5.6 miles (9 km) past Vivario you enter the village of **Vizzavona**, consisting of only a few houses, which lies at an altitude of about 3,270 feet (1,000 m). The village, framed by the silhouette of Monte d'Oro, is an important "filling station" for the athletic GR 20 hikers needing provisions, and of course it's also a resting spot, because their 15-day tour only rarely takes them through settled villages.

Next to the beautiful train station in Vizzavona there are several bars offering refreshments; while the Grand Hotel has modest lodgings for hikers and other visitors. In the last few years, some rich Corsicans, trying to flee the sultry heat on the coast, have added some new vacation houses to the old buildings.

You can take wonderful walks from Vizzavona's train station. A lengthy hike goes along the GR 20 to **Bocca Palmente** and takes you up almost another 2,289

feet (700 m). At first you walk up the small street from the train station to the N 193 and then take this road another 1,300 feet (400 m) towards Ajaccio. There the national highway crosses the GR 20 trail, marked in red and white, which you take heading east. You can also take a beautiful walk on the GR 20 in the opposite direction to the **Cascades des Anglais** ("Waterfall of the English"). You should allow about one hour for the pleasant hike there and back.

You can also depart from Vizzavona for an ascent of **Monte d'Oro** (7,812 feet/2,389 m); however, this is only recommended for experienced hikers, as the arduous ascent alone requires 6 hours.

Leading toward Ajaccio, the N 193 goes over the Vizzavona Pass (3,800 feet/1,163 m), a stomping-ground of the wild domesticated pig, which will try to snare any and all of the food supplies of any visitors who happen to be in the area. You can also go on a small excursion from the next train station, at **Bocagnano**, to the **Cascade du Voile de la Mariée** (Bridal Veil Waterfall). If you want to do this, go to the left at the southern end of the village onto the D 27; from here, another 15 minutes or so on foot will bring you to the point from where you can see the highest waterfall on Corsica as it cascades 490 feet (150 m) to the pool below.

The "Corsican TGV"

Corsicans affectionately call their unique island train *Micheline*; visitors have also ironically dubbed it *TGV*, referring to the French rapid train (*Train à Grande Vitesse*). After riding on the Corsican rails, however, you will soon become convinced that the letters could only possibly stand for *Train à Grande Vibration* (Train of Great Vibration).

Before they replaced the cars in 1989, the trip through the magnificent island landscape was more like a mule ride than

a pleasure trip. The proud occupants of the window seats, although secure in the metal cars, often closed their eyes in order to pray after seeing their dangerous proximity to the abyss.

The Corsican railway has been transporting island natives and visitors between Bastia and Ajaccio since 1893. The *Micheline* climbs from sea level to an altitude of more than 3,600 feet (1,100 m) by the Col de Vizzavona, crosses the pass and rolls on down to the sea, arriving at busy Ajaccio. You pass through many tunnels and over several train viaducts on the way. The most well-known is **Pont de Vecchiu** by Vivario, constructed by none other than the French engineer Gustave Eiffel, who, as we know, gave Paris the Eiffel Tower.

The other track runs from Bastia to Calvi via Ponte Leccia and is called the *Balagne Line.* In summer, the cars are

Above: Above Vizzavona, the railway line from Bastia to Ajaccio reaches its highest point.

filled mainly with swimmers, because in the high season the train stops at every one of the beautiful beaches – if you're in a hurry, forget it!

In constructing the line between Bastia and Porto-Vecchio, they set an record in slowness that has yet to be beaten. The workers needed 42 years to lay the 10.5 miles (17 km) of track between Solenzara and Ghisonaccia. Someone calculated that this comes to 1.8 inches (46 mm) per hour. This stretch was so badly damaged in World War II that it had to be dismantled in 1950.

In 1984, the French federal train system SNCF bought the entire track system of the thereto-autonomous CFC (*Chemin de Fer de la Corse*). They started to replace the cars, which were ready for a museum rather than a functioning train line, with new ones five years later.

Therefore, you often see disappointed faces these days when you travel through the mountains of Corsica, because the train trip is no longer the big adventure it used to be.

CORTE AND VENACO
Accommodation
CORTE: *MODERATE:* **De la Paix**, Avenue Général-de-Gaulle, tel. 95460672. **Auberge Restonica**, at one end of the Restonica valley, very stylish, quiet location, pool, tel. 95460958. **Sampiero Corso**, Avenue Président-Pierucci, tel. 95460976. *BUDGET:* **De la Poste**, 2, Place Padoue, tel. 95460137. **Du Nord et d'Europe**, 22, Cours Paoli, tel. 95460068. **H.R.Hotel**, 6, Allée du 9-Septembre, very cheap, tel. 95451111.

VENACO: *MODERATE:* **Paesotel e Caselle**, Le Vallon, swimming pool, tennis, lovely group of bungalows on the Vecchiu brook, very quiet, tel. 95470201. *BUDGET:* **Le Bosquet**, member of the Logis de France chain, excellent food, tel. 95470011.

Campgrounds
CORTE: **L'Alivettu**, Faubourg Saint-Antoine, tel. 95461109. **Restonica**, Faubourg Saint-Antoine, tel. 95461159. **Tuani**, Restonica Valley, 4 mi/6 km from Corte, tel. 95461165. **Santa Barbara**, N 200-Route d'Aléria, pool, tel. 95462022. **U Sognu**, Route de la Restonica, on the river, tel. 95460907. **VENACO: La Ferme de Peridundellu**, 2.5 mi/4 km from Venaco, toward Aléria, tel. 95470472.

Restaurants
CORTE. *CORSICAN:* **Pascal Paoli**, Place Paoli, tel. 95461348. **A Scudella**, Place Paoli, tel. 95462414. Both of these restaurants serve very good Corsican food and have small outdoor terraces (as well as indoor ones) in the middle of the activity.
VENACO: Paesotel e Caselle, good, typical Corsican food, cozy, tel. 95470201.

Hospital
Hôpital civil, Corte, tel. 95460536.

Transportation
CORTE: *TRAIN:* Station, N 193 toward Ajaccio, continuation of the Allée du 9-Septembre, tel. 95460097. *BUS:* **Société des Autocars Cortenais**, Route de Saint-Pancrace, tel. 95460212/95462289. *TAXI:* **Taxis Corte**, tel. 95460488/95460790/ 95610141. *CAR RENTAL:* **Europcar**, Cours Paoli, tel. 95460279. *MINIBUS:* Minibus, running through the Restonica valley, Joe Rinieri, tel. 95460212

Travel Agent
CORTE: Cyrnea Tourisme, 9, Avenue Xavier-Luciani, tel. 95462462.
VENACO: Loisirs et Nature, le Vallon, tel. 95470022.

Sports
CORTE: *BIKES/MOTORCYCLES:* **Corte Location Service**, tel. 95460713. **Tomasi Location**, on the N 200 toward Aléria, tel. 95460713.
FLYING: **Aeroclub de Corte**, Aérodrome centre Corse, N 200, tel. 95462100.

RIDING: **Ferme Equestre L'Albadu**, Ancienne Route d'Ajaccio, tel. 95462455.

Museum
CORTE: Salles du F.R.A.C., Citadelle de Corte, exhibition of modern art: summer: open daily except Su, 10 am-8 pm; winter: daily except weekends and holidays, 10 am-noon and 2-6 pm, tel. 95462218.

Entertainment
CORTE: *NIGHT LIFE:* **L'Arc-en-ciel**, 14, Cours Paoli-Corti, Corsican guitar music, daily after 10 pm.
CINEMA: **Cinema Aprile**, Quartier St-Antoine, just behind the Restonica bridge, to the right as you come from the Restonica valley.
RADIO: The Corsican radio station **Radio Corti Vivu** broadcasts on the frequency FM 92,6.

Tourist Information
La Citadelle, Corte, tel. 95462420.

NIOLO
Accommodation
ALBERTACCE: *BUDGET:* **Castel di Vergio**, near the Col de Vergio, frequented by skiers and hikers, tel. 95480001.
CALACUCCIA: *MODERATE:* **L'Acqua-Viva**, New building, open all year round, tel. 95480690/ 95480008. **Des Touristes**, tennis, tel. 95480004.
BUDGET: **La Scala**, new building at the intersection with the road to Casamaccioli, tel. 95480276.

Campgrounds
LOZZI: U Monte Cintu, at the southern foot of Monte Cinto, small shop, tel. 95480445/ 95480183.

Restaurant
Castel di Vergio, in the hotel of the same name, good Corsican cooking, homemade ham, tel. 95480001.

Museum
ALBERTACCE: Musée Archéologique, summer: 10 am-noon and 2-6 pm, tel. 95480522.

Tourist Information
CALACUCCIA: Route de Cuccia, tel. 95480522.

FOREST OF VIZZAVONA
Accommodation
VIVARIO: *BUDGET:* **Macchje Monte**, tennis, tel. 95472200.
VIZZAVONA: *MODERATE:* **Monte d'Oro**, Col de Vizzavona, tennis, tel. 95472106/95472344. **Modern**, simple, small hotel, tel. 95472112.

Campgrounds
VIVARIO/TATTONE: Le Soleil, simple, tel. 95472116/95472308. **Savaggio**, north of Tattone, located by the train station and on the GR 20, shady, cheap, and very clean, tel. 95472214/95472009.

Hospital
Centre Hospitalier, Tattone, tel. 95472099.

CORSICA NOSTRA

In recent years, many would-be travelers to Corsica have heard tales of bomb attacks on the Isle of Beauty and wondered whether or not to postpone their vacation. Usually, however, it transpires that attacks on holiday complexes owned by foreign investors haven't harmed a hair on a single tourist's head, as the terrorists – Corsican autonomists – generally choose the winter months for their attacks, when visitors are scarce.

Other minority groups in France, such as the Basques or the Catalonians, also give expression to their discontent through similar attention-getting moves. But what exactly is it that the Corsicans want? And what are the roots of this Corsican malaise?

If you look at French affairs after World War II, you may notice that *la*

Preceding pages: Shepherds' dinner. Hiking route Tra Mare e Monti. Above: The Moor's head – symbol of the Corsican nation.

grande nation didn't initially do much for its Mediterranean island. The large clan families once again held sway on Corsica, and the island was threatened by a depopulating wave of emigration, which went hand in hand with a decline in agricultural activity. In 1945, the French simply assigned Corsica to the economic *département* of Provence, although the island was France's sole true "natural region." Not until 1970, in response to vociferous protest from the islanders, did Paris recognize Corsica as an independent region in its own right.

But even before this, in 1957, de Gaulle had enacted the *Plan d'Action Régional*, designed to help those French regions which were particularly badly off.

Representing a first ray of light for Corsica were two societies that were founded in the same year, ostensibly to ensure fair distribution of government monies: SOMIVAC (*Société pour la Mise en Valeur Agricole de la Corse*), which was responsible for promoting agriculture, and SETCO (*Société pour l'É-*

quipement Touristique de la Corse), which was supposed to help bring about a resurgence of tourism to the island.

However, France's good intentions of offering the help the island so desperately needed were ultimately of little help to the Corsicans, for France had, in the meantime, created another problem.

After the Independence Treaties of Evian (1962), some one million French Algerians were forced abruptly to leave Algeria. Most of these *pieds noirs*, – as the Algerians have called the French since French soldiers arrived in Algeria in the 19th century, when the local population dubbed them "black feet" because of their unfamiliar leather footwear, or shoes, which the natives had never seen before – settled in the south of France, mainly in Nice and Marseilles. Some 16,000 of them also settled in Corsica. To the disgust of the island's natives, these returnees from Algeria received the state support and low-interest SOMIVAC loans to which the Corsicans themselves were entitled. It's thus understandable that the native Corsicans tended to look askance at the new arrivals.

The industrious Algerian Frenchmen settled along the island's fertile eastern coast and, using the generous loans from SOMIVAC and the knowledge they'd brought back with them from Algeria, established vineyards with low-quality grapevines. The wine production of 1959 – 13,750 acres (5,500 ha) of vineyard producing 20,000 liters a year – was outstripped tenfold within a mere ten years: in 1969, there were 75,000 acres (30,000 ha) of vineyard and 2 million hectoliters of wine. The new entrepreneurs on the east coast could only produce wine in such vast amounts by adding sugar to the grape harvest. This method, which artificially increases a wine's alcohol content, had actually been legal since 1926, when a grape disease in France laid waste to the country's vineyards. But now, the Corsican vintners feared for the good reputa-

tion of their own wines, and protested. In 1971, sugaring of wines was once again legally banned. 600 small Corsican vintners were saved from ruin – or so, at least, it seemed at first. But the sudden leap in the wine yield, combined with the increase in sugar imports, had already awakened the suspicions of the controllers, and soon veritable "wine laboratories" could be opened in the maquis.

On August 21, 1975, moderate Corsican autonomists, members of the ARC party (Action for the Rebirth of Corsica), led by the doctor Edmond Simeoni, occupied the vineyards of Henri Depeille in Aléria. All of the occupiers' efforts at negotiation were blocked; instead, police stormed the wine-cellars. In this action, two policemen were killed and two of the occupiers badly injured, and Simeoni surrendered in order to prevent further bloodshed. He was sentenced to five years' imprisonment with two years' probation. His party, the ARC, was officially dissolved on August 27. The big "wine-waterers," however, who had been accused of a financial scandal, were only given sentences of between six and twelve months, on probation.

The wine scandal of Aléria heated up the political conflict. Protest against discrimination against the island, foreign infiltration, and the suppression of the Corsican language brewed in the underground for a good ten years.

During the 1960s, a number of small Corsican groups began to form. At first, many of them were merely protesting bad decisions in agriculture. At the end of the 60s and in the early 70s, however, parties developed which also had political aspirations. The ARC, for example, which was founded in 1967, got a lot of attention with its book *Autonomia*. These moderate autonomists wanted more autonomy in Corsican affairs, but distanced themselves from total separatism from France. As the ARC was proscribed after the incident in Aléria, Simeoni's fol-

lowers founded the APC (*Associu di Patrioti Corsi*, or Association of Corsican Patriots), which also advocated a generally moderate course.

Meanwhile, however, the radical FLNC (*Fronte di a liberazione nazionale di a Corsica*, or National Corsican Liberation Front) was also forming in the underground. Its demands were clear: this party wanted *independenza*, pure and simple; and its members were willing to resort to increasingly radical, even terrorist, tactics to draw attention to their goal. In 1977, they carried their war across to mainland France, blowing train stations, police cars, or banks sky-high. While they contented themselves with a mere 40 attacks in 1973, the number had climbed, by 1980, to more than 400. Most of these attacks were ascribed to the extremist FLNC; although this movement has since splintered into two

*Above: Nationalism is a way to win votes.
Right: FLNC – a disputed nationalistic liberation movement.*

groups: the *canal historique* and the *canal habituel* are the armed factions of the legal "socialist" Cuncolta and the legal "capitalist" MPA, which engage in bitter warfare against each other.

President Valery Giscard d'Estaing seemed to deal with the Corsican question by simply ignoring it; he failed to act on any of his initial promises. The election of François Mitterand as President in 1981 awakened new hopes in the breasts of many Corsicans. He campaigned with promises of decentralization programs, an amnesty for militant Corsican nationalists, and a special status (*statut particulier*) for the island.

In 1982, Corsica was the first French region to receive its own regional parliament (*Assemblée Corse*), based in Ajaccio. At first, the Corsicans placed great faith in their Parliament, but they were soon disappointed. On the one hand, powerful family clans continued to influence events within parliament, and diverted much of the subvention money from Paris into their own pockets; on the other hand, some of the policies seemed virtually incomprehensible; and to cap it all, there was massive election fraud. The *Assemblée Corse* was therefore dissolved after only two years, in 1984.

So Corsica was left with all of its original problems, which led, in 1989, to a new period of crisis. Weeks of strikes drew attention to the critical position of the island's economy: the fact that the price of living was 10-15% higher than on the mainland, and the massive unemployment. In addition to these strikes and discontent, there was a wave of new attacks under the slogan *I Francesi fora*, out with the French! In response, French interior minister Pierre Joxe went on the offensive and began negotiating with Corsican special-interest groups.

In November, 1990, the French National Assembly finally passed a statute of autonomy for the island. Article 85 explicitly states, "The French Republic guarantees the historic, living cultural community which the Corsican people represents...the right to preserve its cultural identity and defend its special economic and social rights."

Since 1990, Corsica has been administered by an executive council elected by the Corsican Assembly, the new regional parliament of the island. Furthermore, the island was granted a special tax status.

In 1992, new elections were held for the regional parliament, and voter registration lists were carefully checked beforehand. Today, there are 51 delegates (in 1981, there were 61) and a 7-member Executive Committee with a President, responsible for transportation, environment, agriculture, economic development, culture, and education.

After a few years, however, it was clear that there weren't yet enough means available, that the clans and election fraud still held sway, and that no truly significant changes had yet taken place. New, isolated attacks gave evidence that not all Corsicans were satisfied with

Paris's concessions. In January 1996 alone, the nationalist "Resistenza" set off 26 explosives in front of offices and banks; no one, fortunately, was injured.

The omnipresent graffiti might lead to the impression that nearly every Corsican is radical and belongs to a group of bomb-throwers or at least demands the independence of her island. In reality, things are a bit different. Estimates place the radical separatist elements of the population at about 2-3%, and these, as a result of extortion in the name of "revolution tax," murders, and the resulting vendettas (39 people died in 1994), are growing less and less popular with the rest of the island's people. Most Corsicans hope for improvements in the island's current situation: more tax breaks, for example, and more autonomy. They also complain that the island is being sold out to the *pinzutti*, or mainland French. But a large part of Corsica's population are more incensed at the people who set off bombs and thereby damage the island's tourism and its reputation.

223

A LINGUA NUSTRALE
"Our Language"

In hardly any other province of France can you sense the clear presence of a unique regional language as you can in Corsica. As Corsican patriots often spray paint over French-language street signs, island officials have adopted the practice of signposting everything in both languages. Especially in whole areas of the island's interior, in the isolated mountain regions, you can see how strong is the influence of Corsican. Whether you're listening to conversation from the small grocery truck which delivers staple supplies to the village residents or are leaning on the counter of the village pub, the soft sounds of Corsican will predominate in your ears. While it's generally the older residents who speak the language most and best, young Corsicans can usually at least understand their parents and grandparents, even if they tend, more and more, to answer in French.

According to a survey of the National Institute for Statistics in the mid-1980s, 86% of the island's population can speak their language fluently, and an amazing 96% claim that they can understand Corsican. These results, which are almost certainly affected as much by the wishes of many Corsicans as by their actual abilities, reveal just how important the *lingua nustrale* (our language) is to local residents. Yet is there actually an independent Corsican language, or is it merely an Italian dialect, as the French government long stoutly maintained?

Corsican is a rich and sonorous language which was neither written nor taught until the 19th century.

Linguists still don't agree on the language's origins. In Corsica, many people are of the opinion that Corsican originally developed in the course of Roman colonialization, deriving from Latin. If you subscribe to this belief, then Corsican, like Sardian or Catalan, should be viewed as an independent Romance language which later came to be strongly influenced by Italian.

Other linguists opine that Corsican is nothing more than an Italian dialect, quite similar to Tuscan and differing from it mainly in the orthography. This was the opinion long held by the French government, as well. Only under pressure from Corsican separatists could they be "persuaded" to change their minds.

When you're listening to the language, you can in fact notice a great deal of similarity to Italian. When writing their language, Corsicans open the Italian word ending -o into -u (Ajaccio becomes Aiacciu) and -e into -i (Corte becomes Corti).

From time immemorial, language has been the sign of a national consciousness; today, it continues to play a significant role in the Corsicans' struggle for their own national identity. *Persa a lingua, persu u populu* (when the language is lost, the people are lost) is a much-cited and relevant maxim.

The tremendous battle of minority languages to prevail in many regions of France (including Brittany, Catalonia, and the Basque country) becomes all the more understandable when you take note of the French government's rigorous language policies throughout the course of the country's history.

During the French Revolution, minority languages were radically suppressed. *Une langue, une nation* (one language, one nation) was the rallying-cry. French was to be the language of instruction and administration; use of any other language, even one's mother tongue, was punishable by law. The real reason for this was to suppress counterrevolutionary forces by nipping them in the bud. Thus, the revolutionary leaders threatened the use of any regional languages other than French with Draconian severity. Not

Right: Let's get it right – Corsicans know their capital as Aiacciu, not Ajaccio!

through a gradual weaning process, but rather through the use of force, French drove Corsican out of the schools and the administration after 1811.

More than a century and a half later, after vociferous protests and attacks in the 1960s, however, Paris finally had to take some kind of counter-action. In 1974, they extended the *Loi Deixonne*, which had been enacted for other minority languages in 1951, to Corsica as well. For more than 20 years, therefore, Corsican has been recognized as a language in its own right (*lingua regionale*), and is taught in universities and schools.

In no other French *département* are students as interested in their regional language as are the students on Corsica. About 15% of all students here choose their native language as an elective course; in France, by contrast, the figure is more like 3%. Even outside of the niversities, the islanders can take steps to keep up their language skills: there are Corsican newspapers, radio stations, and even Corsican-language TV broadcasts.

It's understandable that there's such a variety of theories about the origins of Corsican, as a unified, codified, written version of the language has yet to be developed. Even within Corsica – on the near and far sides of the mountains, for example – there are considerable differences. Lacking any form of binding orthography and syntax, Corsican authors and politicians (such as Pasquale Paoli) are forced to express themselves in Italian.

Until 1974, there were still major problems in teaching the language. However, the Institute for Corsican Studies in Corte is now working on developing a unified form of Corsican with rules of orthography and usage, and is bringing out dictionaries and a Corsican grammar.

A Corsican journalist has written, *In ogni lingua, c'è un'anima e, ind'a nustra c'è l'anima corsa; e salva un'anima è sempre opera pia* (Within every language, there is a soul; within our language, this is the Corsican soul; and saving a soul is always a holy work).

VENDETTA

"It's best to keep your mouth shut – otherwise the mosquitos might fly in." Such are the pearls of wisdom with which people on the island equipped their children early on to arm them for their passage through an uncertain life. Yet blood revenge, called vendetta, and the banditry which accompanies this tradition, are by no means exclusive to Corsica. They are equally prevalent among other cultural groups, such as the Sardinians, the Calabrians, the Albanians, or, most famously, the Sicilians.

According to Seneca, this barbarous practice was quite well developed on Corsica even in the days of the Romans. It became all the stronger when the island came under the rule of a foreign power, the Genoese, and it became clear that Ge-

Above: A crime against a member of one's family was often the spark that ignited the fuse of blood revenge. Right: Sartène – from vendetta capital to tourist stronghold.

noese law was all too seldom able to make just decisions when Corsicans were involved. Vendetta, therefore, developed into a form of "fair" self-justice. Between 1789 and 1811, the list of deaths reached its greatest magnitude. In this space of time, there were nearly 30,000 vendetta victims on Corsica alone.

Two great passions dominate the Corsican soul: love of one's country, and love of one's family. Grotesquely enough, this latter allegiance has wiped out entire families.

Blood revenge begins with the murder of a member of an enemy family. As soon as his relatives have identified the perpetrator and his family, they begin to plot their revenge.

Fearing the Genoese (later the French) authorities and the relatives of the dead man, the murderer flees into the impenetrable undergrowth of the maquis. From now on, he calls himself a *bandit d'honneur*, a bandit of honor, exiled by the law. Only his relatives know where his hiding-place in the maquis is located. His family, and perhaps a local goatherd or two, provide him with what he needs to survive, including ammunition for his gun, without which no self-respecting Corsican bandit would take a step.

From here on in, he has only two options. Either his relatives manage to wipe out the enemy family, in which case he can return home, or he will spend the rest of his life in the Corsican wilderness. Stories are told of bandits who, returning after 16 or even 20 years, were shot in the back on the day they dared to return.

How does life proceed for the family of the murder victim? After mourning the death of their relative, the male members of the family know full well that they have to avenge the death of their father, brother, or other relative in order to salvage their family's honor. They're under strong social pressure from their family clan, for anyone who balks at avenging a murder is taken to task, a process known

in Corsican as *rimbeccare*; the coward himself is called the *rimbecco*. The family no longer respects him, and he may even be turned out of the family, something akin to a sentence of death.

Life in a vendetta situation is anything but pleasant. The family who fears the revenge of the other family has to barricade its house. Doors and windows are locked, and windows are further defended with straw and mattresses (inceppar le fenstre). In fact, the forbidding-looking Corsican style of architecture (see Sartène) has developed as a result of vendetta wars. Houses are built like towers and like fortresses, with a narrow flight of stone stairs that are far from easy to climb; the windows do double duty as firing-holes.

In a worst-case scenario, a family can shut itself up like this in this kind of fortress for months, even for years, leaving their fields lying fallow.

In Sartène, in the southwest of the island, these bloody feuds used to go so far that entire city districts were at war with one another. Not until 1840 was a peace treaty finally drawn up in the church.

The classical vendetta continued into the 20th century. At the beginning of this century, there were still some 60 to 100 deaths recorded.

This form of revenge with fatal consequences did, however, very nearly die out in recent years, until militant rival separatists with machine guns "revived" it in the 1990s.

Forms of self-justice administered by unpolitical Corsicans are generally somewhat less severe: slashed tires, or damaging a business rival with a small load of gunpowder, can be every bit as effective. If you should chance to hear of one of the extremely rare shoot-outs or knife fights at a village festival somewhere back in the mountains, you can bet that alcohol and jealousy played considerable roles. But here, too, in the case of such "personal" fights, the police don't have much effect. Nor should strangers try to get involved in any dispute when someone's honor is at stake.

VOCERI AND LAMENTI
The Origins of Corsican Song

On December 18, 1821, two friends brought the corpse of 51-year-old Luigi Culioli back to his house. The first action of the lady of the house, his wife, Vanina Culioli, was to display his bloody shirt, demanding that her son and their nearest relatives seek revenge. She fastened a bloody bit of the dead father's shirt to the clothing of her shocked son. The next step was to lay out the respected Luigi Culioli on a table, called the *tola*. A number of hastily summoned women then threw themselves on the corpse, arms outstretched, and began to utter the heart-rending *voceri*, or lament for the dead, which also served the function of reminding all male relations within earshot of the need for vendetta. As they intoned monotonously, they tore at their hair; some of the women, those who had been particularly close to the dead man, even rent their clothing and scratched their faces until they bled, as, according to heathen tradition from time immemorial, the sight of blood pleases the dead and placates the inhabitants of the world of shadow.

It was thus that on Corsica in the early 19th century, the glory days of the tradition of blood revenge, a family could have prepared itself for vendetta, a summons which the women often staged with veritably dramatic force. The *voceri* songs, sung exclusively by women, bear the stamp of improvisations. The women lament the great misfortune that has fallen upon the family with this death, praise the murdered man and his good deeds, pledge eternal revenge, and thus remind the men of their bloody duty to vendetta.

The *lamenti* are also songs of mourning, and are also sung by women by the

Right: Paghjella songs and guitar music in "Au son des Guitares" in Ajaccio.

bed of someone who has died. But in this case the women tear their hair for someone who has died a natural, rather than a violent, death. *Lamenti* may also be sung to ease the pain of separation.

Voceri and *lamenti* are generally regarded as the origins of the local popular songs, today so widely varied, and generally performed by men.

In addition, there are also the gentle cradle songs which grandmothers (*nanne*) once sang to lull Corsican progeny to sleep; love serenades, sung on mild evenings under the beloved's window; and ancient shepherds' ditties.

At the beginning of the 20th century, these traditional songs were only seldom heard. In lieu of these, popular French songs of love tended to hold sway. Tino Rossi, still beloved of many, who died and was buried in Ajaccio in 1984, moves some people to tears even today. No one pays much attention to the fact that his songs come more from a French than from a Corsican tradition.

Traditional Corsican music seemed to be falling into oblivion. Not until the CORSITUDE movement in the 1970s, which tried to reanimate Corsican culture and traditions, did people start to rediscover Corsican music, with considerable success.

Today, with a bit of luck, you might get to witness a *chjama è rispondi* (call and answer) in a village bar; this is an improvised, sometimes mischievously needling antiphonal song between two men. These songs are usually performed wholly spontaneously; but a *chjama è rispondi* competition is held every year at the beginning of September in the Niolo, in Casamaccioli.

There, too, you can hear the polyphonal *paghjella*; these *a capella* songs, performed with heart and soul, can give even non-Corsicans goose-bumps. The origins of the melancholy *paghjella* music probably lie in pre-Gregorian days. Musicologists have also recognized influences

from Berbers, Ligureans, and old Italian madrigals.

Best of all, however, is to happen upon such a song by chance. In isolated regions, Corsicans of all ages, depending on their mood (and, perhaps, on how much pastis they've drunk), are apt to sing these songs, which can really get under your skin.

Some good Corsican groups who perform only in their own language and come across with a lot of flair in their concerts include *A Filetta*, who perform polyphonic songs perfectly; *Canta u Populu Corsu*, with traditional hunting and fishing songs; and *I Chjami Aghjalesi*, who sing their own compositions about the country and its politics.

One exceptional phenomenon is the group *I Muvrini* (the little mouflons), who are known far beyond the borders of Corsica. Founded in 1980 by the Bernardini brothers, they initially drew attention to themselves with their pointed political texts, so that the leaders of some communities forbade their performances

altogether. Today, with more toned-down lyrics, modern instruments, and major success, they fill huge concert halls not only in Corsica, but also in Italy, Spain, Holland, Belgium, and recently even in Quebec and Japan – even, let it be said, in Paris; they play to some 80,000 Corsicans a year on their native island, and sold 35,000 records in one year. Their best recordings are *A Voce Rivolta* and their newest CD, *Noi*.

Jean-François Bernardini is not surprised at his group's popularity. "The Corsican people experienced a long period of silence, of oppression... We have dared to sing a song of hope in a desperate and disappointed country. Songs about subjects from every area, about solidarity with political prisoners, about the depopulation of the interior, about arson, but also about love. About all those things, in short, which make up our Corsican identity."

Attending an *I Muvrini* concert has got to be a highlight of anyone's visit to Corsica.

NIELLUCCIU, COPPA, BROCCIU
Pleasures for the Palate

After the difficult voyage to the island, every visitor to Corsica has earned, by his or her first evening – if not at lunchtime – a good glass of Corsican wine.

Wine production on Corsica can look back at a remarkably long tradition: as early as 570 B.C., Phoenecian seafarers had settled down in Aléria and started to cultivate grapevines in the area, as well as along Corsica's east coast.

Today, there's a remarkable selection of red, white and rosé wines available in Corsica's cafés, bars, and even roadside snack bars. You don't have to be an oenophile to notice that three grape varietals which are not cultivated on mainland France are dominant on the island, and are either bottled pure or cut with wines of other varietals. The three are the white

Above: Patrimonio was the first wine-producing region to win the designation AOC.
Right: Prizuttu – tasty way to "pig out."

vermentinu (cultivated in dry areas, preferably grown in granitey soils, yielding a full, even fruity dry wine); the rosé *sciacarellu* (ranging from smooth to full-bodied); and the deep red *niellucciu*, a variety of the Tuscan *sangiovese*.

Seven Corsican wines are permitted to bear the official title Vin de Corse on their labels; they also number among the privileged members of the Appellation d'Origine Contrôlée (AOC). AOC regulations stipulate that a maximum of 50 hectoliters can be pressed from the harvest of one hectare (2.5 acres). In 1968, Patrimonio was the first Corsican wine region to win this seal of approval; today, there are a total of eight. The other seven, generally named after their place of origin, are Calvi, Ajaccio, Sartène, Figari, Porto Vecchio, Coteaux du Cap Corse, and finally Vin de Corse from the east coast, around Aléria.

But man does not live by wine alone; to accompany your glass, why not sample a Corsican meal with all the trimmings? After all, you're on vacation.

A typical Corsican aperitif might be a *Cap Corse*, distilled from a wine base, served with an ice cube; or a heavy *vin de noix* (nut wine), reminiscent of a port. You might also try a glass of Corsican *vin d'orange*, orange wine. And adherents of the typical French style don't have to forego their obligatory *pastis* on Corsica, either.

Now, your palate and stomach have been adequately prepared for the delicacies of Corsican cuisine, and you can turn your full attention to the menu, at your leisure.

The very appetizers of the island are enough to make a gourmand's mouth water. A classic *charcuterie de Corse* will generally come with the tasty ham known as *lonzu*, the smoked ham *prizuttu*, or the rolled ham *coppa*. This three types of ham from the "domesticated wild boar," also known as the "wild domesticated pig," are first salted, then marinated in wine, garlic and herbs, and finally smoked over a fire of maquis branches; in restaurants they are, like any good Italian prosciutto, served with slices of juicy melon.

Another specialty of the Corsican kitchen is *brocchiu*, which, like Italian *ricotta*, has the consistency of a mild cottage cheese; it's made by heating fresh milk in a warm whey until it forms curds, then straining out the liquid.

Corsicans like to eat *brocchiu* in the form of a kind of fried cruller (*fritelle au brocchiu*), with sugar, fruit, honey, or herbs. It's also used as a filling for ravioli, canelloni, zucchini, peppers, or even trout. Brocchiu manufacture is strictly regulated; it's even developed its own *appellation controlée*.

If you're not yet full after these tasty hors-d'oeuvres, you can focus your attention on selecting one of the delicious main courses.

Fans of seafood are in for a great time on Corsica, although their lives will be made difficult by being forced to choose

between trout from the clear mountain streams and lakes or salt-water fish from the Mediterranean, including shrimp, oysters, *loup de mer* (sea perch), squid (calamari), *dorade* (bream), *rouget* (mullet), or *zinzi* (a kind of sea urchin that's eaten raw). The local version of bouillabaisse is called *aziminu*.

But anyone who favors hearty meat dishes will find plenty to eat on Corsica. A juicy, crackling roast of wild boar (*ciughjale*), grilled over a wood fire and served with a chestnut sauce flavored with some of the island's countless herbs (thyme, sage, bay, marjoram, borage, fennel, rosemary, mint, or juniper berries) is worth a special trip to the south all by itself.

Cabri or *cabrettu*, goat's meat served in a ragout or grilled on a spit; *riffia*, a spit of roasted lamb offal; or *figatelli*, small, spicy pork liver sausages, should all be sampled at least once, for the experience if nothing more. Classic side dishes include roasted sweet chestnuts from the Castagniccia; fresh steamed ve-

getables in season; or various kinds of pasta.

After you've ordered another bottle of wine or a glass of *niellucciu* to aid your digestion and have taken a bit of a breather, you should give some serious attention to the Corsican cheese platter. Some visitors see this not as the termination of a successful local meal, but rather as its highlight.

Even for die-hard cheese lovers, the extremely aromatic sheep's- and goat's-milk cheeses (*casgiu*) are guaranteed to be unforgettable, both for their taste and their consistency. These cheeses don't come cheap, because the method of production is fairly labor-intensive: it takes a lot of intuition and talent to bring the huge drained cheeses, weighing several pounds, through the long process of salting and turning in a damp, cool cellar, to the point where they're ready for sale and consumption. The cheese platter is often accompanied by a selection of fresh Corsican fruit, which isn't only a treat for visitors who are counting their calories or trying to eat healthily: red and green grapes, ripe red cherries, and fresh-picked wild figs are a perfect balance to the heavy flavors of the cheese.

Some people with a particular sweet tooth want more than just a cheese platter; if there's enough room left in their bellies, they abandon themselves to the sweet temptations of the island's desserts. In this realm, too, Corsica has plenty of treats to offer: a Corsican version of *crème caramel* or *flan*, which uses chestnut flour (*à la farine de chataignes*), or chestnut crêpes (*crêpes de chataignes*). *Canistrelli* are a typical island cookie, flavored with lemon or anise. To top off all of this culinary bounty, you can sip at a digestif: a glass of Corsican myrtle liqueur, or, to accompany your obligatory cup of coffee, an *eau de vie*, a clear brandy distilled from grape pressings.

Above: Goats-milk cheese from organic farmers (market at Basia). Right: The rock rose (mucchiu) gave maquis its name.

THE SCENT OF THE MAQUIS

During his exile on Saint Helena, Napoleon looked back wistfully on "his island": "With what happiness do I remember her mountains, her lovely landscapes; and with closed eyes, I could recognize her even by her smell!"

Visitors with a fine sense of smell who line up expectantly along the railing of the ferry deck and sniff the air to catch the first whiff of the perfume of Corsica will at first be bitterly disappointed – literally so, as what they'll scent are not heavenly aromas, but the bitter odor of diesel and gas from the cars below them.

Not until you get on land and into the countryside will you be able to perceive the intoxicating smell of Corsica's wild herbs and flowers. This spicy aroma issues from the evergreen stems, leaves, or twigs of the maquis in the form of an essential oil, particularly during hot spells, but also after a refreshing rainfall followed by sunshine.

The island's flora is surprisingly varied, encompassing some 2,000 different species. 78 of these are Cyrno-Sardian, found, that is, nowhere but on Corsica and Sardinia. Notable, too, are the 40-odd different kinds of orchid.

This wide variety can be explained by the island's wealth of different geographical regions, from ocean flora to Alpine zones, which result in a variety of different soils and extreme changes in climate.

You can make a rough distinction between three levels of vegetation; the lowest level, up to around 1,650 feet (500 m); the higher level, between 1,650 and 49,00 feet (500-1,500 m), and the Alpine level, above 4,900 feet.

The lower regions are dominated by the characteristic Corsican vegetation known as *macchia*, or maquis. This growth covers nearly one-third of Corsica's total area, and it's to it that the island owes its distinctive, intense aroma.

The maquis extends from the coast inland; no vacationer here, therefore, will be able to leave the island without having encountered it in some form, or having captured it in a variety of moods in the fore- and backgrounds of countless snapshots.

But what, exactly, is meant by this oft-used term *macchia*?

Maquis is a collective term for a group of wild plants that grow up to some 20 feet (6 m) high, including bushes, herbs, flowers and trees. This rough growth often grows to cover entirely the rusting hulks of wrecked cars, or serves as an ideal concealment for meetings of radical Corsican autonomists.

The vegetation takes its name from its predominant plant, the rock rose (Corsican *mucchju*); the French call it *le maquis*. Once, this term applied not only to undergrowth, but also to the resistance movement in World War II. A *maquisard* was a heavily-armed guerilla who sought a safe hiding place in the maquis undergrowth.

The best time to experience the intoxicating odor and the colorful blossoms of the macchia is in May. Most striking, and most common, plant here is the rock rose with its yellow, white and pink blossoms. None of the 20 species of this plant in the Mediterranean grow higher than three feet or so (1 m); all exude an intense odor. But this small bush is not, in fact, an evergreen; it does lose its leaves, although the next generation of leaves grows in immediately to replace them.

Two creatures dwell in or on the rock rose. One is the scaly, yellow-red hypocist, a parasite that feeds off the plant's roots. You can find the other one in springtime under the small balls of foam that seem to spread over all the plants at this time of year. If you carefully blow the foam away, you can see a small green caterpillar, which has, as it were, "boiled

Above: The strawberry tree, a typical element of maquis vegetation. Right: In spring, spurge and lavender provide bright splashes of color.

over" in the heat and produced the foam as a way to prevent drying out. This innocuous-looking animal eventually develops into the chirping cicada.

Equally widespread is the strawberry tree (French *arbousier*, Latin *arbutus unedo*), which is a member of the heather or erica family, and ca grow up to 20 feet (6 m) in height, although it usually stays at around 6-10 feet (2-3 m). Its shining, light green leaves are not unlike those of the bay tree, except that they have serrate edges. Resembling strawberries (hence the tree's name), the round, knobby fruit, which ripens in late September and October, is edible, although the flavor is rather bland – a fact indicated in its Latin name: *unedo* indicates "I [only] eat one." A more popular way to consume these "strawberries" is to make them into jelly, or distill them into an aromatic strawberry *eau de vie.*

Another plant which attains tree-like proportions is the evergreen bay laurel. Its lancet leaves have a dull, matte shine and exude an aromatic oil from their fine

pores. In June, the bay laurel blooms with white flowers, after which it bears fruits which resemble blueberries, but taste extremely bitter. Make sure, however, to sample some of the clear brandy distilled from this plant, which is a great improvement. In perfume manufacture, as well, heavy use is made of the essence distilled from the bay laurel oil, known as "angel's water." Since Antiquity, a laurel branch has symbolized peace and love.

Other maquis plants include tree heather, mastic bushes, clematis, juniper, various kinds of spurge (euphorbia), and the gorse bush with its yellow flowers. And the herbs which grown throughout the maquis – rosemary, thyme, fennel, and marjoram – play a major role in the island's flavorful cuisine.

Another source of "local color" is the purple-flowering shrub of the lavender bush, which has been used for medical purposes since Antiquity.

Because of the devastating fires which break out every year, which even the hardiest of the *macchia* plants is unable to withstand, the most common form of maquis on the island now is a degenerate one, *garigue*. It features fewer species, and is lower-growing, than the original *macchia* family which used to flourish here. Its name derives from the Provencal term for the plant which dominates it, the scarlet or crimson oak (*garoulio*).

The scarlet oak is an evergreen, bushy shrub with silvery-gray bark. Its small leaves are shiny on both sides, and edged with spines. The oak is often accompanied by the rock rose. Resident on the oak's leaves is the pea-sized female of the scaly insect known as the cochineal insect; dried and pulverized, its body was once used in the manufacture of a brilliant crimson red dye (cochineal).

To a visitor, some of the evergreen oak species on Corsica – the "regular" oak and the cork oak, which occurs mainly in the south, in the region around Porto-Vecchio – might not seem related to the Central European or American varieties, were it not for the acorns they bear, which look the same the world over.

LONG-DISTANCE HIKES

The GR 20

Internationally famous, the Alpine route GR 20 crosses the entire inland region of Corsica and nearly every mountain range on the island. "20" is Corsica's zip code, and GR stands for *Sentier de la Grande Randonée*. This route offers you the unique experience of passing on foot, within two weeks, the most varied assortment of different landscapes, getting to know them all first-hand, surrounded by clear mountain air and perfect silence. Views of steep, rugged, rocky cliffs and deep gorges give way to gentle meadows paving the floors of rolling valleys. Unforgettable views of isolated mountain villages, wild mountain streams, trickling brooks, lakes and ponds are a perfect antidote to the hectic pace of daily life in the big cities that most visitors are trying to escape. No traffic jams will force you to stop against your will; at most, you may be held up by a herd of goats who have decided to take over the path for a while. And time and again, panoramic views open out over the Mediterranean Sea. There's no question about it: get out of your car and into your hiking boots for a truly unforgettable experience!

From North to South, or South to North?

If you want to hike from north to south, the GR 20 starts at the Auberge de la Forêt or in Calenzana near Calvi, and ends in Conca at Ste-Lucie-de-Porto-Vecchio. But you can also take the GR 20 from south to north. If you start from the north, you have to deal with 4,250 feet (1,300 m) of ascent on your first day out, and you pass the 6,500-foot mark (2000 m) on the second day – carrying, mind

Right: On the first leg of the GR 20, you have to ascend 4,250 feet (1,300 m).

you, provisions for several days on your back. If you begin in the south, however, you start out in the Bavella region at a more comfortable pace, gradually hitting your stride, and only reach the real mountains on the second half of your trip.

The two-week island crossing on the GR 20 involves some demanding hiking, with several places where you have to climb with ropes or cross rickety suspension bridges: it's not just a pleasant little stroll along old shepherds' trails. Many of the approximately 3,000 hikers who complete this route every year (as opposed to the 10,000 or so people who walk only parts of it) have grossly underestimated the GR 20, thinking it would be comparable to France's other major hiking routes, and place similar physical demands on them. But you'd better be in pretty good physical shape if you want to take on the GR 20. Furthermore, you have to allow for unpredictable weather conditions, even more extreme than you'd find elsewhere in Europe. In a matter of minutes, the blazing sunshine in the mountains can suddenly vanish behind an impenetrable wall of cloud.

Essential, if you want to essay the GR 20, is a good hiking guide. The official times given here are generally calculated for someone walking at a moderate pace, without stopping. Best seasons for setting out are the months between June and October. If you start in May or June, you may still encounter snow in the highest mountains, especially on shady northern slopes; in these conditions, you may even need pitons to complete the route.

It's also important to observe basic rules of environmental and nature conservation: always leave huts, mountain refuges, and picnic spots clean, which helps the route to preserve its unspoiled beauty for others. This holds especially true for the refuges in the *Parc Régional de la Corse*, which are exclusively self-catering huts, meaning that you have to bring and prepare your food yourself.

As the GR 20 isn't a Sunday stroll, but rather a challenging mountain hike, don't stint on your equipment. Useful items include a backpack with an interior frame (weighing about 33 pounds/15 kg when full), sturdy mountain hiking boots with firm soles, a large rain poncho, a cooker, and utensils. Mountain equipment for the GR 20 includes a coil of rope, bandages, emergency foil, a compass, a good hiking guide, and the most detailed map you can find (such as the folding IGN 1:50 000 map with the trail marked in red). Also important are a tent and sleeping bag, as some huts haven't got any blankets and may well be full in the high season, so you could be forced to set up lodging outdoors. A sun hat, sunglasses, and sun-tan lotion with a high UV protection factor are also obligatory. As far as provisions are concerned, think in terms of light objects such as powdered drinks, tea bags, freeze-dried meals, nuts, and cereal, because along this route you only have three opportunities to come down into civilization and stock up on supplies.

It's essential to be able to read the trail markers. Marked from top to bottom, a white-red-white-red arrow means a change of direction, while a red-and-white cross means the wrong direction. Smaller paths branching off to a village, inn, or interesting sight are marked like a change of direction with the addition of a diagonal white bar above the arrow. The frequent "regular" trail markings, which simply indicate that you're still going the right way and appear along the whole length of the trail, are white and red.

There are 14 stages of the GR 20. In the north, you begin at Calenzana and proceed to the refuge Piobbu, thence to the Carozzu hut, on to Haut-Asco and the ruins of the Altore hut, and from there to the hut of Ciottuli di i Mori (under the Paglia Orba). From here, you press on to the Manganu hut, then to the self-catering hut Pietra Piana in the Manganello Valley, and continue on by way of the Onda hut to Vizzavona, a small mountain village with a train station. On past the Capanelle hut, the self-catering Prati hut,

and the Usciolu hut, the route leads to the isolated self-catering hut of Asiano. On the penultimate evening, you sleep in the Paliri hut, and reach, the next day – perhaps tired, but certainly happy – the east coast village of Conca, the final destination.

The Trail Tra Mare e Monti

In eight to ten stages you can get to know the varied west coast of Corsica on foot on your way along the route "between the sea and the mountains." The trail leads through lush, flowering maquis growth, studded with thousands of rock roses, and through shady forests with chestnuts, oaks, pines, and beeches. In July and August you can work up a lot of sweat along this route, particularly when you get near the coast, because of

Above: Obscure object of desire – the refuge at Piobbu, end of the first leg of the GR 20. Right: Author Heike Mühl tests the Spasimata bridge.

the extreme heat. Unlike the GR 20, however, the *Tra Mare e Monti* brings you to small villages every day, where you can pick up food and drink. Normal hiking equipment is sufficient for this path, which is marked in orange; you won't need mountaineering tackle. In spring and autumn, the weather can be very changeable, dousing you with sudden rain showers, but you won't suffer as much from the heat. Each of the *Gîtes d'Etape* (simple inns or hostels, often with restaurants and near to the villages) which house the 1,500 or so hikers who follow the Tra Mare e Monti every year can sleep 10 to 15 people.

Starting at the southeastern edge of Calenzana, the hiking trail initially follows an old mule path; but Tra Mare e Monti branches off from this after about 40 minutes. Passing through the mountain villages of the Balagne region and the forest of Bonifatu, the route ascends to the Bocca di Bonassa, 3,770 feet (1,153 m) high, then leads down through the Fango Valley to the beach of Galeria.

Past several Genoese towers, over two mountains around 2,290 feet (700 m) high, the path now runs to Girolata, located on the gulf of the same name in the popular nature preserve La Scandola. From the jutting cliffs along the coast, you can see the nests of white-tailed eagles, or watch cormorants fishing. After the muted colors of the mountains, the strong blue of the sea in La Scandola comes as a welcome change.

Tra Mare e Monti continues on south through the mountains to the villages of Curzu and Serriera. As soon as you've traversed the rocky landscape of red granite cliffs, you're rewarded with a breathtaking view opening up over the stunning Gulf of Porto. In Porto, you can have an interlude of "civilized life" in the hotels and discos; soon thereafter, by the mountain village Ota, begins the ascent into the Spelunca Gorge. When you've reached Evisa, you have only another two or three days to go until you reach the former Greek settlement of Cargèse, where the trail ends – right on the water.

Da Mare a Mare

Three different hiking routes are lumped together under the term *Da Mare a Mare*. All three are marked in orange, and each leads from one coast of the island to the other, leading from east to west over the mountains (but not the highest or hardest Corsica has to offer) to the rocky cliffs and secluded bays of the west coast. Unlike the GR 20, this route requires no more equipment than your regular hiking gear.

The northernmost of the three routes leads in 7 days from the singers' capital of Sermano through the former island capital of Corte and the Tavignano valley to the dam of Calacuccia. It continues on through Albertacce, past the foot of the highest mountain on Corsica, Monte Cinto, over the Col de Vergio (a ski area in winter) and Aitone to Evisa. From

here, the route follows the last 3 days of the *Tra Mare e Monti*, ending in Cargèse.

For the middle route, you'll need six days. It starts in the vacation center of Aquacitosa, near Ghisonaccia, on the east coast. This trail leads through shady pine forests. You can stop off in the thermal spa of Guitera, either to take the waters for your health or simply to relax, before going on with renewed energy through the Ornano region, the old bishop's seat of Vico, and over the Col St. Georges to Ajaccio, city of Napoleon's birth.

Newest of the *Da Mare a Mare* routes is the southernmost trail, which leads in six days from Porto-Veccio through Alta Rocca, Ospedale, Cartalavonu, and Levie to the Bavella group, the romantic mountain villages of Zonza and Quenza, and finally leading, via Fozzano, to the popular resort Propriano. Here, you're welcomed by the Gulf of Valinco with its deep blue water; along its edge, a promenade, lined with cafés, excellent restaurants, and luxurious hotels, offers you a perfect spot to put up your feet and rest.

TRAVEL PREPARATIONS

Entering the Country

There is no longer any customs or passport control for people travelling within the European Union. Sometimes, however, officials do run spot checks. Make sure, therefore, to bring an identity card or passport.

For citizens of non-EU countries, the entrance requirements for Corsica are the same as those for entering any other part of France. If you're uncertain, ask at the French Embassy, or check with the consulate in your native country.

Exchanging Money / Currency

The unit of currency in Corsica is the French franc, which is abbreviated as FF (or simply F). One franc is subdivided into 100 *centimes*. Banknotes come in denominations of 500, 200, 100, 50 and 20 francs, coins in 20 (these are new: watch out, they look a lot like the 10-franc coins!), 10, 5, 2, and 1 franc, and 50, 20, 10 and 5 centimes. There's no limit on the amount of foreign currency you can bring into Corsica. You can take up to 12,000 French francs out of the country without a declaration.

Best place to change cash is at a bank or post office; you can also change money at exchange offices and in a number of hotels. For travelers checks, which are certainly a safer way to travel, a number of banks charge high commissions.

You can write *Eurochecks* in amounts of up to 1,400 FF, but you'll have to pay extra commissions when you get home – the same is true if you use your EC card at an automatic teller maching. The exchange rate at EC automats, however, is generally very good.

Credit cards, another safe form of payment, cannot be used everywhere on Corsica. But you can be sure they'll be accepted in good hotels, at rental car agencies, in the better restaurants, at large gas stations, and on ferry boats.

Clothing

Because the island boasts such extreme geographical and climatic differences, you'll need a wide range of clothing.

Along the coast, you'll need lighter garments; best bet is cotton. A hat, suntan lotion and sunglasses serve as protection from the hot and very bright rays of the sun. For evenings on the seashore, you should have a sweater or blazer along; and there'll be opportunity to get dressed up if you want to go to a good restaurant or just stroll around.

When visiting churches, make sure you're wearing appropriate clothing.

Best gear if you want to hike in the maquis relatively unharmed is a pair of long, sturdy, but light-weight cotton pants.

In the mountains, you should always have long pants and a good windbreaker or anorak along in your day pack. Equally important are some form of thin raingear and good, sturdy hiking shoes.

Climate / When to Go

High tourist season on Corsica is during the hottest months of the year, in July and August, when schools in France and Italy have their vacations and most small businesses close. For driving tours around the island, however, these months are not really ideal: first, it's much too hot; second, all of the beaches and seaside resorts are filed to overflowing. If you want to go off into the mountains, however, and hike the famous GR 20 without snow and with some guarantee of optimal weather conditions, then these two months are an excellent time to go – and they're also perfect for anyone who prefers ocean swimming only when the water is at around tbe temperature of a warm bath.

Most tourist facilities are open between early May and the end of September; some of them are even open between April and October. The only hotels that are open year-round are those in ski areas or in the cities. Loveliest time of year is

May and early June, when the weather is comfortable and fairly stable (daytime temperatures 70-77°F/21-25°C, nighttime temperatures 50-60°F/10-15°C) and the famous maquis of Corsica spreads a carpet of flowers across the island. At this time of year, the beaches are at their cleanest, but the water is still refreshingly cool. May is still a bit too early for mountain hikes, as some of the trails may still be covered with snow.

Second-best time of year is the post-season period from early September to early October. By this time, the prices have already gone down a bit, and water temperatures are around 64-73°F (20-23°C). Because of the hot summer months just past, the island is dry as tinder, and September often sees devastating forest fires. For hikers, the first two weeks of September are excellent; after this, there are often afternoon thunderstorms in mountain regions.

Customs Regulations

Between France and all other EU countries, there are no longer any import and export restrictions or customs regulations. For citizens of non-EU countries, however, the old conditions still hold; that is, you can bring in the following goods: valuables worth up to 250 $, 200 cigarettes or 100 cigarillos or 50 cigars or 250 g of tobacco, 2 liters of wine and 1 liter of spirits.

TRAVELING TO CORSICA

By Plane

Corsica has three international airports: Ajaccio, Calvi and Bastia. In the high season, several charter lines also service the small airport of Figari, between Propriano and Porto-Vecchio. *Air France* and its subsidiary, *Air Inter*, operate regular direct service from all major French airports.

From European airports, a number of different airlines offer direct flights (often charter flights, often only offered in the high season of July and August) from Amsterdam, Barcelona, Brussels, Cologne, Düsseldorf, Frankfurt, Genoa, Hamburg, Innsbruck, London, Milan, Munich, Pisa, Rome, Salzburg, Stuttgart, Vienna, and Zürich. There are also direct flights to and from Morocco: *Royal Air Maroc* offers service from Casablanca and Oujda.

If you'd like to fly to the island in the off season, you generally have to change in Marseilles, Nice, or Paris. Most flights go through Paris, and from there you usually continue on *Air Inter*. From Marseilles or Nizza, you'll change to a plane of the airline *Compagnie Corse Meditérrannée*.

Airline offices on Corsica:

Air France/Air Inter: 3, Boulevard du Roi Jérôme, Ajaccio, Tel: 95294545. 6, Avenue Emile-Sari, Bastia, tel. 95545495. Aéroport Sainte-Catherine, Calvi, tel. 95652009.

Compagnie Corse Meditérrannée, B.P.505, Ajaccio, tel. 95290500.

Airport Information:

Ajaccio: Campo dell'Oro airport, tel. 95210707.

Bastia: Poretta airport, tel. 95545454.

Calvi: Sainte-Catherine airport, tel. 95650354.

Figari: airport, tel. 95710022.

By Boat

You can reach Corsica by boat from harbors in Italy, Sardinia, and France, taking any of a number of ferry lines to do so. Ports of embarkation include Marseilles, Toulon, Nice, Genoa, La Spezia, Livorno, Piombino or Santo Stefano.

From early May to the end of September, there are several ferries a day between the mainland and Corsica. During the rest of the year, there are at least two ferries a week. A simple ferry trip lasts from 4 to 9 hours, depending on your port of embarkation or on whether you've opted for the longer night trip. On night ferries, you can rent cabins in every possible price category. Ferry reservations are necessary in the main season if you want to take your car with you. Motorcyclists, however, can risk trying to get aboard without a prior reservation.

Since June, 1995, there's a new vessel on the Corsica Ferries line, the "Corsica Express." This high-speed boat (which also accommodates cars) takes 3 hours for the Nice-Bastia route, and 2 hours 45 minutes for Nice-Calvi. The boat, with its 350,000-horsepower engine, services both Corsican harbors every day.

For information and reservations, ask any travel agent. On the island, the offices of the ferry lines can also give information and accept reservations:

S.N.C.M.: Quai l'Herminier, Ajaccio, tel. 952966-99/88. Nouveau Port, Bastia, tel. 955466-99/88. Quai Landry, Calvi, tel. 95650138. Avenue J.-Calizi, Ile Rousse, tel. 95600956.

Corsica Ferries: 5, Boulevard Chanoine-Leschi, B.P.239, Bastia, tel. 95311809. Port de Commerce, Ajaccio, tel. 95510639. Port de Commerce, Calvi, tel. 95654321. Esplanade de la Gare, Ile Rousse, tel. 95604411.

Navarma Lines / Moby Lines: S.A.R.L. Colonna d'Istria et Fils, 4, Rue Commandant-Luce-de-Casabianca, Bastia, tel. 95314629/95316247. S.A.R.L., J. Gazano, Port, Bonifacio, tel. 95730029.

By Car

If you want to explore the inland regions of Corsica, as well as the coast, and plan to spend at least two weeks on the island, it's worthwhile to bring your own car if you can arrange it, as the bus and railway networks are only adequate along the coast, and rental cars on Corsica are quite expensive. If you're driving from England, you can come down through France to Marseilles, Toulon or Nice. If you opt to go through Italy, note that you can pay tolls on the Autostrada with a credit card. If you've reserved a ferry, re-

member to allow for traffic jams on the expressway when you're figuring out how much time you'll need to get there.

TRAVELING ON CORSICA

Bus

Corsica has an extensive bus network which links all of the island's major cities. For the west coast stretch between St-Florent and Bonifacio, you should allow at least three days; a second line links Ajaccio, Corte and Bastia with one another, and the third route leads along the east coast from Bonifacio to Bastia.

If you're planning to travel all around the island on public buses, you'd better have loads of time. Buses run only once or twice a day, and, along the west coast, often need as much as four hours to cover a stretch of 60 miles (100 km). Because of these long travel times and the infrequency of service, it's almost impossible to take a day trip, such as that from Ajaccio to Porto and back, by bus. As buses only run along the national highways, you see hardly anything of the lovely little villages inland. The bus system, therefore, is only recommended for single transfers or for those who are planning lengthy stays on the island.

Train

Train travel on Corsica is a tourist experience. Because of the beautiful settings of the tracks, which lead straight through the mountains, you shouldn't miss the chance to take a day trip from Ajaccio to Corte. There is a rail link between the three major cities Ajaccio, Corte, and Bastia; the island's other route links Bastia, Ponte Leccia, and Calvi. Depending on the time of year, trains run two to four times a day. Hikers (GR 20) without cars often make use of this means of transportation. You only need reservations for groups, in which case an extra car is added to the train. Timetables and information are available from any train station. **Ajaccio**, tel. 95231103. **Bastia**, tel. 95326006. **Calvi**, tel. 95650061. **Corte**, tel. 95460097. **Ile-Rousse**, tel. 95600050. **Vizzavona**, tel. 95472102.

Rental Car

The international rental car companies have branches in all the larger coastal cities, as well as at the airports; inland, you can only find them in Corte. There are also some Corsican firms, which offer lower prices and have, like their larger competitors, cars (usually French) in mint condition. You'll need a national or international driver's license, which you must have had for at least three years.

Boat

Sailing around Corsica's coast is a marvelous experience. The island has 13 marinas, some beautifully situated; these also rent boats. To rent a large yacht, you have to show a sailing certificate.

Organized Excursions and Tours

Several bus lines offer various excursions, lasting one or several days, on Corsica: *Eurocorse Voyages*, bus station, Ajaccio, tel. 95210630. 1, Rue Maréchal-Sébastini, Bastia, tel. 95310379. Quai Comparetti, Bonifacio, tel. 95731507. *Autocars Ceccaldi*, bus station, Ajaccio, tel. 95202976/ 95210124/95213806. *Autocars Santoni*, Z.I. du Vazzio, tel. 95226444/ 95212956.

You can also book organized tours and excursions through the local travel agencies on the island.

Ajaccio: *Kallistour Voyages*, 11, Place Général-de-Gaulle, tel. 95211736. *Nouvelles Frontières*, 12, Place Foche, tel. 95215555. *Ollandini*, 3, Place Général-de-Gaulle, tel. 95211012.

Bastia: *Kallistour Voyages*, 6, Avenue Maréchal-Sébastini, tel. 95317149. *Nouvelles Frontières*, 33 bis, Rue César-Campinchi, tel. 95320162. *Ollandini Voyages*, 40, Boulevard Paoli, tel. 95311171.

Calvi: *Corse Voyages*, Boulevard Wilson, B.P.6, tel. 95650047.

Corte: *Corte Voyages*, 14, Cours Paoli, tel. 95460035.

Porto-Vecchio: *Corsicatours*, 7, Rue Jean-Jaurès, tel. 95701036. *Riva Corse Voyages*, 13, Rue du Général-de-Gaulle, tel. 95701231.

PRACTICAL TIPS

Accommodations

On Corsica, there aren't any luxury hotels, and only a few 4-star hotels, but there are countless 3- and 2-star hotels. For further information, contact: **G.I.E. Étapes Hotelières Corses**, Rue de L'Ancienne-Poste, 20231 Venaco, tel. 95470022. **G.I.E. Corsica Hotels**, B.P.3, 20166 Porticcio, tel. 95254234. **G.I.E. Ilotel**, Route de Pineto, 20290 Lucciana, tel. 95360963. **Casa Toia la Route des Auberges**, Auberge L'Aghjola, 20259 Pioggiola, tel. 95619048.

Youth hostels: Résidence les Lauriers, 20110 Propriano, tel. 95762981. **Hôtel des Jeunes BVJ Corsotel**, 20260 Calvi, tel. 95653372.

Holiday apartments in the countryside (*Gîtes Ruraux*): **Relais Régional des Gîtes Ruraux**, 6, Avenue Pascal Paoli, 20000 Ajaccio, tel. 95205154.

Rural accommodation (*Fermes Auberges*): **Association Régionale des Fermes Auberges et des Structures Agri-Touristiques**, Maison de l'Agriculture, 19, Avenue Noël-Franchini, B.P.319, 20178 Ajaccio, tel. 95294231/ 95294225.

Association of Holiday Residences: **Fédération Régionale des Résidences de Tourisme**, La Sauvagie, 20137 Porto-Vecchio, tel. 95700742.

Banks

Banks are open weekdays 9 am-noon and 2:30-5 pm, closed Saturdays and Sundays. Not all banks are open on Monday. In tourist centers, you'll find banks that are open to exchange money until 6 pm, throught the lunch hour, and on Saturdays. The post office, exchange offices, and good hotels will also exchange French francs for foreign currency.

Camping

Camping in the wild is absolutely forbidden throughout Corsica. As independent campers are often responsible for the devastating fires which sweep the island, it's understandable that the Corsicans are quite strict about this. Besides, given the range and numbervof lovely campgrounds scattered over the whole island, everyone is sure to find something to his or her taste. Depending on the facilities, campgrounds, like hotels, are awarded one to four stars.

You can get information and addresses from:

Campground Association: **Fédération Française de Camping Caravaning**, Chemin de Toretta, Route du Salario, 20000 Ajaccio, tel. 95214790.

Reserving your stay: **GIE Corsica Camping**, 20, Rue St-Charles, 20000 Ajaccio, tel. 95211447.

Crafts

Lana Corsa, wool articles, Saliceto, tel. 95476437/95484379. **I Bancalari**, woodcarving and furniture, Cuttoli Cortichiato, tel. 95256472. **Arte di Musica**, musical instrument making, Pigna/Balagne, tel. 95617715/95617781. **L'Artigiani di Pigna**, ceramics, wood, and agricultural products, Pigna, tel. 95617056/95617781. **Case di L'Artigiani**, associaion of crafts shops, Rue Bonaparte, Sartène, tel. 95770734/95770226.

Electricity

Corsican plugs have a voltage of 220 Volt. If you're coming from overseas, therefore, you'll need a transformer for any appliances you bring, as well as an adapter to make sure the plug fits Corsican sockets; as these can vary, you might want to bring an adapter in any case.

Emergency

Fire department (*Pompiers*), tel. 18. **Ambulance** (*Samu*), tel. 15. **Police, emergency line** (*Police Sécours*), tel. 17. **Police**: Ajaccio, tel. 95292147. **Bastia**, tel. 95545022. **Calvi**, tel. 95650017. Corte, tel. 95460481. **Ghisonaccia**, tel. 95560017. **Porto-Vecchio**, tel. 95700017. **St-Florent**, tel. 95370017. **Sartène**, tel. 95770117.

Festivals and Holidays

Official holidays throughout France, including Corsica, are: **January 1**, New Year's Day; **Easter Monday**; **May 1**, Worker's Day; **May 8**, German capitulation in 1945; **Ascension Day** (June); **Whit Monday** (June); **July 14**, Bastille Day (1789), national holiday; **August 15**, Assumption Day; **November 1**, All Saints' Day; **November 11**, Armistice Day (1918); **December 25**, Christmas.

During Good Friday week (March/April), you can witness some spectacular processions on Corsica. In Bonifacio: *Les Cinq Confreries*, in Calvi: *La Granitola*, in Corte: *Le Christ Roi*, in Erbalunga: *La Cerca*, in Bastia: *Le Christ Noir* and in Sartène: *Le Catenacciu*.

In Good Friday week, there are also special Easter ceremonies in the Greek Orthodox church in Cargèse, such as a candle-lighting ceremony on the Saturday before Easter at midnight.

June 2: *Saint-Erasme*, processions through the cities of Ajaccio, Bastia, Propriano and Calvi in honor of the patron saint of fishermen.

June 24: *Saint-Jean Baptiste* in Bastia. Birthday of John the Baptist, celebrated with a with procession and festival.

July 14: The French national holiday of Bastille Day is celebrated all over Corsica with fireworks and festivals. In Porto, there's also a large public fair.

September 8-9: *Santa di u Niolo* in Casamaccioli. Festival and religious service to honor patron saints of the Niolu.

September 8: *Notre-Dame*, Bonifacio. Festivals are generally held in the summer months. From the middle to the end of June, Calvi hosts a large **jazz festival** (tel. 95651667). In the governor's palace in Bastia from mid-July to mid-August, you can hear classical and modern music at the **Festival d'Été** (tel. 95310912 or 95323361). Film fans shouldn't miss the film festival **La Corse et le Cinéma** in July (Cinémaffiche, tel. 95703502). In September, a similar film festival is held in Bastia, with entries from throughout the Mediterranean region: **the Festival du Film des Cultures Méditerranéennes** (tel. 95320832 or 95320886). In August, there are theater performances in Ajaccio (tel. 95215090) as well as at the large Citadel Festival in Calvi (tel. 95652357).

Hiking

Corsica is a paradise for hikers and climbers. In addition to the well-known and well marked trails of the *GR 20, Tra Mare e Monti*, and the three *Da Mare a Mare* routes (see p. 236-239), there are countless other, smaller trails, which are not always very well marked. In general, it holds true in the mountains of Corsica that you're moving in high Alpine regions. Good equipment and detailed, accurate maps are essential.

For general information about walking and hiking trails: **Parc Naturel Régional de la Corse**, Rue Général-Fiorella, B.P.417, Ajaccio, tel. 95215654.

Guided hikes on Corsica are organized by: **Office National des Forêts**, Rés. La Pictrina, Avenue de la Grande Armée, Ajaccio, tel. 95201427. Guided forest walks in July and August. **I Muntagnoli Corsi**, Centre de montagne et de loisirs, Quenza, tel. 95786405, organizes hikes, climbing excursions, and cross-country ski tours. **Muntagne Corse in Liberta**, Immeuble Le Rond Point, 2, Avenue de la Grande Armée, Ajaccio, tel. 95205314. Hiking, fishing, and cross-country skiing. **Move**, Speloncato, tel. 95615146/ 95627083.

Literature

Asterix on Corsica is perhaps the most entertaining introduction to Corsica's history and the Corsican mentality.

The book *Corsica – Historic Sketches and Walks in the Year 1852*, by Ferdinand Gregorovius reports in great detail on the island's landscapes, and is filled with informative narrations of the island's history and eye-witness accounts of Corsican traditions.

Also of great interest to English readers is James Boswell's 18th-century account *Corsica*. Boswell gives descriptions of Corsica, as well as a goodly amount of important news and anecdotes about Pasquale Paoli, General of the Corsicans, and quite a bit of information about the island's history.

For readers who are interested in French literature, the following novellas make ideal vacation reading:

Alphonse Daudet: Letters from my Mill (*Lettres de mon Moulin*), short stories, 1869. One story deals with the lighthouse on the Iles Sanguinaire, near Ajaccio.

Gustave Flaubert: *Voyage dans les Pyrénées et en Corse.*

Guy de Maupassant: A Life (*Une Vie*), 1883.

Prosper Mérimée: *Colomba*, 1840 and *Matteo Falcone*, 1840.

Maps

One good road map, which you can also buy cheaply on Corsica, is the **Carte Michelin** Nr. 90 on a 1:200 000 scale.

The best maps for hikers are published by the *Institut Géographique National* (IGN): **Itinéraires Pédestres**, Map 20 (Corse Nord) and 23 (Corse Sud) on a scale of 1:50 000. The **Série Top 25** covers the whole island in a series of maps on a scale of 1:25 000. These maps are distinguished by their good reliefs, which seem almost three-dimensional, as well as by their reliable markings of hiking trails (including the GR 20), bergeries, and mountain huts (refuge).

Opening Hours

There's no law about opening hours on Corsica, as there is in some European countries; but most stores are closed between 12 and 2 pm, and after 7 or 8 in the evening. Stores are open all day Saturday, but many stores stay closed on Monday (and Sunday, of course, is a free day almost everywhere in Europe). Fresh bread is sacred to the Corsicans, so that a number of bakeries are open on Sunday and Monday, as well.

Post Office / Telephone

Opening hours of post offices can vary. In general, they're open from 9 am-noon and and 2:30-6 pm. You can recognize them by the yellow rectangular sign bearing the legend **PTT** *(Poste, Télé-phone, Télégraphe)*.

A few of the yellow mailboxes in the towns have two mail slots, one with the label *Corse* and the other for *Autres Destinations* (other destinations), which are the ones to use for mail sent abroad.

You can buy stamps at tobacconists as well as at the post office; another place to get them is from post-card stands.

If you're having anything sent to *Poste Restante*, it will, if there's no other indication on the envelope, be sent to the main post office and held there for pick-up. However, letters and packages are only held for 15 days; if unclaimed by then, they're returned to the sender. You can pick up mail for a small fee after showing some form of identification.

You can place phone calls on Corsica from any telephone booth, and these are nearly all equipped to receive calls, as well. Almost all of the coin-operated phones have been replaced by ones that accept telephone cards, or **Télécarte**, which you can buy for 40 francs (50 units) or 96 francs (120 units) at the post office or in tobacconists.

Many bars and restaurants have a *Point Phone*, which is still coin-operated (you can even use 10-franc coins). Calling from your hotel room can be up to 40% more expensive than the public rate.

As of October 18, 1996 Corsica has the area code 04 (when calling from abroad: ++33 4).

International dialling prefixes from Corsica:
- to Australia, 19 61 and area code.
- to Great Britain, 19 44 and the local area code, without the 0.
- to Ireland, 19 353 and the local area code.
- to the U.S.A. and Canada, 19 1 and area code.

Press

The largest Corsican newspaper (circulation 40,000) is the liberal right-wing paper *Corse-Matin*, a regional edition of Nice-Matin, which appears along the Côte d'Azur. 12,000 copies of the liberal left-wing *la Corse* (a regional edition of the Marseilles-based newspaper *le Provençal*) are published on Corsica every morning. Both papers contain plenty of useful information about local events, emergency medical service, and the weather. Vacationers who are interested in Corsican culture, poltics, and economy should take a look at the French-language news magazine *Kyrn*.

Tipping

A service charge is included in all hotel and restaurant bills. If you're content with the service, it's customary to add a tip of another 5-10%.

Theft

Moped-driving purse-snatchers are a rare, if not extinct, breed on Corsica: this isn't a "dangerous" island. While you can, in mountain villages, count on the honesty of the inhabitants, things look quite different in tourist centers along the coast. So leave your expensive jewelry at home, and lock valuables in your hotel safe (some campgrounds also offer this service). If you've got an expensive high-tech bicycle with you, make sure to write down the serial number before you go. In Bastia, motorcycles have been known to be stolen from in front of hotels while the biker was inside asking about room availability. Never leave camera equipment or cash unattended in your car, even for five minutes, as "car-crackers" tend to work quickly, with the benefit of experience. If you notice that the surface of a parking lot – expecially in the mountains or near a beach – is littered with shards of windshield glass, you should only park your car there after completely emptying it, and leaving the windows open. It's not a bad idea to get some kind of luggage insurance before you go (cameras are only half covered).

Tourist Information

On Corsica, tourist information offices go by the names *Office du Tourisme or Syndicat d'Initiative*. Here, you can pick up free city maps, listings of hotels and campgrounds, and other information.

Headquarters for the **north** are located in Bastia: Union Départementale des Offices de Tourisme et Syndicats d'Initiative de la Haute Corse, Nouveau Port, 20200 Bastia, tel. 95310204.

In the **south**: Union Départementale des Offices de Tourisme et Syndicats d'Initiative de la Corse du Sud, 1, Place Foch, B.P.21, 20176 Ajaccio, tel. 95214087.

French Government Tourist Offices abroad:

AUSTRALIA: BNP Building, 12th floor, 12 Castlereagh Street, Sydney NSW 2000, tel. (61) 2231 5244, fax (61) 2221 8682.

CANADA: 1981 Av. McGill College Suite 490, Montreal, Quebec H3A 2W9, tel (514) 288 4264.

GREAT BRITAIN: 178 Piccadilly, London W1V OAL, tel. (0891) 244 123 or (0171) 493 6594.

IRELAND: 35 Lower Abbey Street, Dublin 1, tel. 1 703 4046, fax 1 874 7324.

U.S.A.: 444 Madison Avenue, 16th floor, New York, NY 10022, tel. (212) 838 7800, fax (212) 838 7855.

9454 Wilshire Boulevard, Suite 715, Beverly Hills, CA 90212-2967, tel. (310) 271 2693, fax (310) 276 2835.

GLOSSARY

(Corsican terms in italics)

Good day . . . . bonjour
. . . . *bonghjornu*
Good evening . . . . bonsoir
. . . . *bonna sera*
Hello . . . . salut
. . . . *salute*
How are you? . . . . comment
allez-vous?
. . . . *cumu sete*?
Goodbye . . . . au revoir
. . . . *a vedeci*
very good . . . . très bien
. . . . *bè bè*
not good . . . . pas bien
. . . . *male*
yes / no . . . . oui / non
. . . . *iè / innò*
please . . . . s'il vous plaît
. . . . *par piacè / par carità*
thank you . . . . merci
. . . . *grazie*
Excuse me . . . . pardon
. . . . *scusa mi / scusate mi*
My name is . . . . Je m'appelle
. . . . *mi chjamu*
What is your name? . . Comment-vous
appellez vous?
. . . . *Cumu vi chijamate*?
okay . . . . d'accord
. . . . *d'accunsentu*
Do you speak... . . . . . . parlez-vous
. . . . *voi parlate*
English . . . . anglais
. . . . *inglese*
German . . . . allemand
. . . . *tedescu*
French . . . . français
. . . . *francese*

Corsican . . . . corse
. . . . *corsu*
I don't understand . . Je ne comprends pas
. . . . *un capiscu micca*
How do I get to...? . . . . . . comment
aller à
. . . . *cumu si va in*
expensive . . . . cher
. . . . *caru*
cheap . . . . bon marché
. . . . a bon *pattu*
How much does it cost? . . . .
ça fait combien?
. . . . *quantu costa*?
I'd like . . . . j'aimerais
. . . . *mi piaceria*
I'm hungry . . . . j'ai faim
. . . . *aghju a fame*
What time is it? . . quelle heure est-il?
. . . . *chi ora è*?
Check, please . . . . . l'addition s.v.p.
. . . . *a nota per piacè*
Do you have a room? . . . . . . Avez
vous une chambre de libre?
. . . . *Avete una stanza libara*?
single room . . . . une simple
. . . . *una simplice*
double room . . . . une double
. . . . *una doppia*
today . . . . aujourd'hui
. . . . *oghje*
tomorrow . . . . demain
. . . . *dumane*
yesterday . . . . hier
. . . . *arrimane*
left . . . . a gauche
. . . . *a manca*
right . . . . a droite
. . . . *a dritta*
cold . . . . froid
. . . . *freddu*
hot . . . . chaud
. . . . *caldu*
open . . . . ouvert
. . . . *apertu*
closed . . . . fermé
. . . . *chjosu*
water . . . . de l'eau
. . . . *acqua*

with / without gas (carbonation) . . .
. . . . avec / sans gaz
. . . . *à / senza gaz*
a glass of wine . . . . . un verre de vin
. . . . *un bicchjeru di vinu*
a beer . . . . une bière
. . . . *una birra*
coffee with milk . . . . . un café au lait
. . . . *u caffè a latte*
black coffee . . . . un cafè
. . . . *u caffè*
bread . . . . pain
. . . . *pane*
meat . . . . viande
. . . . *carne*
vegetables . . . . legumes
. . . . *urtaglia*
salad . . . . salade
. . . . *insalata*
fruit . . . . fruits
. . . . *frutta*
sugar . . . . sucre
. . . . *zuccheru*
harbor . . . . port
. . . . *molu / portu*
train station . . . . gare
. . . . *gara*
bus station . . . . gare routière
. . . . *gara stradale*
bus . . . . car
. . . . *caru*
train . . . . train
. . . . *trenu*
beach . . . . plage
. . . . *piagia / marina*
sea . . . . mer
. . . . *mare*
doctor . . . . docteur
. . . . *duttore*
hospital . . . . hôpital
. . . . *spidale*
Monday . . . . lundi
. . . . *luni*
Tuesday . . . . mardi
. . . . *marti*
Wednesday . . . . mercredi
. . . . *mercuri*
Thursday . . . . jeudi
. . . . *ghjovi*

Friday . . . . vendredi
. . . . *vennari*
Saturday . . . . samedi
. . . . *sabatu*
Sunday . . . . dimanche
. . . . *dumenica*
1 . . . . un / *unu*
2 . . . . deux / *dui*
3 . . . . trois / *tré*
4 . . . . quatre /*quattru*
5 . . . . cinq / *cinque*
6 . . . . six / *sei*
7 . . . . sept / *sette*
8 . . . . huit / *ottu*
9 . . . . neuf / *nove*
10 . . . . dix / *dece*
11 . . . . onze / *ondeci*
12 . . . . douze / *dodeci*
13 . . . . treize / *tredeci*
14 . . . . quartorze / *quattordeci*
15 . . . . quinze / *quindeci*
16 . . . . seize / *sedeci*
17 . . . . dix-sept / *dicesette*
18 . . . . dix-huit / *diciottu*
19 . . . . dix-neuf / *dicenove*
20 . . . . vingt / *vinti*
30 . . . . trente / *trenta*
40 . . . . quarante / *quaranta*
50 . . . . cinquante / *cinquanta*
60 . . . . soixante / *sessanta*
70 . . . . soixante-dix / *settanta*
80 . . . . quatre-vingt / *ottanta*
90 . . . . . quatre-vingt-dix / *novanta*
100 . . . . cent / *centu*
1000 . . . . mille / *mille*

Menu
(Corsican terms in italics)

ail . . . . garlic
aliolu . . . . cold garlic sauce
anguille . . . . eel
bouillabaisse / *aziminu* . . . . fish soup
brebis . . . . . . sheep's-milk cheese
brocciu . . . . Corsican cottage cheese
brochet . . . . pike
brochette . small skewer of grilled meat
cabri . . . . goat
cabri/cabrettu a l'istrettu . goat ragout
in a zesty sauce

caille . . . . partridge
canard . . . . duck
canistrelli . . . . Corsican cookie
with anise, almonds, and nuts
cassoulet . . . . a casserole with
. . . . white beans and pork
concombre . . . . cucumber
courgettes . . . . zucchini
côte d'agneau . . . . lamb cutlet
côte de veau . . . . veal cutlet
côte de boeuf . . . . beef cutlet
côte de porc . . . . pork cutlet
crudité . . . mixed raw vegetable plate
coppa . . . . . . smoked rolled ham
cuisse de grenouille . . . . frogs' legs
dinde, dindon . . . . turkey
dorade . . . . dorado
entrecôte . . . . cutlet
escargots . . . . snails
farine de châtaigne / *farina pisticcina* . . .
. . . . chestnut flour
fèves / *fasgioli* . . . . . . white beans
figues . . . . figs
flageolets . . . . green beans
fiadone . . . . brocciu cake
figatellu . . . . . . pork liver sausage
foie . . . . liver
fromage / *casgiu* / *frumagliu* . . cheese
fritelle . . . . small fried cakes
. . . . filled with brocciu
friture du golfe . . . . little fish
fried in an egg-based dough
gibier . . . . game
gigot . . . . leg
glace . . . . ice cream
huitres . . . . oysters
langouste / *arigosta* . . . . . crayfish
limande . . . dab (a flounder-like fish)
lonzu . . . . . a kind of smoked ham
lotte . . . . burbot
loup de mer . . . . sea-perch
miel / *mele* . . . . honey
migliacci (nicci, flaculelle) . . *brocciu-*
cakes on chestnut leaves
oie . . . . goose
olive / *aliva* . . . . olive
pan bagnat . white bread sandwich with
lettuce, tomato, egg, olives, anchovies,
drenched with oil (*bagnat* = bathed in)

pâté de merle . . . . blackbird paté
piverunata . . . goat stew with peppers
potage . . . . soup
poulet / *poulastrou* . . . . chicken
prizuttu . . . . . a kind of smoked ham
pulenta . . . . . . thick chestnut puree
raie . . . . ray, skate
raisins . . . . grapes
rascasse . . . . hogfish
riffia . . . . . . skewer of lamb offal
rouget . . . . red mullet
sanglier / *cinghjale* . . . . . . wild boar
stufatu . . . . . beef ragout served with
brocciu ravioli
tarte tatin . . . . caramelized apple tart
terrine de sanglier . . . . . wild boar paté
thon . . . . tuna fish
truite . . . . trout
oursin / *zini* . . . . sea urchin
volaille . . . . poultry
zuppa corsa . Corsican vegetable soup
(not unlike Italian minestrone)

AUTHORS

Heike Mühl, author of this book, studied Romance languages and art history in France and Germany, and assembled and published a detailed study of the *Grand Projets* in Paris. On her countless, months-long visits to Corsica, she's had a chance to develop her expertise on what is – in her opinion – the loveliest island in the Mediterranean. As a tour leader for hiking and study tours, as well as in her capacity as a travel guide writer, she visits Corsica several times a year.

Dr. Klaus Boll, a cultural historian, has been visiting Corsica since 1981. A passionate hiker, he's completely at home in the mountains of Corsica, and as hikers can work up quite an appetite, he's also gotten to know Corsica's culinary specialties and wines. For this volume, he wrote the features on Corsican cuisine and the GR 20. Klaus Boll is also the author of the *Nelles Guide Costa Rica*.

PHOTOGRAPHERS

Archiv für Kunst und Geschichte,
Berlin: 23, 29, 30, 34, 37, 38, 144L, 226
Begsteiger, A.M.   54
Fuhrmann, Mara (Photo-Press) 16, 112,
156, 162, 200, 235
Galikowski, Elisabeth 33, 176/177, 202
Gassner, Andreas   207, 211
Hinze, Peter   80/81, 91, 128,
132, 150, 187, 189
Janicke, Volkmar E. 27, 40/41, 59, 101,
127, 178
Jerrican, Labat (Mainbild)   109
Kirst, Detlev   cover, 196/197
Messner, Sabine   35, 198
Mühl, Heike and **Boll**, Klaus   21, 28,
32, 48, 66, 71, 72, 75, 76, 78, 84, 86,
89, 94/95, 105, 114, 118, 125, 126,
133, 142, 143, 145, 154, 157L, 157R,
170, 181, 191, 192, 205, 214, 216/217,
222, 223, 225, 229, 231, 239
Müller, Barbara   165
Radkai, Marton   92
Schmidt, Friedrich   82, 90
Schröder, Dirk   10/11, 26, 39, 55, 60,
64/65, 74, 77, 96, 98, 104, 108, 122,
136/137, 144R, 147, 168, 171, 173,
180, 184, 185, 193, 209, 218/219,
220, 233, 234, 237, 238
Schwarz, Berthold   42/43, 49, 61, 73,
116/117, 129, 134, 138, 146, 151, 153,
155, 174, 182, 230, 232
Stadler, Otto (Mainbild)   50, 208
Stadler, Otto (Silvestris) 8/9, 12, 15, 25,
44, 123
Stuhler, Werner 18, 19, 24, 68, 87, 131,
194, 227
U. W. E. (Silvestris)   36
Volz, H. (Mainbild)   106
Wojciech, Gaby   57, 100, 111, 113,
160/161, 164

Explore the World

NELLES MAPS

AVAILABLE TITLES

Afghanistan 1 : 1,5 M
Australia 1 : 4 M
Bangkok - *Greater Bangkok, Bangkok City* 1 : 75 Th / 1 : 15 Th
Burma - Myanmar 1 : 1,5 M
Caribbean Islands 1 *Bermuda, Bahamas, Greater Antilles* 1 : 2,5 M
Caribbean Islands 2 *Lesser Antilles* 1 : 2,5 M
Central America 1 : 1,75 M
Crete - Kreta 1 : 200 Th
China 1 - *Northeastern* 1 : 1,5 M
China 2 - *Northern* 1 : 1,5 M
China 3 - *Central* 1 : 1,5 M
China 4 - *Southern* 1 : 1,5 M
Egypt 1 : 2,5 M / 1 : 750 Th
Hawaiian Islands 1 : 330 Th / 1 : 125 Th
Hawaiian Islands 1 *Kauai* 1 : 125 Th
Hawaiian Islands 2 *Honolulu - Oahu* 1 : 125 Th
Hawaiian Islands 3 *Maui - Molokai - Lanai* 1 : 125 Th
Hawaiian Islands 4 *Hawaii, The Big Island* 1 : 330 Th / 1 : 125 Th
Himalaya 1 : 1,5 M
Hong Kong 1 : 22,5 Th
Indian Subcontinent 1 : 4 M

India 1 - *Northern* 1 : 1,5 M
India 2 - *Western* 1 : 1,5 M
India 3 - *Eastern* 1 : 1,5 M
India 4 - *Southern* 1 : 1,5 M
India 5 - *Northeastern - Bangladesh* 1 : 1,5 M
Indonesia 1 : 4 M
Indonesia 1 *Sumatra* 1 : 1,5 M
Indonesia 2 *Java + Nusa Tenggara* 1 : 1,5 M
Indonesia 3 *Bali* 1 : 180 Th
Indonesia 4 *Kalimantan* 1 : 1,5 M
Indonesia 5 *Java + Bali* 1 : 650 Th
Indonesia 6 *Sulawesi* 1 : 1,5 M
Indonesia 7 *Irian Jaya + Maluku* 1 : 1,5 M
Jakarta 1 : 22,5 Th
Japan 1 : 1,5 M
Kenya 1 : 1,1 M
Korea 1 : 1,5 M
Malaysia 1 : 1,5 M
West Malaysia 1 : 650 Th
Manila 1 : 17,5 Th
Mexico 1 : 2,5 M
Nepal 1 : 500 Th / 1 : 1,5 M
Trekking Map *Khumbu Himal / Solu Khumbu* 1 : 75 Th
New Zealand 1 : 1,25 M
Pakistan 1 : 1,5 M
Philippines 1 : 1,5 M

Singapore 1 : 22,5 Th
Southeast Asia 1 : 4 M
Sri Lanka 1 : 450 Th
Tanzania - Rwanda, Burundi 1 : 1,5 M
Thailand 1 : 1,5 M
Taiwan 1 : 400 Th
Vietnam, Laos, Cambodia 1 : 1,5 M

FORTHCOMING

Colombia - Ecuador 1 : 2,5 M
Trekking Map *Kathmandu Valley / Helambu, Langtang* 1 : 75 Th
Venezuela - Guyana, Suriname, French Guiana 1 : 2,5 M

Nelles Maps in european top quality!
Relief mapping, kilometer charts and tourist attractions.
Allways up-to-date!

Explore the World

NELLES GUIDES

AVAILABLE TITLES

Australia
Bali / Lombok
Berlin and Potsdam
Brittany
California
  Las Vegas, Reno,
  Baja California
Cambodia / Laos
Canada
  Ontario, Québec,
  Atlantic Provinces
Caribbean
  The Greater Antilles,
  Bermuda, Bahamas
Caribbean
  The Lesser Antilles
China
Corsica
Crete
Cyprus
Egypt
Florida
Greece - *The Mainland*
Hawaii
Hungary
India
  Northern, Northeastern
  and Central India

India
  Southern India
Indonesia
  Sumatra, Java, Bali,
  Lombok, Sulawesi
Ireland
Israel - with Excursions
  to Jordan
Kenya
London, England and Wales
Malaysia
Mexico
Morocco
Moscow / St Petersburg
Munich
  Excursions to Castels,
  Lakes & Mountains
Nepal
New York - *City and State*
New Zealand
Paris
Philippines
Portugal
Prague / Czech Republic
Provence
Rome
South Africa
Spain - *North*

Spain
  Mediterranean Coast,
  Southern Spain,
  Balearic Islands
Sri Lanka
Thailand
Turkey
Tuscany
U.S.A.
  The East, Midwest and
  South
U.S.A.
  The West, Rockies and
  Texas
Vietnam

Nelles Guides – authorative, informed and informative.
Allways up-to-date, extensivley illustrated, and with first-rate relief maps.
256 pages, appr. 150 color photos, appr. 25 maps